OXFORD ENGLISH MONOGRAPHS

General Editors

CHRISTOPHER BUTLER   STEPHEN GILL
DOUGLAS GRAY   EMRYS JONES
ROGER LONSDALE

Original frontispiece for Olive Schreiner's 1897 *Trooper Peter Halket of Mashonaland*. Titled 'photograph', it was taken by an unknown photographer in Bulawayo during the Imperial campaign. This brutal hanging scene is described in the novella. The photograph was suppressed from all subsequent editions of the novella until 1974 AD. Donker edition. By kind permission of the Special Collection library, Brown University, Providence, Rhode Island.

Rereading the Imperial Romance

*British Imperialism and
South African Resistance in
Haggard, Schreiner, and Plaatje*

LAURA CHRISMAN

CLARENDON PRESS • OXFORD

OXFORD
UNIVERSITY PRESS

Great Clarendon Street, Oxford, OX2 6DP
Oxford University Press is a department of the University of Oxford.
It furthers the University's objective of excellence in research, scholarship,
and education by publishing worldwide in

Oxford New York

Athens Auckland Bangkok Bogotá Buenos Aires Calcutta
Cape Town Chennai Dar es Salaam Delhi Florence Hong Kong Istanbul
Karachi Kuala Lumpur Madrid Melbourne Mexico City Mumbai
Nairobi Paris São Paulo Singapore Taipei Tokyo Toronto Warsaw

and associated companies in Berlin Ibadan

Oxford is a registered trade mark of Oxford University Press
in the UK and certain other countries

Published in the United States
by Oxford University Press Inc., New York

British Library Cataloguing in Publication Data

Data available

Library of Congress Cataloging in Publication Data

Data available

ISBN 0-19-812299-3

1 3 5 7 9 10 8 6 4 2

Typeset by Regent Typesetting, London
Printed in Great Britain
on acid-free paper by
T.J. International Ltd,
Padstow, Cornwall

For Benita

Acknowledgements

THIS book began as a doctoral thesis at University of Oxford, in 1986. For their generous input, I thank my supervisor Kate Flint, Paul Kenny, my examiner Graham Pechey, Brian Willan and his family. For funding this doctoral study my abundant thanks to the Scottish Education Department. Thanks also to the Beit Fund of Oxford, the British Academy, and the School of African and Asian Studies at the University of Sussex, for further financial support along the way. Without the extensive labour of librarians, this book could not have materialized. In particular I would like to thank Cathy Henderson of the Harry Ransom Humanities Research Center, University of Texas at Austin. A special thanks to Brenda Cooper for being so warm and generous a Director of Cape Town's Centre for African Studies. Her personal support, and the institutional support of the Centre, contributed considerably to this research.

For inspiration, solicitude and assistance as this project slowly developed from thesis to book, my deep gratitude to John Barrell, Elleke Boehmer, Gale Chrisman, Saul Dubow, Denise deCaires Narain, Isabel Hofmeyr, Ian and Penny Gibson, Ralph Grillo, Rochelle Kapp, Sybil Oldfield, Lawrence Phillips, Karen Lazar, Neil Lazarus, Alan Sinfield, Kelwyn Sole, Jane Starfield, Jenny Taylor, Vincent Quinn, and Norman Vance. Thanks to the Victorian Studies graduate seminar at Oxford; Sussex University's English Subject Group and School of African and Asian Studies; Peter Hulme at the University of Essex and Rachel Holmes at Queen Mary and Westfield College for giving me the opportunity to present early versions of this work. Robert Chrisman and Scott McCracken read drafts of several chapters; their thoughtful, astute feedback has helped more than I can say. I owe an especial debt to Benita Parry, to whom this book is dedicated with love. Her extraordinarily generous and invaluable critical input, scholarship, encouragement and stimulation have accompanied each stage of this project. The book's flaws are, of course, mine alone.

L. C.

Contents

Introduction

THIS book explores the historical experience of British imperialism in South Africa, as mediated through the works of three novelists: the imperialist H. Rider Haggard, the liberal anti-imperialist Olive Schreiner, and the African nationalist Sol Plaatje. South Africa currently occupies a marginalized place in cultural studies of British imperialism. With the single exception of the Anglo-Boer War, South Africa's literary impact on the British metropolis during the 'Age of Empire' receives scant critical attention when compared to India, which continues to be seen as 'the jewel in the crown', the land that colonized British imaginations at every point in its colonial and imperial history. The work of post-colonial critic Gayatri Spivak is indicative of the dominant theoretical and literary place accorded to India. Her analysis of *Jane Eyre*, which continues to have paradigmatic significance, articulates a notion of imperialism as a highly abstracted will-to-power.[1] It is simultaneously identified with the highly specific ideology, historical period and region selected by Spivak: Christian missionary ideology, early to mid-nineteenth-century Britain, and the terrain of India. Though she presents these topics as strategic, Spivak's lack of acknowledgement of alternative regions and periods, and her regular allusions to 'allegory', mean that this region and period assume theoretical primacy. Thus the critic can be caught in a double bind: imperialism's theoretical definition as the totality of Western history/knowledge/power is effectively at one with its definition as mid-Victorian missionary ideology.[2]

It is in part to counteract this emphasis on India as the defini-

[1] Gayatri C. Spivak, 'Three Women's Texts and a Critique of Imperialism', in *Postcolonial Criticism*, ed. Bart Moore-Gilbert, Gareth Stanton, and Willy Maley (London: Longman 1997), 145–65.

[2] Analysis of the implications of the privileging of India within the practice of postcolonial theory and discourse analysis is found in Arif Dirlik, 'The Postcolonial Aura: Third World Criticism in the Age of Global Capitalism', *Contemporary Postcolonial Theory: A Reader*, ed. Padmini Mongia (London: Arnold 1996), 294–321. For critical discussion of the theories of imperial culture by Gayatri Spivak, Edward Said, and Fredric Jameson see Laura Chrisman, 'Imperial Space, Imperial Place: Theories of Culture and Empire in Fredric Jameson, Edward Said and Gayatri Spivak', *New Formations*, 34 (summer 1998), 53–69.

tive site of British imperial culture that my study was undertaken. This is not to suggest that individual writers of and about
imperial South Africa are critically neglected; the attention
given in recent years to H. Rider Haggard and Olive Schreiner
is considerable, and growing. But outside South African
academia, in the critical metropoles of the UK and the USA,
these writers' works tend to be analysed less as products of a
historically particular, distinctive geo-political region and more
as representative of the African continent.[3] The preference for a
version of Haggard and Schreiner as general Africanists conditions which texts of theirs get taken into the post-colonial
critical canon. Thus, Haggard's *King Solomon's Mines* (1885)
and *She* (1886)—which can yield to a general continental and
romantic classification—regularly receive attention, but his
'Zulu epic' *Nada the Lily* (1892) receives scant attention, since
its regional and historical particularity make it ineligible for this
same treatment. Similarly, Schreiner's *Story of an African Farm*
(1883) is preferred to her *Trooper Peter Halket of Mashonaland*
(1897), since the former can be transposed into a level of
colonial generality while (as the title alone suggests) the latter
remains stubbornly local.

But South Africa came to hold a particular importance for the
British empire and its metropolitan populations during this
period.[4] Hannah Arendt notes its movement into political, eco-

---

[3] Some examples of this approach to Haggard and Schreiner include Sandra
Gilbert and Susan Gubar, *No Man's Land: The Place of the Woman Writer in the
Twentieth Century* (London: Yale University Press 1989); Anne McClintock,
Imperial Leather: Race, Gender and Sexuality in the Colonial Contest (London:
Routledge 1995); Anne McClintock, '*Maidens, Maps and Mines*: *King Solomon's
Mines* and the Reinvention of Patriarchy in Colonial South Africa', in *Women and
Gender in Southern Africa to 1945*, ed. Cheryll Walker (London: James Currey
1990), 97–124; Rebecca Stott, 'The Dark Continent: Africa as Female Body in
Haggard's Adventure Fiction', *Feminist Review*, 32 (summer 1989), 69–89. For a
critique see Laura Chrisman, 'Gendering Imperial Culture: Problems in Feminist
Post-Colonial Criticism', in *Cultural Readings of Imperialism: Edward Said and the
Gravity of History*, ed. Keith Ansell-Pearson, Benita Parry, and Judith Squires
(London: Lawrence and Wishart 1997), 290–304.

[4] See Mary E. Chamberlain, *The Scramble for Africa* (London: Longman 1974)
for a useful general outline of the period. For detailed discussions of South African
imperial developments see Jeff Guy, *The Destruction of the Zulu Kingdom: The
Civil War in Zululand. 1879–1884* (London: Longman 1979); Shula Marks and
Richard Rathbone, eds., *Industrialisation and Social Change in South Africa.
African Class Formation, Culture, and Consciousness 1870–1930* (London: Long-
man 1982); Shula Marks and Stanley Trapido, eds., *The Politics of Race, Class and
Nationalism in Twentieth Century South Africa* (London: Longman 1987); Jack

nomic and cultural centrality as 'the culture-bed of Imperialism'.
The reason for its rapid move from imperial margins to centre
was not complicated: 'diamond fields were discovered in the
seventies and large gold mines in the eighties. The new desire for
proft-at-any-price converged for the first time with the old
fortune hunt'.[5] Arendt analyses South Africa's impact on the
British empire primarily in terms of the new forms of racist
ideology and monopoly financial capitalism that it generated.[6]
She situates this within a broader analysis of imperialism as 'the
political emancipation of the bourgeoisie', marking a transformation of the relationship between British state and economy
as the bourgeoisie entered the political sphere to pursue economic expansion.[7]

My study applies Arendt's analysis to the examination of the
literary subjectivities produced through these political and economic transformations. South Africa, I find, was formative in
pushing metropolitan and colonial subjectivities into new and

and Ray Simons, *Class and Colour in South Africa 1850–1950* (London: International Defence and Aid Fund for Southern African 1983).

   [5] Hannah Arendt, *The Origins of Totalitarianism* (1951; London: André Deutsch
1986), 151. See also John A. Hobson, *Imperialism: A Study* (London: J. Nisbet
and Co. 1902); V. I. Lenin, *Imperialism, the Highest Stage of Capitalism* (1917;
Peking: Foreign Languages Press 1975); Rosa Luxemburg, *The Accumulation of
Capital*, trans. A. Schwarzschild (1913; London: Routledge and Kegan Paul 1951).
Useful discussions are Anthony Brewer, *Marxist Theories of Imperialism: A Critical
Survey* (London: Routledge and Kegan Paul 1980); Roger Owen and Bob Sutcliffe,
eds., *Studies in the Theory of Imperialism* (London: Longman 1972). For provoca-
tive analysis of imperialism as a progressive force, see Bill Warren, *Imperialism:
Pioneer of Capitalism* (London: Verso 1980). See also Richard Koebner and
H. D. Schmidt, *Imperialism: The Story and Significance of a Political Word 1840–
1960* (Cambridge: Cambridge University Press 1964), and Joseph Schumpeter,
Imperialism and Social Classes (1919; New York: Meridian Books 1955), for non-
economic political and sociological discussions, respectively, of imperialism of this
period.

   [6] On Victorian racism, see Christine Bolt, *Victorian Attitudes to Race* (London:
Routledge and Kegan Paul 1971); Michael D. Biddiss, ed., *Images of Race*
(Leicester: Leicester University Press 1979).

   [7] On British imperial history of this period see C. Eldridge, *Victorian Imperialism*
(London: Hodder and Stoughton 1981); H. John Field, *Toward a Program of
Imperial Life: The British Empire at the Turn of the Century* (Westport: Greenwood
Press 1982); Eric Hobsbawm, *The Age of Empire. 1875–1914* (London: Weidenfeld
and Nicolson 1987). A useful documentary history is Herman Ausubel, *The Late
Victorians: A Short History* (London: Anvil 1955). See also John A. Hobson, *The
War in South Africa: its Causes and Effects* (London: J. Nisbet and Co. 1900);
Michael Freeden, ed., *J. A. Hobson: A Reader* (London: Unwin Hyman 1988);
Mary Langan and Bill Schwarz, eds., *Crises in the British State 1880–1930*
(London: Hutchinson 1985).

increasingly contradictory forms, and I explore four important moments of South African transformation which forced new kinds of ideological and literary responses: the emergence of gold and diamond mining; the emergence of British Zululand through the Anglo-Zulu War; the emergence of Rhodesia through war against, and resistance by, Shona and Ndebele people; the emergence of the Union of South Africa, the subsequent dispossession of Natives' Lands and formation of the ANC.

Gayatri Spivak takes mid-Victorian missionary 'subject' and 'soul' making discourse as indicative of imperial narrative in general. But the writers examined here reveal that it is precisely the uncertain relation *between* that mid-Victorian ideology and its late nineteenth-century anti-liberal opposite, an essentialist social Darwinism, that exercises so much of their literary energy.[8] Likewise, their writing registers the attempt to comprehend the relation of free trade with late nineteenth-century monopoly capitalism. Even for Rider Haggard this obtains: he feels compelled to add the trading, mid-century generation of Allan Quatermain to the representatives of his own generation, Sir Henry and Captain Good, in order to produce an ideal synthetic British imperial subject with which to lead late nineteenth-century imperial romance and mineral wealth accumulation. In Schreiner and Plaatje, the liberal paternalism of mid-Victorian imperial ideology is forced into scrutiny even as they seek to utilize its resources against the advent of openly oppressive forms of expansionism they witness in Rhodes and the Natives' Land Act respectively. In other words, the analysis of late nineteenth-century imperial subject-constitution needs to

---

[8] Representative imperialist ideologues of this period include: J. A. Cramb, *Reflections on the Origins and Destiny of Imperial Britain* (London: Macmillan and Co. 1900); C. de Thierry, *Imperialism*, introduced by W. E. Henley (London: Duckworth and Co. 1898); Benjamin Kidd, *Social Evolution* (1894; London: Macmillan and Co. 1898); Lord Alfred Milner, *The Nation and the Empire* (London: Constable 1913); Karl Pearson, *National Life from the Standpoint of Science* (London: Adam and Charles Black 1901); Lord Rosebery, *Questions of Empire* (London: Arthur L. Humphreys 1900). Useful critical discussions of late 19th-cent. imperialist ideology and related social science are Richard Faber, *The Vision and the Need: Late Victorian Imperialist Aims* (London: Faber and Faber 1966); Greta Jones, *Social Darwinism and English Thought: The Interaction between Biology and Social Theory* (Brighton: Harvester Press 1982); Bernard Semmel, *Imperialism and Social Reform: English Social-Imperial Thought 1895–1914* (London: Allen and Unwin 1960).

recognize the self-conscious way this subjectivity differentiates itself from, and engages with, mid-Victorian ideological, economic, and political formations.[9]

ROMANTIC ENCHANTMENT AND CRITIQUE

The postcolonial critic Benita Parry observes that :

Not until the late nineteenth century and the massive land expropriations in Africa, intensified capitalist interventions in Asia, and the incorporation of Latin American republics as economic dependencies of western capital, did imperialist rhetoric invent an exorbitant and anomalous idiom of messianic utilitarianism and bellicose mysticism, where the positivist and aggressive phraseology of compulsory universal modernization is joined with the anachronistic and chimerical lexicon of chivalry, 'a mandate of destiny', and 'a high and holy mission' serving as ideological pillars of the west's planetary ambitions.[10]

My book reads this conjunction of utilitarianism and mysticism in Frankfurt School terms: I see in the ideological structures of New Imperialism the legacy of Enlightenment scientific positivism turned into a cult.[11] The conjunction of rationality with mythic forms of consciousness that Adorno and Horkheimer ascribe to fascist modernity is evident in the genre of Haggard's imperial romance.[12] In Haggard an evolutionary

[9] For examples of contemporary imperialist poetry see W. E. Henley, *Poems* (London: David Nutt 1898); William Watson, *Selected Poems* (London: The Bodley Head 1903); Chris Brooks and Peter Faulkner, eds., *The White Man's Burdens: An Anthology of British Poetry of the Empire* (Exeter: University of Exeter Press 1996). Elleke Boehmer, ed., *Empire Writing: An Anthology of Colonial Literature 1870–1918* (Oxford: Oxford University Press 1998), is a useful anthology of primary texts. For discussions of popular culture, see Robert Colls and Philip Dodd, eds., *Englishness: Politics and Culture 1880–1930* (London: Croom Helm 1985); John M. MacKenzie, ed., *Imperialism and Popular Culture* (Manchester: Manchester University Press 1986); John M MacKenzie, *Propaganda and Empire: The Manipulation of British Public Opinion, 1880–1960* (Manchester: Manchester University Press 1984). See also Hugh Ridley, *Images of Imperial Rule* (London: Croom Helm 1983).

[10] Benita Parry, 'Narrating Imperialism: *Nostromo*'s Dystopia', in *Cultural Readings of Imperialism: Edward Said and the Gravity of History*, ed. Keith Ansell-Pearson, Benita Parry and Judith Squires (London: Lawrence and Wishart 1997), 230–1.

[11] Max Horkheimer and Theodor Adorno, *Dialectic of Enlightenment*, trans. J. Cumming (1944; New York: Continuum 1972).

[12] On imperial romance see John A. McClure, *Late Imperial Romance* (London: Verso 1994). See also Thomas Richards, *The Imperial Archive: Knowledge and the Fantasy of Empire* (London: Verso 1993).

ideology combines with a model of romantic primitivism; the operations of science and magic fuse within the romance to produce an authoritarian style of imperial legitimation. The imperial romance form assumed a particular prominence during Britain's political and economic expansion in Southern Africa, as a mode that both articulated and attempted to resolve the socio-economic contradictions brought on by rapid capitalist expansion in the region. The dynamics that cultural critic Fredric Jameson and Benita Parry discern in Joseph Conrad's fraught responses to reification occur also in Haggard's self-conscious and structured deployment of romance.[13] It is not only Conrad's *Nostromo* that features a troubled exploration of 'material interests' and 'saving ideas', condensed in the refractory and indeterminately physical/idealist figure of the mines. Haggard's *King Solomon's Mines* also evinces a complicated mystificatory/demystificatory approach to capitalist accumulation, a subtlety in its techniques of 'staging' oppositions between values in order to contain them, *ressentiment*, a subtle deployment of ontological discourse to fix racially divided categories of political authority, and an equally underhand rhetorical technique to affirm strictures against inter-racial sex. Furthermore, Haggard's romance narrative is structured on the logic of commodities, the abstract exchange value that its surface ideology so stridently disclaims.[14] Through the bodies of Africans, especially through the commodified bodies of African women, the complex mediation of an abstract 'value' becomes evident.

In *King Solomon's Mines* African dead bodies exhibit their value through the symbolic 'trade-offs' they receive: in exchange for providing the men's food the body of Foulata is buried with the treasure, endowed with its tribute and 'eternalized'. But in *Nada the Lily* no such trade-off operates; the narrative performs an entirely one-sided economy of capitalist consumption. This is revealed through the thematic preoccupation with cannibalism.

---

[13] Parry, 'Narrating Imperialism'; Fredric Jameson, ch. 5 'Romance and Reification: Plot Construction and Ideological Closure in Joseph Conrad', in *The Political Unconscious: Narrative as a Socially Symbolic Act* (London: Methuen and Co. 1981), 206–80. See also Gail Fincham and Myrtle Hooper, eds., *Under Postcolonial Eyes: Joseph Conrad after Empire* (Cape Town: University of Cape Town Press 1996).

[14] See Thomas Richards, *The Commodity Culture of Victorian England: Advertising and Spectacle, 1851–1914* (London: Verso 1991).

The more Haggard attempts to render the imperial spirit of Zuluness as one that equates killing with consuming, the more he underscores cannibalist and capitalist impulses at work in his own imperial fiction. Haggard ultimately has an interest in casting the militaristic Zulu as a corpse—only if seen to be dead can they be safely 'eaten'—while at the same time paradoxically he wants to recuperate something of their 'live' spirit, because only if this spirit is alive can it animate the degenerate spirit of the British body that consumes it. By 'eating up' the bodies of brave Zulu warriors, the enervated modern British soldier body, and the reified reader, can ingest and be revived by the spirit, culture, and potency of the Zulu.

Plaatje's *Mhudi* was a direct response to the Haggardian historical romance of *Nada*. Point for point, the novel concerns itself with the same historical period as *Nada*, with the same model of native 'imperialism', and with the same inaugural moment of Boer colonialism. But Plaatje uses the model for entirely different ends: the articulation of an emergent African nationalism. Where Haggard seeks to escape, Plaatje seeks to explore, the complex origins and consequences of white colonialism and imperialism. In the process Plaatje dismantles the tight fit of romantic and rationalist modality that Haggard's aesthetic creates: Plaatje sets the two in creative, mutually ironizing tension, and thereby exposes as ideology what Haggard seeks to establish as mythic truth.

DISAGGREGATING THE METROPOLIS

Edward Said sees the imperial metropolis as unified, contending that 'there was scarcely any dissent, any departure, any demurral from them: there was virtual unanimity that subject races should be ruled . . . With few exceptions, the women's as well as the working-class movement was pro-empire'.[15] My reading of Olive Schreiner concludes otherwise. I assume that metropolitan dissent was theoretically possible and actually practised.[16] The metropolis needs to be disaggregated, seen not

[15] Edward Said, *Culture and Imperialism* (London: Chatto 1993), 62. See also 'Edward Said's *Culture and Imperialism*: A Symposium', *Social Text*, 40 (1994).

[16] Liberal metropolitan anti-imperialists include Leonard Hobhouse, *Democracy and Reaction* (London: T. Fisher Unwin 1904); Charles Masterman, ed., *The Heart*

as a homogeneous unit but, as the work of art historian Annie Coombes suggests, composed of different and competing interest groups, institutions, and classes, whose ideological relationship to imperialism was not determined solely on the basis of their spatial residence.[17] Gayatri Spivak too conceives of metropolitan opposition as a possibility; her conception stems from her deconstructive tenets and her primarily philosophical focus on Kantian notions of subject-formation. Thus she reads Mary Shelley's *Frankenstein* as an example of anti-imperialist critique. This is manifest in its representation of Victor Frankenstein, which criticizes his substitution of theoretical for practical reason and his attempt to invent 'a putative human subject out of natural philosophy alone'.[18] In criticizing the epistemological violence performed by an inappropriate application of scientific reason, Shelley effectively opposes the 'subject-making and territorial' project of imperialism.

My reading of Schreiner likewise sees her as offering a critique that targets an instrumental rationality that reduces everything and everyone to a means. She presents Peter's colonial and colonized psyche as a site of contradiction; the unconscious is construed a potential zone of resistance.

of Empire (London: T. Fisher Unwin 1901). A late Victorian socialist critique of imperialism can be traced in William Morris, *News From Nowhere or an epoch of rest*, ed. James Redmond (1891; London: Routledge and Kegan Paul 1970). See Bernard Porter, *Critics of Empire: British Radical Attitudes to Colonialism in Africa 1895–1914* (London: Macmillan 1968). For discussions of English radical patriotism, see Hugh Cunningham, 'The Language of Patriotism', in *Patriotism: The Making and Unmaking of British National Identity*, i: *History and Politics*, ed. R. Samuel (London: Routledge 1989), 57–89. For useful historical discussions see Diane Paul, ' "In the Interests of Civilization": Marxist views of Race and Culture in the Nineteenth Century', *Journal of the History of Ideas*, volume 42, number 1 (Jan.–Mar. 1981), 115–38, and her 'Eugenics and the Left', *Journal of the History of Ideas*, volume 45, number 4 (Oct.–Dec. 1984), 567–90. See also Henry Pelling, ch. 5 'British Labour and British Imperialism', *Popular Politics and Society in Late Victorian Britain* (London: Macmillan 1979), 82–100. For discussion of a later period of the British left's relationship to empire, see Stephen Howe, *Anticolonialism in British Politics: The Left and the End of Empire 1918–1965* (Oxford: Oxford University Press 1993). And see Paul Gilroy's seminal *There Ain't No Black in the Union Jack* (London: Unwin Hyman 1978).

[17] See her 'The Recalcitrant Object: Culture Contact and the Question of Hybridity', *Colonial Discourse/Postcolonial Theory*, ed. Francis Barker, Peter Hulme, and Margaret Iversen (Manchester: Manchester University Press 1994), 89–114, and *Reinventing Africa. Museums, Material Culture and Popular Imagination in Late Victorian and Edwardian England* (London: Yale University Press 1994).

[18] Spivak, 'Three Women's Texts', 156.

Schreiner challenges the notion of economic rationality as sovereign, suggesting a rearticulation of the subject from reason to ethics and/or the affective spheres. At the same time she attempts to reformulate the notion of rationality itself, from an instrumental to a transcendental form that seeks to grasp the workings of the capitalist system as a whole, a structure of political economy that straddles metropole and colony.

A Spivakian critical project might stop there, with the analysis of Schreiner's philosophical deconstruction of the 'epistemic violence' of the imperial subject. But this would be to miss much of the import of Schreiner's intervention. Her analysis of the subject is a materialist confrontation of the class structure that feeds and is fed by this subject. This is most evident in the hypothetical speeches that Christ gives Peter to appeal to an imaginary British metropolitan audience. These speeches target intellectuals, women, and workers as potential opponents of Rhodesian expansionism, and in the process rewrites a symbolic and moral national narrative, an imaginary England in which these three groups constitute its vanguard. Schreiner's materialist awareness however foregrounds the impossibility of such a narrative realization. Peter refuses to bear these speeches; existing intellectuals, women, and workers of England, he explains, will refuse him a hearing because of his low class status. Schreiner upholds the possibility of an oppositional anti-imperial metropolis but at the same time exposes it for what it is, a fiction that cannot be realized until the British class structure, with its impoverishment, degradation, and snobbish exclusivity of its own subjects, its destroyed.

REPRESENTING BLACK SOUTH AFRICA:
POLITICAL RESISTANCE

Fredric Jameson recognizes the particularity of imperial capitalism of this period and its cultural consequences:

Colonialism means that a significant structural segment of the economic system as a whole is now located elsewhere, beyond the metropolis, outside of the daily life and existential experience of the home country . . . Such spatial disjunction has as its immediate consequence the inability to grasp the way the system functions as a whole . . . no

scientific deductions on the basis of the internal evidence of First-
World data, can ever be enough to include this radical otherness of
colonial life, colonial suffering and exploitation, let alone the structural connections between that and this, between absent space and
daily life in the metropolis.[19]

Viewing the economy and the body as primary determinants of
subjectivity, Jameson presumes that colonized peoples cannot
have any metropolitan sensory impact; they are conceivable
only as an extension of the economic system that controls them.
This underlies his suggestion that 'the other pole of the relationship, what defines him [the "imperial type"] fundamentally
and essentially in his "imperial" function,—the persons of the
colonized—remains structurally occluded, and cannot but so
remain, necessarily, as a result of the limits of the system' (17).
The human sense of existence is, for Jameson, entirely and
directly constituted by the sensations of the physical body.
And since he views the nation as the natural limit of the
existential–sensory subject, then whatever occurs outside of that
national space must consequently be unbridgeably 'other' to
it. Thus, however discrepant metropolitan people's social,
economic, political and intellectual positions, their phenomeno-
logical experience of imperialism is singular.

My readings follow Jameson's interest in the subjective
effects visited on the metropolis by imperial capitalism, and
their mediation through creative literature. But I dissent from
Jameson's definition of metropolitan existence as structurally
precluded from an existential access to the global scale now
claimed by imperialism. The cognitive and physical boundaries
between metropolis and colony were all more mobile than
Jameson's scheme can allow for; the writers studied here, both
in their lives (trafficking across metropole/colony) and in their
writings (mediating both perspectives) were fairly typical of
this period. Jameson is curiously non-dialectical in his con-
ceptualization here: for the metropole to be existentially non-
self-identical it seems, it has to be isolated and static.

Another problem with Jameson's argument is the way it
precludes the possibility that political resistance by colonized
peoples could have any human impact on metropolitan subjects.

[19] Fredric Jameson, 'Modernism and Imperialism', *Field Day Pamphlet number
14* (Derry: Field Day Theatre Co. Ltd. 1988) 11–12.

Indeed, Jameson here writes the category of the political altogether out of the constitution of human subjectivity, so intent is he to emphasize the constitution of the subject through the economy and the body. For Haggard, Schreiner, and Plaatje, formal structures of government such as despotism, democracy, and chiefdoms are, like the political activities that surround them, vital elements in their sensory, aesthetic and intellectual apprehension of empire. With few exceptions, literary criticism of Haggard and Schreiner has tended to overlook this in its overeagerness to read imperialism as synomymous with the way race and gender are represented. I seek instead to restore the category of the political; it mediates and is mediated by, these categories of race and gender. This book then has affinities with the materialist work on Victorian imperial literature of Patrick Brantlinger, Deirdre David, Benita Parry, Jenny Sharpe, and Mrinilini Sinha.[20]

The density of political dynamics can be seen in the interestingly uneven relations between metropolitan home government and colonial administrations in South Africa. The variability of these relations was pronounced in the case of the Anglo-

---

[20] See Patrick Brantlinger, *Rule of Darkness: British Literature and Imperialism, 1830–1914* (Ithaca: Cornell University Press 1988); Deirdre David, *Rule Britannia: Women, Empire, and Victorian Writing* (Ithaca: Cornell University Press 1995); Jenny Sharpe, *Allegories of Empire: The Figure of the Woman in the Colonial Text* (Minneapolis: University of Minnesota Press 1993) and 'The Unspeakable Limits of Rape: Colonial Violence and Counter-Insurgency', in *Colonial Discourse and Post-Colonial Theory: A Reader*, ed. P. Williams and L. Chrisman (Hemel Hempstead: Harvester Wheatsheaf 1993), 196–220; Mrinalini Sinha, *Colonial Masculinity: The 'Manly Englishman' and the 'Effeminate Bengali' in the Late Nineteenth Century* (Manchester: Manchester University Press 1995). Benita Parry's work on imperial literature includes: *Conrad and Imperialism* (London: Macmillan 1983); *Delusions and Discoveries: Studies on India in the British Imagination 1880–1930*, foreword by Michael Sprinker (London: Verso 1998); 'Materiality and Mystification in *A Passage to India*', *Novel. A Forum on Fiction*, volume 31, number 2, spring 1998, 174–94; 'Conrad and England', in *Patriotism: The Making and Unmaking of British National Identity*, iii: *National Fictions*, ed. Raphael Samuel (London: Routledge 1989), 189–98; 'The Content and Discontents of Kipling's Imperialism', *New Formations*, 6 (winter 1988), 84–112; '*Tono-Bungay*: Modernisation, Modernity and Imperialism, or the Failed Electrification of the Empire', *New Formations*, 34 (summer 1998), 91–108. See also Peter Hulme, 'The Locked Heart: The Creole Family Romance of *Wide Sargasso Sea*', in *Colonial Discourse/Postcolonial Theory*, ed. Francis Barker, Peter Hulme, and Margaret Iversen (Manchester: Manchester University Press 1994), 72–88; Sally Ledger and Scott McCracken, eds., *Cultural Politics at the Fin de Siècle* (Cambridge: Cambridge University Press 1995); Nicholas Thomas, *Colonialism's Culture: Anthropology, Travel and Government* (Cambridge: Polity Press 1994).

Zulu War. It is borne out too in the ways that Schreiner and Plaatje continue to construct the metropolitan government and populace as a humanitarian and democratic alternative court of appeal to the legislature and economy of Southern Africa. A colonial discourse analysis that obscures these distinctions, or interprets imperial culture exclusively as the projection of either colonial or metropolitan activities, ideologies, and anxieties— would do well to reread Hannah Arendt here, on the administrative and ideological conflicts that were structural to the New Imperialism's governmental arrangements.[21]

Contra Jameson, the colonized were not absent from metropolitan horizons: in fact, in high as in popular literature, their political agency proved to have considerable impact on metropolitan senses. One example is the Zulu people, who offered formidable resistance to the British when invaded in 1879. The Zulu often function in British popular representations of this period less as metonym of blackness and more as the exemplar of a particular class and/or national–political subject: they indicate an African 'aristocracy' and indigenous structure of 'imperialism'. This was often expressed through the fixation on Shaka, the early nineteenth-century ruler and founder of the Zulu kingdom. In Shaka's 'empire' British metropolitan discourses find an outlet for their own political fantasies of autocratic power, militarism and a centralized hierarchical state organization. For colonial administrators, as my analysis suggests, the story is different: the Zulu feature as political threat to the colony Natal, and as potential labourers to be instrumentalized for production.

Haggard, onetime assistant to Natal's Theophilus Shepstone, reveals the fault-lines of a metropolitan–colonial 'hybridity'; his conflicted loyalties to both metropolitan desire and colonial instrumentality eventually produces a series of contradictory

---

[21] I am using the phrase 'colonial discourse analysis' to refer to the critical field established after Said's *Orientalism*, which follows a loosely Foucauldian notion of 'discourse' and analyses a range of textual materials for its illustration of colonial knowledge/power dynamic. Travel writing has been a favoured genre for 'colonial discourse analysis'. Examples for this period include Sara Mills, *Discourses of Difference: An Analysis of Women's Travel Writing and Colonialism* (London: Routledge 1993); Mary Louise Pratt, *Imperial Eyes: Travel Writing and Transculturation* (London: Routledge 1992); David Spurr, *The Rhetoric of Empire: Colonial Discourse in Journalism, Travel Writing and Imperial Administration* (Durham: Duke University Press 1993).

writings, culminating in *Nada the Lily*. Haggard's turn to
historical fiction about Shaka and his successor Dingane here
needs to be seen as a legitimation crisis, produced by the death
of the Zulu kingdom; it attempts to chronicle the Zulu people
in a way that removes the British from responsibility for this
death. *Nada* rewrites the Zulus as victims, not agents, of
history. Through his emphasis on the fatal destructiveness of
heterosexuality, and femininity, Haggard diminishes the importance of white colonialism as a contributory factor in the decline
of the Zulu nation. And by associating the ruler Dingane's
lechery with his political motivations, Haggard effectively
diminishes the force of Dingane's anti-colonial resistance. A discourse analysis of gender and colonialism needs to recognize
Haggard's manipulation of sexuality to serve as political alibi.
If the novel is read as simply expressive of homosocial desire or
misogyny, this dimension gets lost.[22]

If Haggard can only feature African political resistance by
transforming it into metaphysics or fatal sexuality, Schreiner in
Trooper Peter clearly registers the 1896–7 *Chimurenga*, the
uprising of the Shona and Ndebele people against Cecil
Rhodes's expansionism. Her novel makes no patronizing claims
to speak 'for' Africans; neither does it exoticize or occlude black
Africans (as Conrad does in *Heart of Darkness*). Schreiner
focuses instead upon an immanent critique, through representing the way a colonial trooper transforms himself into an
opponent of colonialism. Yet Schreiner acknowledges the
African people as active agents of resistance, not as pathetic
victims of Peter's liberal charity. And, most striking, Schreiner
situates African women as primary bearers of resistance. The
women are for Schreiner members of a collective movement.
Her trooper Peter, whose opposition stems from his radical
Christian conversion to humanitarianism, operates instead as an
isolated individual who for setting free an African prisoner is
shot by his own captain. Rather than celebrating this for its

---

[22] Gender and sexuality studies of imperial culture are multiplying. See e.g.
Joseph Bristow, *Empire Boys: Adventures in a Man's World* (London: Harper
Collins 1991); Graham Dawson, *Soldier Heroes: British Adventure, Empire and the
Imagining of Masculinities* (London: Routledge 1994); Reina Lewis, *Gendering
Orientalism: Race, Femininity and Representation* (London: Routledge 1995);
Christopher Lane, *The Ruling Passion: British Colonial Allegory and the Paradox
of Homosexual Desire* (Durham: Duke University Press 1995).

individual heroism or turning this into the narrative of a Christian martyr, Schreiner suggests the limited utility of individual resistance within a capitalist social and economic structure. The necessity for *collective* colonial and metropolitan oppositional action is promoted through its very absence. Schreiner presents colonial discourse analysis here with the challenge of accounting for a discourse that is simultaneously idealist and materialist, liberal and radical, both deconstructive and affirmative in its articulation of political action.

For ANC founder member Plaatje, the Union of South Africa and subsequent Natives' Land Act impel a dense meditation on the meanings, forms, and values of African political agency. Plaatje's *Mhudi* selects as catalyst for the novel's action the historical unilateral decision by a chief of the colonized Rolong to murder two imperial Ndebele tax collectors. This murder is presented as both a legitimate act of anti-imperial resistance and a dubiously undemocratic gesture. Plaatje then presents the subsequent alliance of the Rolong with the Boers against the Ndebele as an act of anti-imperial resistance, in which the Rolong have a star role. Plaatje thus contests, and reverses, established white historiography, in which the Rolong were relegated to a merely auxiliary role in this battle. Yet at the same time, this very alliance is also presented as a fundamentally mistaken collusion with the emergent forces of colonialism, and a betrayal of potential pan-African solidarity. Against a Haggardian (and later African nationalist) equation of national history with masculine warfare, Plaatje's novel argues for the central place of African women—as political agents, not static domestic icons of tradition—in building a national narrative.[23] And it is through the women that Plaatje's pan-Africanist ideology emerges, contrasting sharply with the interracial model of male–male bonding which his novel more openly foregrounds.

[23] For theoretical discussion of gender, nationalism and empire (that uses the example of India) see Gayatri C. Spivak, 'Can the Subaltern Speak? Speculations on Widow Sacrifice', in *Colonial Discourse and Post-Colonial Theory: A Reader*, ed. Patrick Williams and Laura Chrisman (Hemel Hempstead: Harvester Wheatsheaf 1993), 66–111, and her 'Subaltern Talk: Interview with the Editors', *The Spivak Reader*, ed. Donna Landry and Gerald MacLean (London: Routledge 1995), 287–308. See also Spivak's 'How to Read a Culturally Different Book', in *Colonial Discourse/Postcolonial Theory*, ed. Francis Barker, Peter Hulme, and Margaret Iversen (Manchester: Manchester University Press 1994), 126–50.

RETHINKING EARLY AFRICAN NATIONALISMS

The Routledge 'New Accents' volume on *The Empire Writes Back*. *Theory and Practice in Post-colonial Literatures* indicates the degree to which theoretical formulations on post-colonial discourse have been taken up at an undergraduate level, and fruitfully conjoined with curricular topics such as 'Commonwealth Literature', 'Post-colonial Literature'.[24] But this recent critical/theoretical spotlight falls almost exclusively on writing and thought of the period of 'independence' and afterwards; lacking is any literary analysis of the writing (non-fictional and fictional) produced by African thinkers, writers, journalists, and politicians during the 'Age of Empire' itself. Such significance as they have been granted is mainly by historians, not cultural critics.[25] Unsurprisingly, perhaps, these early nationalist, pan-Africanist, anti- and 'post'-colonial intellectuals have generally been considered as the territory of antiquarians. These intellectuals produced a considerable body of work, from West and South Africa. From South Africa, in addition to Sol Plaatje, this list includes S. M. Molema; Pixley Seme; the poets I. W. W. Citashe, A. K. Soga, Robert Grendon, John Dube, Mrs A. C. Dube.[26] West Africa produced nineteenth-century thinkers such as James Africanus Horton, J. E. Casely Hayford, Adelaide Casely Hayford, and Edward Wilmot Blyden.[27]

[24] Bill Ashcroft, Gareth Griffiths, and Helen Tiffin, *The Empire Writes Back: Theory and Practice in Post-colonial Literatures* (London: Routledge 1989).

[25] These historians include Hollis R. Lynch, *Edward Wilmot Blyden: Pan-Negro Patriot 1832–1912* (New York: Oxford University Press 1967); Thomas W. Livingston, *Education and Race. A Biography of Edward Wilmot Blyden* (San Francisco: The Glendessary Press 1975); Peter Fryer, ch. 9 'Challenges to Empire', in *Staying Power: the History of Black People in Britain* (London: Pluto Press 1984), 237–97. See V. Y. Mudimbe, ch. 4 'E. W. Blyden's Legacy and Questions', in *The Invention of Africa: Gnosis, Philosophy, and the Order of Knowledge* (London: James Currey 1988), 98–134. Elleke Boehmer, *Colonial and Postcolonial Literature* (Oxford: Oxford University Press 1995) acknowledges this earlier generation of writers, and her *Empire Writing: An Anthology of Colonial Literature 1870–1918* (Oxford: Oxford University Press 1998) includes some extracts.

[26] S. M. Molema, *The Bantu Past and Present: An Ethnographical and Historical Study of the Native Races of South Africa* (Edinburgh: W. Green and Son 1920); Pixley Seme, *The Regeneration of Africa* (New York: Columbia University Press 1906). I. W. W. Citashe, A. K. Soga, Robert Grendon, John Dube, Mrs A. C. Dube, have been collected in Tim Couzens and Essop Patel, eds., *The Return of the Amasi Bird: Black South African Poetry 1891–1981* (Braamfontein: Ravan Press 1982).

[27] James Africanus Horton, *West African Countries and Peoples, British and native: with the requirements necessary for establishing that self-government*

On the whole, these writers have been featured as precursors of the national and cultural liberation movements whose proper birth began in the second half of the twentieth century. Their constitutional reformism has been construed as deriving from a middle-class self-interest; their cultural practices as illustrating anti-colonial thinker Frantz Fanon's 'first stage' of 'native' intellectual development, an 'assimilationist' stance that imitates European codes.[28] Alternatively, their adherence to nationalism itself has been analysed as a version of imperialism itself. By embracing a 'derivative' discourse (nationalism) these nationalists merely repeat the epistemology of imperialism.[29] But Sol Plaatje's novel challenges such assessments. The socio-economic and political consequences of the Union of South Africa in 1910 and the Natives' Land Act of 1913 forced on Plaatje an awareness of the overdetermined dissonances within the formation he knew as British imperialism.[30] *Mhudi* sees him making creative use of these dissonances—in particular, the semantic confusions stemming from the divisions between ideology and practice—as resources for fiction. Plaatje suggests both the

recommended by the Committee of the House of Commons, 1865; and a vindication of the African race (London: W. J. Johnson 1868) and *Letters on the Political Condition of the Gold Coast* (London: W. J. Johnson 1870); Edward W. Blyden, *Christianity, Islam and the Negro Race* (London: W. B. Whittingham 1887); *African Life and Customs* (London: C. M. Phillips 1908); *Africa and the Africans* (London: C. M. Phillips 1903); *West Africa Before Europe* (London: C. M. Phillips 1905); J. E. Casely Hayford, *Gold Coast Native Institutions. With Thoughts upon a Healthy Imperial Policy for the gold Coast and Ashanti* (London: C. M. Phillips 1903) and *Ethiopia Unbound. Studies in Race Emancipation* (London: C. M. Phillips 1911).

[28] Such characterizations of this period are found in Frantz Fanon, *The Wretched of the Earth*, trans. Constance Farringdon (1961; Harmondsworth: Penguin 1985), 166–99. See also Ngugi wa Thiong'o, *Decolonising the Mind: The Politics of Language in African Literature* (London: James Currey 1986).

[29] On this argument see Partha Chatterjee, *Nationalist Thought and the Colonial World: A Derivative Discourse* (London: Zed Books 1986), and his *The Nation and Its Fragments: Colonial and Postcolonial Histories* (Princeton: Princeton University Press 1993). See also *Selected Subaltern Studies*, ed. Ranajit Guha and Gayatri Spivak, foreword by Edward Said (Oxford: Oxford University Press 1988). For important critiques of this approach see Neil Lazarus, *Nationalism and Cultural Practice in the Postcolonial World* (Cambridge: Cambridge University Press 1999) and 'Disavowing Decolonization: Fanon, Nationalism, and the Problematic of Representation in Current Theories of Colonial Discourse', *Research in African Literatures*, volume 24, number 3 (winter 1993), 69–98.

[30] See Sol Plaatje, *Native Life in South Africa Before and Since the European War and the Boer Rebellion*, ed Brian Willan, foreword by Bessie Head (1916; Athens: Ohio University Press 1991).

fluidities of socio-economic, political power and the fixities of race to function as motors of imperial history. It is important to note the precise nature of these historical and conceptual determinants of Plaatje's multilayered and radically decentred national narrative, with its reversible, divided, and deferred signification codes, its irreducibility to a single hermeneutic dynamic or allegorical interpretation.

The models for interpreting anti-colonial literature based on 'writing back to the centre', 'mimicry' or 'hybridity' do not adequately account for the formal, linguistic and ideological textures of his novel.[31] Neither should Plaatje's achievement be taken as evidence of a 'transculturation' process through a cultural 'contact zone'.[32] And *Mhudi* does not simply subvert Western imperialism by reversing the negative valuation placed on Africans, nor does it simply supply an ambassadorial presentation of the equality and parallels of African with English cultures. The triangulated elements of the historical situation on which Plaatje bases his narrative, together with the semantic contradictions of British imperialism of the 1910s, mean that his representations are multiply mediated and more complex than any of the above approaches can suggest.

Similarly, the objective and subjective complexities of Plaatje's African nationalism preclude the interpretation of this narrative as the demonstration of a nationalist subjectivity that repeats the totalizing subjectivity of British imperialism. The nationalism Plaatje articulates is constitutively multiple: its designators, like its constituents, shift. The diverse ethnic, gender and political inflections of Plaatje's nationalism here give rise to diverse temporalities for the African nation (past, utopian/ potential, thwarted, achieved in future Ndebele). This multiplicity is like Plaatje's range of imperialist definitions: historically specific in origin, its literary mediation overdetermined.

---

[31] On 'writing back' as a model, see Ashcroft, Griffiths, and Tiffin, *The Empire Writes Back*. On 'hybridity' and 'mimicry' as models, see Homi Bhabha, 'Of Mimicry and Man: The Ambivalence of Colonial Discourse', *The Location of Culture* (London: Routledge 1994), 85–92.

[32] On transculturation, see Mary Louise Pratt, 'Transculturation and Auto-ethnography: Peru 1615/1980', in *Colonial Discourse/Postcolonial Theory*, ed. Francis Barker, Peter Hulme, and Margaret Iversen (Manchester: Manchester University Press 1994), 24–46. For a critique, see Laura Chrisman, 'Local Sentences in the Chapter of the Postcolonial World', *Diaspora. Journal of Transnational Studies*, volume 7, number 1 (spring 1998), 87–112.

The implications of my analysis of Plaatje's fiction extend to this period of black nationalist writing in general. Such writers need re-examination; their work constitutes a far more radical, complex and ambivalent critique of imperialism than has been recognized. Instead of being conquered by the 'master-narratives' of imperialism, Plaatje's example suggests that these writers may have deliberately exploited the contradictions produced by the political, intellectual and economic activities of the West, developing a polyphonic discourse that addresses and mediates simultaneously an African readership, a Western public, a Western parliament. Future reassessment would involve not only a revision of this particular set of nationalists, nor this period of nationalism alone: it involves a radical retheorization of the nature of nationalism itself, and a major retheorization of black colonial subjectivity.

It is not only the relationship of nineteenth- and early twentieth-century African intellectuals to a metropolitan, white, imperial Europe that demands to be reviewed. Paul Gilroy's *The Black Atlantic* suggestively provides a transnational perspective for the analysis of African-American intellectuals, among them the nineteenth-century Martin Delany, who travelled in Africa, and the young W. E. B. Du Bois, who visited Europe.[33] Gilroy's study stimulates further examination of counter-Atlantic relationships between Africans and African-Americans. Plaatje was

[33] See Paul Gilroy, ch. 1 'The Black Atlantic as a Counterculture of Modernity', 1–40, and ch. 4 ' "Cheer the Weary Traveller": W. E. B. Du Bois, Germany, and the Politics of (Dis)placement', 111–45, *The Black Atlantic: Modernity and Double Consciousness* (London: Verso 1993). W. E. B. Du Bois, *The Souls of Black Folk* (1903; Harmondsworth: Penguin 1989); Martin Delany, *Official Report of the Niger Valley Exploring Party* (New York: T. Hamilton 1861). Another important African-American traveller was Alexander Crummell. See his *Africa and America* (1891; New York: Negro Universities Press 1969) and *The Future of Africa* (New York: Charles Scribner 1862). See Gregory U. Rigsby, *Alexander Crummell: Pioneer in Nineteenth-Century Pan-African Thought* (London: Greenwood Press 1987). For a suggestive discussion of the black Atlantic connections of South Africa and the USA, see Ntongela Masilela, 'The "Black Atlantic" and African Modernity in South Africa', *Research in African Literatures*, volume 27, number 4 (spring 1997), 88–96. For a critique of Gilroy, see Laura Chrisman, 'Journeying to Death: Paul Gilroy's *The Black Atlantic*', *Race and Class*, volume 39, number 2 (Oct.–Dec. 1997), 51–64. For an analysis of black intellectuals in the British metropolis in the 1930s, see Bill Schwarz, 'Black Metropolis, White England', in *Modern Times: Reflections on a Century of English Modernity*, ed. M. Nava and A. O'Shea (London: Routledge 1996), 176–207. For discussion of African-American thought of this period, see Wilson Jeremiah Moses, *The Golden Age of Black Nationalism, 1850–1925* (Oxford: Oxford University Press 1978).

friendly with Du Bois and his *Native Life in South Africa* was partly modelled on Du Bois's *The Souls of Black Folk* (1903). When Plaatje visited the USA and Canada for a two-year speaker tour, he shared public platforms, and developed relationships, with an impressive range of some of the most prominent and influential black activists, thinkers and artists of the day, including Ida B. Wells, Marcus Garvey, James Weldon Johnson, Jessie Fauset, as well as Du Bois. And Du Bois was responsible for the US publication of *Native Life*. The possible two-way influences of Plaatje's relations with these activists and intellectuals needs to be researched. The study of British imperialism and its meanings for African nationalist intellectuals thus demands a comparative and an oppositional reading: the countercurrents of transnational African/American cultures may well transform our understanding of the British empire itself.

UNEVEN TEXTUAL RELATIONS

The readings that follow are close textual studies, guided by three concerns: the uncovery of the novel's internal logic, its ideological 'raw material' and mediatory mechanisms; the contextualization of the novel as a product of, and at times an intervention against, precise contemporary imperial politico-economic processes; the discursive relationship of the novel to other contemporary and earlier literary, social-scientific discourses.

Thus I aim to provide readings that suggest the density of the literary, intertextual relationships among Haggard, Schreiner, and Plaatje, most pronounced in Plaatje's modulation of Haggard's literary genre of the imperial romance, but evident also in a variety of cross-cutting influences and ideological concerns. The local complexity of this trio's interrelations is evident in Haggard's appropriation of a passage from Schreiner's *Story of an African Farm*. Schreiner uses a barter metaphor here in the service of a psychic economy profoundly opposed to principles of exchange; Haggard steals the metaphor for opposite ends, to legitimate capitalist exchange, and break down the very opposition Schreiner establishes between noumenal and phenomenal spheres.

Haggard's appropriation of women's anti-imperialist sentiments was not confined to Schreiner; he does the same with
Lady Florence Dixie's pro-Zulu pronouncements, and this
suggests just how important it is to read imperialist texts as
reactive, derivative, and assimilative, rather than as texts that
precede and totally determine 'reaction' by opponents. If
Schreiner's writing serves in complicated ways as a kind of
matrix for Haggard, it has a similar role in Plaatje's production
of a pro-feminist discourse in *Mhudi*. But Plaatje—who named
his daughter Olive after Schreiner—radically revises Schreiner's
feminism by offering a social-constructionist theory of gender
subjectivity and by applying Schreiner's eurocentric concepts to
African ends, namely an argument for pan-African women's
gender emancipation and solidarity as the means to racial
emancipation from white subjugation.

This local example suggests the larger methodological
challenge of reading imperial culture through its contemporary
contestations, and rethinking the theorization of imperial
hegemony and resistance accordingly. The three writers in this
book do not neatly illustrate a dialectical synthetic relationship.
Haggard's contradictory but ultimately affirmative imperialist
articulations, Schreiner's unevenly materialist and idealist
strains of anti-imperialist critique, and Plaatje's simultaneously
liberal-assimilationist and radical pan-Africanist articulations,
are each too complex to yield to a formula of 'thesis–anti-
thesis–synthesis'. This is not to cast doubts on the value of dia-
lectical analysis itself, but to argue against a Hegelian, idealist
version and for more situated, immanent, and materialist appli-
cations.

As this may suggest, my approach in these critical readings
derives from a conception of authorial—and political—agency;
these writers were not passive vehicles but actively involved in
interpreting, revising, and intervening within and against the
dominant imperialist 'structures of feeling'. Although agents,
these writers do not entirely control the meanings of the writing
they produce. I have not selected them to press them into the
service of an allegorical reading; their representations of British
imperialism need to be seen as significant illuminations, not
microcosms, of the period's cultural political formations. My
approach resists the assumptions of a colonial discourse

analysis that sees different textual genres as interchangeable modes of discourse. What emerges from a study of these three writers is the particular currency of fiction as a distinctive practice for the consolidation and contestation of imperialism. Fictionality, and its relationship with ideology, rather than discursivity, is the concern of this book.

This book issues at a time when the postcolonial theory industry has never been greater.[34] Sceptics and critics have also become increasingly vocal.[35] While some materialist critics see

[34] See e.g. Homi Bhabha, *The Location of Culture*; Gayatri C. Spivak, *A Critique of Postcolonial Reason: Toward A History of the Vanishing Present* (London: Harvard University Press 1999), and *The Post-Colonial Critic: Interviews, Strategies, Dialogues*, ed. Sarah Harasym (London: Routledge 1990). Anthologies of postcolonial theory include Padmini Mongia, ed., *Contemporary Postcolonial Theory: A Reader* (London: Arnold 1996); Patrick Williams and Laura Chrisman, eds., *Colonial Discourse and Post-Colonial Theory: A Reader* (Hemel Hempstead: Harvester Wheatsheaf 1993). Students' guides to the field include Leela Gandhi, *Postcolonial Theory: A Critical Introduction* (Edinburgh: Edinburgh University Press 1998); Ania Loomba, *Colonialism/Postcolonialism* (London: Routledge 1998); Bart Moore-Gilbert, *Postcolonial Theory: Contexts, Practices, Politics* (London: Verso 1997).

[35] Critics and critiques include Aijaz Ahmad, *In Theory: Classes, Nations, Literatures* (London: Verso 1992), and 'The Politics of Literary Postcoloniality', in *Contemporary Postcolonial Theory: A Reader*, ed. Padmini Mongia (London: Arnold 1996), 275–93; David Scott, *Refashioning Futures: Criticism after Postcoloniality* (Princeton: Princeton University Press 1999). Others include Laura Chrisman, 'Inventing Post-Colonial Theory: Polemical Observations', *Pretexts: Studies in Writing and Culture*, volume 5, numbers 1 and 2 (1995), 205–12; 'Questioning Robert Young's Postcolonial Criticism', *Textual Practice*, volume 11, number 1 (spring 1997), 38–45; Neil Lazarus, 'National Consciousness and the Specificity of (post)Colonial Intellectualism', in *Colonial Discourse/Postcolonial Theory*, ed. Francis Barker, Peter Hulme, and Margaret Iversen (Manchester: Manchester University Press 1994), 197–220 and 'Postcolonialism and the Dilemmas of Nationalism: Aijaz Ahmad's Critique of Third-Worldism', *Diaspora. A Journal of Transnational Studies*, volume 2, number 3 (winter 1993), 373–400; Ania Loomba, 'Overworlding the Third World', *Oxford Literary Review*, volume 13, numbres 1 and 2, 1991, 164–92; Anne McClintock, 'The Angel of Progress: Pitfalls of the Term "Post-Colonialism"', in *Colonial Discourse and Post-Colonial Theory: A Reader*, ed. Patrick Williams and Laura Chrisman, 291–304; E. San Juan, Jr, 'On the Limits of "Postcolonial" Theory: Trespassing Letters from the "Third World"', *ARIEL: A Review of International English Literature*, volume 26, number 3 (1995); Ella Shohat, 'Notes on the Post-Colonial', in *Contemporary Postcolonial Theory: A Reader*, ed. Padmini Mongia, 322–34. Benita Parry's critiques include 'Problems in Current Theories of Colonial Discourse' *Oxford Literary Review*, volume 9, numbers 1 and 2 (1987), 27–58; review article of Ahmad's *In Theory*, *History Workshop Journal*, 36 (1993), 232–41; 'Signs of Our Times: A Discussion of Homi Bhabha's *The Location of Culture*', *Third Text*, 28 and 29 (autumn–winter 1994), 5–24; The Postcolonial: Conceptual Category or Chimera?', *Yearbook of English Studies: The Politics of Postcolonial Criticism*, volume 27, Modern Humanities Research Association (London 1997), 3–21. For

no value in claiming allegiance to a domain that includes idealist post-structuralist versions of critical or theoretical analysis, I demur. The challenge as I see it is to create methodologies that fuse the strengths of anti-colonial national liberationist theory, Marxism, feminism, and cultural materialism, to provide dynamic literary practice that is also 'postcolonial'.

critical discussions of postcolonial studies in relation to contemporary South Africa, see David Johnson, 'Literature for the Rainbow Nation: The Case of Sol Plaatje's *Mhudi*', *Journal of Literary Studies*, volume 10, numbers 3 and 4 (1994), 345–58; Kelwyn Sole, 'Writing South Africa', *Alternation*, volume 5, number 1 (1998), 256–66, 'South Africa Passes the Posts', *Alternation*, volume 4, number 1 (1997), 116–51.

Manufacturing Mystery from Mining:
King Solomon's Mines (1)

HAGGARD'S imperial romance *King Solomon's Mines* was composed during a transitional period; South Africa was beginning to assume a major position in the British empire. The emergence of South Africa's mineral industries transformed the country from a service station en route to India to a global centre of industrial production. Historians Shula Marks and Richard Rathbone remark that this transformation created a striking unevenness of socio-economic relations as evident in

the dominance of a highly advanced form of monopoly capital on the gold and diamond fields, with the most sophisticated capital structure and technology, based on a mass of unskilled migrant labour, still dependent on pre-capitalist social formations for its reproduction and controlled by a series of coercive devices such as the compound and pass laws.[1]

A distinctively brutal system of forced labour thus developed. In 1886, John X. Merriman, later to be Prime Minister of the Cape colony, wrote 'The misery of this place [Kimberley] grows on one, the appalling crime and the utter hollowness of our civilization which tolerates such things. I verily believe that never was there a labouring population so utterly debased or treated with such complete disregard of their moral and physical welfare'.[2]

---

[1] Shula Marks and Richard Rathbone, eds., *Industrialisation and Social Change in South Africa: African Class Formation, Culture and Consciousness 1870–1930* (London: Longman 1982), introd., 9–10. See also the volume's three essays on the mining industry by Rob Turrell, 'Kimberley: Labour and Compounds, 1871–1888', 45–76; Kevin Shillington, 'The Impact of the Diamond Discoveries in the Kimberley Hinterland: Class Formation, Colonialism and Resistance among the Tlhaping of Griqualand West in the 1870s', 99–118; Peter Richardson and Jean Jacques Van-Helten, 'Labour in the South African Gold Mining Industry, 1886–1919', 77–98. For a more general history of the region's development, see Deryck M. Schreuder, *The Scramble for Southern Africa. 1877–1895* (Cambridge: Cambridge University Press 1980).

[2] Quoted in Marks and Rathbone, *Industrialisation and Social Change in South Africa*, Introd., 13.

King Solomon's Mines is a contemporary response to this emergence of imperial capitalism.[3] It is also a response to recent archaeological investigations into the nearby ruins of Great Zimbabwe. Haggard conflates these two phenomena to mythologize imperial history and its extraction of mineral wealth. In this chapter, I explore the mechanisms whereby Haggard rewrites the narrative of modern capitalism in South Africa.[4] His reinvention derives from complex dialectics of science and romance, factuality and fantasy (or in Frankfurt School terms reason and myth).[5]

ROMANTIC DOMINATION

Haggard was formative in the development of the imperial romance. His manifesto 'About Fiction' articulates a contradictory rationale for this genre.[6] His antipathy towards bour-

---

[3] *King Solomon's Mines* (London: Longmans, Green and Co. 1885). The edition used here is Penguin (Harmondsworth: Penguin 1972).

[4] See Laura Chrisman, 'The Imperial Unconscious? Representations of Imperial Discourse', *Critical Quarterly*, volume 32, number 3 (autumn 1990), 38–58. Some recent interpretations of *King Solomon's Mines* also allude, in passing, to the book's relationship to capitalist accumulation. See Deirdre David, *Rule Britannia: Women, Empire, and Victorian Writing* (Ithaca: Cornell University Press 1995), 190; Anne McClintock, *Imperial Leather: Race, Gender and Sexuality in the Colonial Contest* (London: Routledge 1995), 257. And see Gail Low, *White Skins. Black Masks: Representation and Colonialism* (London: Routledge 1996), 79–83, for a discussion of how Haggard's fiction creates 'a mythic "interior" space which allows the acquisition of treasure without also having to explain the contemporary history of the diamond boom . . . the narrative allows Haggard to mystify the treasure quest and limit the impact of the white men's discoveries', 83.

[5] I am here using 'myth' as a term to denote a form of thought which is conceived of by modern commentators as the opposite to 'Enlightenment' scientific positivism and rationality, in other words, associated with subjectivism, non-reflection and faith. This notion of myth is central to the arguments of Frankfurt School theorists Max Horkheimer and Theodor Adorno in their *Dialectic of Enlightenment* (1944) which argues that the historical development of reason has culminated in a situation in which rationality itself is inextricable from the condition of myth against which it originally reacted. This inextricability is what animates Haggard's literary project. Patrick Brantlinger's Frankfurtian analysis of Haggard's fiction shares this interest in the mythic, occult subjectivist elements of his writing but sees these as being in uneasy relation to realism. For Brantlinger, Haggard is a writer who 'hesitates at defending his tales as truer than realistic fictions or even as somehow true . . . Haggard often suggests that his stories refer more to his own—or perhaps to universal—dream states than to outward reality' (*Rule of Darkness. British Literature and Imperialism, 1830–1914* (Ithaca: Cornell University Press 1988), 245).

[6] 'About Fiction', *The Contemporary Review*, 51 (Feb. 1887), 172–80. For

geois control of commerce, urban industrialism, and democracy produces Haggard's anti-populist populism, expressed through a commercial cultural medium and a corresponding hatred of the literate masses on which it depends. Romance, for Haggard, opposes the very technology of print-capitalism upon which it constitutes itself. Haggard's aesthetic is functional in idealizing the colonies as sites to rejuvenate a degenerate imperial race and divert potential proletarian insurgence.[7]

The contemporary reviews of *King Solomon's Mines* give a clear indication of the social and political stakes of Haggard's romantic aesthetic.[8] That Haggard succeeds in establishing an unthreatening outlet for popular desires is suggested by an enthusiastic article in *The Spectator*, titled 'Modern Marvels'.[9]

Haggard's later comments on the genre see ch. 16 'Romance Writing', *The Days of My Life,* ii (London: Longmans, Green and Co. 1926), 83–105. See Wendy Katz, ch. 2 'The Politics of Romance', in *Rider Haggard and the Fiction of Empire: A Critical Survey of British Imperial Fiction* (Cambridge: Cambridge University Press 1987), 30–57. Jerome Buckley, *William Ernest Henley: A Study in the 'Counter-Decadence' of the 'Nineties* (Princeton: Princeton University Press 1945) provides a thorough discussion of the romance activist ethic of writers like Henley. Henry Miller is an heir to this romance activist ethic. His account of *The Books in My Life* (London: Peter Owen 1952) devotes two chapters to Haggard's books: ch. 4 'Rider Haggard', 81–99 and ch. 8 'The Days of My Life', 140–6.

[7] Attacks on Haggard as a writer include: 'The Fall of Fiction', *Fortnightly Review*, 44 (1 Sept. 1888), 324–36; 'Culture of the Horrible', *Christian Quarterly Review*, 125 (Jan. 1888), 389–411; 'H Rider Haggard and the New School of Romance', *Time*, 16 (May 1887), 513–24; 'King Plagiarism and His Court', *Fortnightly Review*, NS 279 (1 March 1890), 421–39. A defence of Haggard is found in 'Modern Men. Mr H Rider Haggard', *The Scots Observer*, volume 1, number 23 (27 April 1889), 631–2. Haggard's piece was itself a contribution to an immense debate over the merits of realism and romance, which ranged through a variety of newspapers and journals through the 1880s and included interventions in 1884 by Henry James ('The Art of Fiction', *Longman's Magazine* 4, September) and Robert Louis Stevenson ('A Humble Remonstrance', *Longman's Magazine* 5, December). See Katz, *Rider Haggard and the Fiction of Empire*, 35–6 on these two interventions. See also Patrick Brantlinger's discussion of theories of romance in the realism/romance debates, *Rule of Darkness*, 231–3.

[8] Contemporary reviews of *King Solomon's Mines* include *The Academy*, 28 (7 Nov. 1885), 304–5; *The Spectator*, 58 (7 Nov. 1885, 1473; *The Saturday Review*, [Andrew Lang], 60 (10 Oct. 1885), 485–6; *Public Opinion*, 48 (30 Oct. 1885), 551; *The Athenaeum*, 86 (31 Oct. 1885), 568; *The Independent*, 37 (3 Dec. 1885), 13; *Queen*, 78 (7 Nov. 1885), 512.

[9] 'Modern Marvels', *The Spectator*, 58 (17 Oct. 1885), 1365–6. Haggard presents contemporary fiction as an outlet for popular frustrations aroused by industrial capitalist reification: 'a weary public calls continually for books, new books to make them forget, to refresh them, to occupy minds jaded with the toil and emptiness and vexation of our competitive existence' ('About Fiction', 174). Katz argues that 'the special quality of romance which satisfied the needs of late-

The piece compares Haggard's imaginary activities with the empirical activities of scientific, geographical, and archaeological investigation.

We wonder, now that the whole earth is being searched as with a microscope, and that we are really approaching its secret places—the centre of Africa, the great unexplored islands like New Guinea . . . that antiquarians are inquiring about really interesting antiquities, the origins of the races and of the States,—whether we shall ever find anything really marvellous, anything which will deflect the whole current of human thought . . . We doubt it greatly. (1365)

Ostensibly an impartial assessment of the capacity of modern science to satisfy the human 'lust for wonder', the article reveals a relentless desire to escape the confines of human evolutionism. The anonymous author thus tellingly observes:

Of intellectual changes we can recognize only one, and that excites no wonder. It is even difficult to perceive, unless you watch children closely; but if they are watched, it becomes perceptible, that the Western mind, for good or evil, is releasing itself by some change in its very structure from dependence on authority . . . men are born with harder brains. (1366)

This forms the basis of the author's disquiet, and his approval of Haggard's fiction. If he implicitly allies scientific rationalism with the dynamics and technologies of capitalist global expansion, he also makes explicit science's association with democracy. More people are gaining access to knowledge of the world, and acquiring greater capacity for critical independent reasoning.[10] The author's commendation of *King Solomon's*

Victorian society . . . was its simple avowal of an existence of absolute truths which could pacify a large number of potentially disaffected people' (*Rider Haggard and the Fiction of Empire*, 32).

[10] Haggard's 'About Fiction', 174, actually finds something to praise in the growth of literacy and demand for books: 'In some ways this demand is no doubt a healthy sign. The intellect of the world must be awakening when it thus cries aloud to be satisfied . . . Day by day the mental area open to the operations of the English-speaking writer grows larger. At home the Board schools pour out their thousands every year, many of whom have acquired a taste for reading, which, when once it has been born, will, we may be sure, grow apace'.

What is praiseworthy about this expansion is the greater increase in commercial profit and power (the writer's opportunity to control an expanding 'mental area'). However in his *A Farmer's Year* (London: Longmans, Green and Co. 1899) he qualifies this perspective on 'mental growth': 'The city breeds one stamp of human beings, and . . . the country breeds another. They may be a little sharper in

Mines takes on rather authoritarian overtones in arguing that the book

> has a charm which is not in itself, but in the appeal it makes to a hungry desire or hope . . . the desire that the lust of wonder should be fully and, so to speak, honestly satiated; the hope that men will discover some day somewhere something that shall leave them sufficiently, or it may be permanently, astonished . . . Mr Haggard, in finding Solomon's mines in Southern Africa and describing the marvels which protected them, sets loose, with rare though peculiar skill, a mental motor that is stronger than imagination, and found among more men, existing as it often does in its highest strength among the dull. (1365)

Haggard manipulates this 'lust for wonder', which carries the potential intensity of oppositional or utopian popular desire, to protect social authority against the threat of independent reason. The author's description equivocates between the yearning for 'sufficient' and for 'permanent' astonishment; or, in other words, between the notion of a finite, fulfillable desire and an infinite desire in which the stimulation is, in effect, the fulfilment. Haggard's fiction apparently succeeds in synthesizing these two: his representation of the mines fulfils a finite desire (the heroes' acquisition of the mines' wealth) through which his readers' infinite desire is 'set loose' and safely diverted. The threat posed by popular desire for knowledge and for social transfiguration is safely contained in this medium: set in a plausibly Southern African terrain, anchored in the pseudo-empirical discourses of the 'editor' and the narrator Allan Quatermain, the book simultaneously renders a 'marvellous' narrative. Fiction's promise as a stimulant of social transformation surrenders to the conservative ideology that it is only within fiction that 'wonderful', regenerative and transformative experience can or should occur.[11]

the towns, but after all it is not mere sharpness that has made Great Britain what she is, it is the thews and sinews of her sons which are the foundation of everything, and the even, healthy minds that well in healthy bodies' (466). Katz argues that 'in the romance, experience does not reveal truth so much as validate it. For this reason, a lack of vigorous intellectual struggle, if not anti-intellectualism, prevails. Accordingly, romance exhibits a logical congeniality with messianic interpretations of Empire and with notions of ruling-class stability, both of which also depend upon *a priori* truths' (*Rider Haggard and the Fiction of Empire*, 34).

[11] Haggard's 'About Fiction' contains an attack on French naturalist writers for the way they, in contrast, unleash passion, warning that 'Naturalism in all its

For the author of 'Modern Marvels', the actual operations of scientific discovery must be disparaged as prosaic. The very emphatic mode of his disparagement, I suggest, attests to the opposite: the exhilarating potential that such scientific knowledge holds. The *Pall Mall Budget* reviewer of Haggard's *She* is, in contrast, not afraid to affirm the 'marvellous' properties of contemporary science:

The materials for such inventions lie at everybody's hand. There is a *Dark Continent in which the imagination can expatiate at ease . . . The miracles of science and the marvels reported from the great debatable land between science and superstition*, incline men to widen indefinitely the bounds of what may be called imaginative belief. We have a Napoleonic contempt for the word 'impossible', and are too sceptical to disbelieve anything.(emphases added)[12]

This reviewer confirms the worst fears of 'Modern Marvels', in endorsing an active imagination as common human property prompted by the 'miracles of science' to dangerously imperious heights, 'a Napoleonic contempt for the word "impossible" '. Nevertheless, even this reviewer is concerned, ultimately, to inscribe readers as passive rather than active. He defines their scepticism as a manipulable credulousness rather than a critical autonomy of thought.

horror will take its root among us' (179). France's threat is more than sexual, as is intimated by Haggard's bombast: 'Society has made a rule that for the benefit of the whole community individuals must keep their passions within certain fixed limits, and our social system is so arranged that any transgression of this rule produces mischief . . . We all know, too, how much this sort of indulgence depends upon the imagination, and we all know how easy it is for a powerful writer to excite it in that direction' (176–7). The threat of sexual chaos is simultaneously the threat of social turmoil, in which the masses are ruled by their anti-social desires (physical appetites) and society is ruled by the masses. Should Britain not allow a properly moderated expression and satisfaction of its people's needs (the social reformist argument advanced by several imperialist ideologues), it will become susceptible to socialist terror. Should it not allow in the medium of fiction a sublimation of these desires and needs, in which the spiritual substitutes for the sensual, then not only fiction but British society itself will fall victim. Both its radical political history and its contemporary status as rival for imperial power in Africa overdetermine that France should be associated with political turbulence. The first makes France an obvious symbol of popular and proletarian insurrection and agitation. France's economic threat to Britain's prosperity—a threat not only of control over colonial labour-power but also colonial markets—takes a literal form, in the image of the British book market being taken over by French products. French ideological control over 'the masses' is equated with political control by those masses; both scenarios constitute a foreign condition that divests Haggard's British writer-hero class of their rightful power.   [12] *Pall Mall Budget*, 25 (6 Jan. 1887), 28.

The metaphor of geography is a recurrent, striking feature of this ideological containment.[13] The human imagination can wander around in a 'Dark Continent' of Haggard's making, stimulated by 'the great debatable land between science and superstition' to believe anything it is introduced to during its travels in Haggard land. The more this imagination surrenders to conquest by Haggard's vision, the more it feels itself, ironically, to be the conqueror, possessed of Napoleonic power. Geographical metaphor also features in the hostile article 'The Fall of Fiction'. Haggard's fiction is alleged to contain

examples of the marvellous brought into arbitrary contact with the familiar, over against which it stands without hope of fusion. *Our own mental posture, as his readers, is in consequence one of grotesque ambiguity; we are kept standing with one foot on the dry land of realism, and the other in the deep sea of preternaturalism*, with the result that we can neither swim nor walk. (330) (emphases added)

All these writers characterize Haggard's fiction as a kind of land into which the reader is transported. The land combines terrestrial realism and an extra-terrestrial marvellousness. The author of 'The Fall of Fiction' objects to this generic indeterminacy as having a disempowering effect on the reader. The authors of the *Pall Mall Budget* and 'Modern Marvels' laud such indeterminacy for, effectively, the same reason—the immobilization of the reader's social and critical agency.

SYNTHETIC MINERAL HISTORY

The temporal and ideological conjunction of Quatermain's generation with that of Sir Henry enables a fictional synthesis of two minerals, each associated with different moments within South Africa's mining history. The diamond industry began in 1867; the gold, in 1885–6, the date of Haggard's romance. The treasure cave in *King Solomon's mines* contains chests of both gold and diamonds; the gold has been manufactured into stamped coins, while the diamonds are uncut. The mines them-

---

[13] See also the review of *She*, in *Public Opinion*, 51 (4 Jan. 1887), 38: 'We are grateful to Mr Haggard for carrying us on a pinion, swift and strong, far from the world of platitudinous dulness, on which most young writers embark, to a region limited only by his own vivid imagination, where the most inveterate reader of novels cannot guess what surprise awaits him'.

selves contain diamonds. This was cause of some concern to
contemporary critics. The reviewer for *The Academy* opines 'it
seems a mistake to make the treasure consist of diamonds rather
than of gold; for any precious stones in such abundance as is
here implied would inevitably fall to the value of painted glass,
while it is scarcely possible to conceive an over-production of
gold' (304). *The Spectator* comments archly 'though we do not
remember that diamonds figure in the Scripture catalogue of
that potentate's wealth, we are ready to believe that his treasury
was rich beyond the dreams of avarice' (1473).

Haggard's substitution of diamond for gold may appear to be
simply a means of giving a hyperreal magnitude to the treasure.
In fact, this substitution belongs to a complicated game of
fictionality and empiricism, sustained through explicit references
to factual South African mining and their simultaneous historical falsification. Quatermain's passing references to his discovery of Witwatersrand gold some thirty years earlier posit a
gold site that was only just being discovered at time of composition.[14] Haggard thus reverses the sequence of actual historical
mineral development in South Africa, so that a (suspended)
South African gold industry predates that of diamonds.

I suggest that the actual discovery of gold in 1885 finally
triggers Haggard's fictional production itself. As in Britain, so in
South Africa: the production of wealth is being controlled, in
Haggard's view, by the wrong classes of an international bourgeoisie.[15] In placing gold as an ancient industry, rediscovered by
Allan Quatermain in 1855, Haggard partially removes it from
that contemporary power structure and associates it instead

---

[14] What prompted Evans's initial disclosure of the legend, thirty years back, was
Allan Quatermain's description of 'some wonderful workings I had found whilst
hunting koodoo and eland in what is now the Lydenburg district of the Transvaal.
I see they have come across these workings again lately in prospecting for gold, I
knew of them years ago', 22.

[15] On Haggard's landed gentry origins and ideological affiliations see Katz, *Rider
Haggard and the Fiction of Empire*, ch. 1 'The Days of His Life', 7–29. Anne
McClintock comments that 'Haggard's anti-semitism, of a piece with his antipathy
to mining capitalists and his conviction that imperialism should be in the hands
of the landed gentry, placed Jews in a region of racial belatedness that they shared
with the Zulus' (*Imperial Leather*, 247). Katz discusses Haggard's anti-semitism,
pp. 149–50. See also her comment (55): '[Haggard] would have it that bankers,
financiers, and shady money lenders are distinct from the Empire itself, wild
aberrations on the imperial scene and enemies of the imperial forces represented by
the good old stock'.

with the 'legitimate' classes represented by his trio. That Quatermain did not act upon his original discovery is itself part of this legitimation process: gold is seen to belong by rights to those who have a prior historical claim and at the same time a higher moral claim as attested through the deferral of gratification. On historical, moral, and as we shall later see racial–national grounds, Haggard's trio is constituted as a counter-hegemonic force to the forces which controlled existing South African mineral wealth.

Even as Haggard constructs the novel as an idealized alternative to, and fictional substitute for, the sordid operations of actual gold mining, he simultaneously exploits mining's actuality to legitimize the fiction. When he first hears it, Quatermain will not believe the diamond legend of Solomon's mines because he has not encountered 'real' diamond reserves; the promotion of a rhetorical empiricism and historical referentiality is fundamental to the romance's ideology as a whole. If the real gold and diamond industries serve Haggard's fiction as one source of (fake) authentication, the Bible serves as another. The reviewer of *The Spectator* comments that 'it was a happy thought . . . to make the treasure King Solomon's. That is a name to conjure with as well in the West as in the East . . . It may even be said that the *Scriptural association of the name gives a certain verisimilitude to the story*' (1463) (emphases added). It is this same reviewer who, as we have seen, sharply commented that 'we do not remember that diamonds figure in the Scripture catalogue of that potentate's wealth'.

Haggard uses the Bible to add empirical foundation to his fiction; yet he also tampers with that source by adding to it the most established gem of the South African mineral industry. Diamonds paradoxically then become indicative of pure fictionality and factuality. This is clearly established as the men encounter the mines for the first time, 'a vast, circular hole with sloping sides, three hundred feet or more in depth, and quite half a mile round' (207). Sir Henry and Captain Good respond with astonished stares; Quatermain remarks to them ' it is clear that you have never seen the diamond mines at Kimberley. You may depend on it that this is Solomon's Diamond Mine; look there, I said, pointing to the stiff blue clay . . . the formation is the same' (207).

The result is a fiction in which the modes of romance and realism are safely intertwined and confined, mediating each other.[16] Haggard uses this fusion of scientific and romantic discourses to mystificatory ends. Understanding of these ends is best arrived at through an analysis of earlier and contemporary discourses surrounding Great Zimbabwe. During the early 1870s, Karl Mauch began archaeological investigations into these ruins. The *Illustrated London News* reported on 11 January 1873:

Strange stories have been told of late about the Ophir of Solomon having been discovered. The recently opened diamond mines of South Africa led to explorations further north, which resulted in the revelation of extensive gold mines. Mr Hartley, the lion-hunter, and Mr Mauch, the German explorer, went further, and made known a more northern auriferous district. It is in the last-discovered gold-field that the real Ophir is supposed to have been seen.[17]

Edward Bacon estimates that this 'is probably the first reference in the West to Zimbabwe'.[18] It takes its place among the emergent archaeological research of Schliemann, Maspero, and the Egypt Exploration Fund during the 1870s and 1880s. This research was concerned to ground classical mythology in history. Schliemann, for example, endeavoured to prove that 'Homer did not describe myths, but real events and tangible realities' by locating Troy in The Troad, in 1877.[19] The concern

[16] *The Spectator* (51, 28 April 1888, 569–71) published an excited article, titled 'Reality and Romance', which congratulates a real-life episode (reported in *The Times*) of an attack by 'Arab slave-hunters' on an English mission station near Lake Nyasa for being 'simply chapters iii to viii in [Haggard's] "Allan Quatermain" rewritten'. The article raises some interesting questions about the practical impact of imperial romance on imperial action: 'A steady siege then begins, the Arabs, just as in the romances, showing by their manner of conducting it that "they had among them men trained in some measure to warfare, and accustomed to attack fortified posts". Doubtless all the defenders were great readers of tales of adventure. Imagine their delight when so correct a symptom of the situation developed itself as this', 571. Haggard's chapter on 'Romance-Writing', *The Days of My Life*, vol. ii, provides a catalogue of events that Haggard invented in his romances and which later occurred in real life. These citations of imagination verified by fact suggest his need for sanction by the real, but also something of a superstitious faith in the 'omnipotence of thought'.
[17] In Edward Bacon, ed., *The Great Archaeologists: The Modern World's Discovery of Ancient Ruins as Originally Reported in the Pages of the Illustrated London News from 1840 to the Present Day* (London: Secker and Warburg 1976), 43.   [18] Bacon, *Great Archaeologists*, 43.
[19] From an *Illustrated London News* article on Mycenae, Greece, 31 March 1877. In Bacon, *Great Archaeologists*, 59.

to ratify ancient Western texts extended to the Bible itself. In 1883, a report on 'A Buried City of the Exodus' stated that excavations at Tell-el-Maskhutah revealed

the city under the mound . . . to be none other than Pithoum, the 'store' or 'treasure city' which the children of Israel 'built for Pharoah' (Exodus, i, 11) . . . The first definite geographical fact in connection with the sojourn in the Land of Egypt has been established . . . One short exploration has upset a hundred theories and furnished a wonderful illustration of the historical character of the Book of Exodus.[20]

The popular urge to identify the Zimbabwe ruins with the King Solomon's mines of Ophir belongs to this ideological imperative, the scientific verification of biblical narrative.[21] At the same time, as *The Spectator*'s review indicates, the biblical basis of 'King Solomon's Mines' itself functions to provide a layer of veracity to the fiction.

Zimbabwe was thus claimed by scientific reason and by romanticism. James Bryce's highly regarded book on South Africa devotes an entire chapter to the ruins.[22] He concludes by constructing them as an emblem of unknowability, the point at which scientific knowledge fails:

It is this mystery which makes these buildings, the solitary archaeological curiosities of South Africa, so impressive. The ruins are not grand, nor are they beautiful . . . It is the loneliness of the landscape in which they stand, and still more the complete darkness which surrounds their origin, their object, and their history, that gives to them their unique interest. Whence came the builders? What tongue did they speak? What religion did they practice? Did they vanish imperceptibly away, or did they fly to the coast, or were they massacred in a rising of their slaves? We do not know; probably we shall never know. We can only say, in the words of the Eastern poet: 'They came like water, and like wind they went'. (82)

The chief value of the ruins apparently lies in their mystery, and the speculative opportunities they afford.[23] Such romanticiza-

[20] Bacon, *Great Archaeologists*, 85.
[21] For an account of the Ophir legend, see Hermann and Georg Schreiber, ch. 6 'Silver from Atlantis and Gold from Ophir', in *Vanished Cities*, trans. Richard and Clara Winston (London: Wiedenfeld and Nicolson 1958), 180–223.
[22] James Bryce, *Impressions of South Africa* (London: Macmillan and Co. 1897), ch. 9, 'Out of the Darkness: Zimbabwye', 70–87.
[23] On the value of ancient ruins as providers of 'mystery' and speculation see J.

tion of the ruins is the flipside of an attempt to subject them to 'scientific' scrutiny; both approaches assimilate the ruins into the epistemological narratives of nineteenth-century European imperialism. These narratives are conditioned on occlusion: notwithstanding the fact that the ruins are located in black Africa, they cannot owe their creation to the indigenous population. The production of a mystery to surround them presumes the impossibility of their African origin; this is, effectively, a suppression of the very possibility of African history itself. Bryce does hypothesize concerning the creators of the ruins that they are of Middle Eastern origin. This was the dominant view; it was challenged only after the turn of the century.[24]

Haggard's own non-fictional discourse of Zimbabwe supplies a populist alternative to the highbrow discourse of James Bryce. In his 1896 preface to A. Wilmot's book on *Monomotapa (Rhodesia). Its Monuments, and its History from the most Ancient Times to the present Century*, Haggard claims that the researches have proved the ruins to be of 'undoubtedly of Phoenician origin'.[25] He additionally argues that Phoenicians worked the neighbouring gold mines. Haggard goes on to reveal the ideological connections between this ancient practice of mining and that of present South Africa, mapping a narrative that articulates contemporary racial anxieties and uneasily equates the imperial English with the mine managers and profiteers of antiquity:

A. Cramb, *Reflections on the Origins and Destiny of Imperial Britain* (London: Macmillan and Co. 1900), 215–62. See also Laurence Goldstein, *Ruins and Empire* (Pittsburgh: University of Pittsburgh Press 1977).

[24] For example by the archaeologist D. R. MacIver in *Medieval Rhodesia* (1906), who concluded that '(1) The Rhodesian ruins were built comparatively recently, the date of the erection of the Zimbabwe temple being "not earlier than the fourteenth century AD" and (2) These buildings are the work of "a negroid or negro race of African stock"', quoted in H. A. Wieschhoff, *The Zimbabwe–Monomotapa Culture in Southeast Africa* (Menasha: George Banta 1941), 12. Wieschhoff endorses MacIver's conclusions. See also Hosea Jaffe, *A History of Africa* (London: Zed Books 1985), 7–39, on Zimbabwe–Mwene Mutapa within the history of African communal despotism.

[25] London: T. Fisher Unwin 1896. Haggard's preface is pp. xiii–xxiv.Wilmot was a member of the Legislative Council, Cape of Good Hope. The book's dedication is to: 'The Right Honourable Cecil Rhodes . . . who has been principally the means of giving a new Empire to Britain, and by whose advice and aid the researches into the history of Monomotapa were undertaken.' The direct connection between present imperialism and archaeological research into past 'empire' is explicit.

Gain and slaves were the objects of the voyaging of *this crafty, heart-less, and adventurous race, who were the English of the ancient world without the English honour* . . . A mere trading expedition [to Eastern Africa] was impossible . . . the servants of Solomon could not accomplish their visit to Ophir and return thence with merchandise . . . in less than three years. *Moreover, as is the case to-day, the development and working of the inland mines by the help of native labour* must have necessitated the constant presence and supervision of large numbers of armed and civilized men. It was therefore necessary that these adventurers, sojourning in the midst of barbarous tribes, should build themselves fortresses for their own protection, as it was natural that in their exile they should follow the rites and customs of their fathers. (pp. xvii–xviii) (emphases added)[26]

Through the trope of the Phoenicians Haggard concedes the commercial and expansionist basis of modern England, but is then obliged to assert a moral difference between them. His discourse continues to waver when he goes on to hypothesize the neighbouring fortresses as highly *defensive* constructions. Mining generates the necessity for protection against one's own workforce. There is an implicit if indirect admission here of the violent and onerous costs of capital production, something *King Solomon's Mines* is desperately concerned to repress. The piece concludes with an evocation of mystery, a rhetorical device it shares with Bryce's account:

At what date this Phoenician occupation began, for how many centuries or generations it endured, and when it closed, no man can say for certain, and it is probable that no man ever will be able to say. The people came, they occupied and built, they passed away, perhaps in some violent and sudden fashion such as might well have been brought about by a successful insurrection of their slaves, or by the overwhelming incursion of Arabian or more savage races. (p. xix)[27]

---

[26] See Martin Bernal, *Black Athena: The Afroasiatic Roots of Classical Civilization*, ii: *The Fabrication of Ancient Greece 1785–1985* (New Brunswick: Rutgers University Press 1987), ch. 8 'The Rise and Fall of the Phoenicians', 337–66, esp. 350–5 on 19th-cent. perceptions of the correspondence between the Victorian English and the ancient Phoenicians. See also ch. 9 'Final Solution of the Phoenician Problem', 367–99.

[27] Even Gillian Caton Thompson in her highly respected book *The Zimbabwe Culture, Ruins and Reactions* (1931) feels obliged to affirm 'Mystery'. On accepting the African basis of the ruins she maintains: 'The interest in Zimbabwe and the allied ruins should on this account, to all educated people be enhanced a hundred fold; it enriches, not impoverishes, our wonderment at their remarkable achievement; it cannot detract from their inherent majesty: for the mystery of Zimbabwe is

Earlier on, Haggard suggests more explicitly that:

A new incursion of barbarians took place—how many such have those ruins witnessed? Probably those savages were of the Zulu section of the Bantu race; at least they stamped out whatever civilization . . . still flickered . . . so completely that even native tradition is silent concerning it, and once more oblivion covered the land and its story. (pp. xiv–xv)

Haggard, like Bryce, turns to the device of poetry to illustrate and signify the 'mystery'; here a poem by Andrew Lang performs this function. Because of the ways in which it illuminates the dogged determination to produce the 'Zimbabweans' as victims of (racial, natural, historical) oppression, and its blatant admission of contemporary British materialism it merits quotation:

> Into the darkness whence they came,
> They passed, their country knoweth none,
> They and their gods without a name
> Partake the same oblivion.
> Their work they did, their work is done,
> Whose gold, it may be, shone like fire,
> About the brows of Solomon,
> And in the House of God's Desire.
>
> *The pestilence, the desert spear,*
> *Smote them: they passed, with none to tell*
> *The names of them who laboured here.*
> Stark walls and crumbling crucible,
> Strait gates and graves, and ruined well,
> Abide, dumb monuments of old,
> *We know but that men fought and fell,*
> *Like us, like us for love of gold.*
>
> (pp. xix–xx) (emphases added)[28]

the mystery which lies in the still pulsating heart of native Africa' (quoted in Schreiber, *Vanished Cities*, 223). One racism is substituted for another.

[28] Andrew Lang, anthropologist, mythographer, fairy-tale collector and man of letters, was a close friend of Haggard. Haggard dedicated *She* to him, and the two men together wrote the romance *The World's Desire* (New York: Ballantyne Books 1890). Lang has received some critical attention (see Roger L. Green's *Andrew Lang: A Critical Biography*, Leicester: Edmund Ward 1946), but critics have tended to address the different aspects of his work as autonomous areas, with little attempt to synthesize those aspects or consider their relation to a late nineteenth-century imperialist milieu. This absence of exploration of Lang's connections with imperialism is surprising, given his friendship with Haggard, and his associa-

Gold, then, is the common denominator of antiquity and the present day. The most direct ideological purpose of Zimbabwe would seem to be their provision of a mythical/historical sanction for the present practice of South African mining. The extraction of gold has a biblical precedent.

For Haggard the dependency of the imperial Phoenician mining company on its native labourers generates a fear of their potential power. This power then doubles to become external as well as internal. Not only might the slaves revolt, marauding 'barbarians' might strike. The physically superior African will overthrow the intrinsically precarious empire. This fear is found in many contemporary discourses of empire and frequently figured in the examples of the decadent Roman empire and the decadent Moorish empire, victims of their own physical enervation and the muscular development of barbarian and subject races.[29] The projected overthrow of Zimbabwean mining frequently includes the notion of a sudden interruption. A. H. Keane, for example, makes the suddenness a central feature:

It is to the irruption of these Bantu hordes into Rhodesia that is to be attributed the sudden suspension of the mining operations, the expulsion or extermination of the Semitic prospectors and settlers . . . we saw that there were found unmistakable indications of conflicts, massacres of the old occupants—unburied remains, torn gold-wire

tion with the Indian imperialist writer A. E. W. Mason (with whom Lang also wrote a novel: *Parson Kelly*, London: Longmans, Green and Co. 1900). Partial exceptions are: Katz, *Rider Haggard and the Fiction of Empire*; Brantlinger, *Rule of Darkness*; and Robert Michalski in his 'Divine Hunger: culture and the commodity in Rider Haggard's *She*', *Journal of Victorian Culture*, volume 1, number 1 (spring 1996), 76–97.

[29] See e.g. the lecture *Degeneration Amongst Londoners* given by Dr James Cantlie (London: Field and Tuer, the Leadenhall Press 1885): 'Spain, only yesterday, as it were, fell from being the leader of nations to the position she holds to-day. The Spaniards, held in bondage by the Moor, were for centuries condemned to slave and toil under their hard peasant. But out of the stout hirelings sprang men with strong frames and indomitable courage, and the Moor had now in turn to succumb', 36–7. James Froude is an example of a highly influential, imperialistic contemporary historian who adhered to a cyclical view of history, (largely derived from Thomas Carlyle), in which politically strong nations, and empires, are doomed to enervation and overthrow by (not infrequently) their subject peoples. See the section on 'Froude's Protestant Island' which forms chs. 9 and 10 of John Burrow, *A Liberal Descent: Victorian Historians and the English Past* (Cambridge: Cambridge University Press 1981), 231–85. Froude's anti-industrialism and nostalgia for the feudal England of 'unambitious agricultural freeholders' is very similar to that of Haggard (Burrow, 281).

bangles, scattered beads, and so on. There was unquestionably a total interruption of the works, and of the traffic in gold.[30]

Haggard's *King Solomon's Mines* reveals a fascination for the idea of interruption inscribed in the ruins themselves. Such an interruption pronounces violence to be an essential attribute of black Africans. This representation both acknowledges and disavows the force of imperialist physical, cultural, and epistemological violence against African peoples. It provides in equal measure an outlet for fears of African resistance, and a reversal of imperial practice, by postulating that Africans have erased imperialist history. Having wiped out the narrative of imperial occupation, the Africans themselves are responsible for creating the mystery of Zimbabwe. In these representations, the languages of history and historical interpretation are inseparable from the language of psychology. We have seen how Haggard's non-fictional account of Great Zimbabwe's history covers the land in 'oblivion', a concept that recurs in Lang's poem. Zimbabwe is 'the scene of so much forgotten history and of so many unwritten tragedies'. In effect, a notion of imperial history is fetishistically personified, endowed with a psyche. Conversely, a mythic, essential and singular imperial psyche is postulated and given a history that can, like the gold itself, be 'mined'. A process of scientific discovery converges with a romantic or mystical principle of structural repetition and determinism. This is intensified in the fiction of *King Solomon's Mines*. In mining the region of Southern Africa Haggard's nineteenth-century imperialists represent themselves as repeating an earlier history. They are also finding it, discovering through this fabrication of a unified transcultural psyche their own buried past and raising it from the imperial unconscious to consciousness. Rendering Great Zimbabwe's mining operations as interrupted serves subjective as well as (pseudo) ethnographic ends: positing interruption invites completion.

The forces of scientific reason and realism are expressed, in Haggard's fiction and in the contemporary discourses I have examined, through the ideological backing given to archaeological discovery, empirical investigation, scholarship, linear historical process, biological and social evolutionism. Yet as the

[30] A. H. Keane, *The Gold of Ophir: Whence Brought and by Whom?* (London: Edward Stanford 1901), 181.

above example reveals even the passage of a linear history can be, and is, rendered mythical through the imposition of a notion of a mysteriously continuous imperial psyche. What in fact we see throughout *King Solomon's Mines* is the instrumentalization of the discourses of science for non-scientific, authoritarian ends. From being a mode of apprehension, science is turned into an aesthetic style and a legitimation device conferring authority upon Haggard's imperial ideological project. In this fiction, Haggard moves beyond the non-fictional writings on Zimbabwe by turning the spotlight on to the imperial knowers/dreamers themselves. It is not just the ruins that are invested with these epistemological and ontological qualities but a fabricated, generalized imperial subjectivity itself, which as manifested through the ruins and the British trio is placed beyond scientific reason and human comprehension.

NATURAL PRECEDENTS

Andrew Lang's poem offers two explanations for Zimbabwe's decline: natural factors ('pestilence') succeed racial factors ('the desert spear'). The threat of nature for Zimbabwe predominates in the fictional text, *The Ruined Cities of Zululand*, by Hugh Walmsley (1869).[31] As this is a novel that is known to have influenced Haggard's writing of *King Solomon's Mines*, it is worth a brief examination.[32] The plot of the first volume has many similarities to Haggard's book. Two men, Captain Hughes and the missionary Wyzinski, set out for the fabled ruins that no European has succeeded in reaching. Like Sir Henry and Captain Good in Haggard's text their motive is emphatically non-commercial; they aim 'to prove that our fathers spoke the truth' (49). As in Haggard's text they are accompanied by a noble African (Masheesh, a 'Matebele' chief), and by some lesser African servants (Noti and the 'Hottentot' Luigi) who meet the same unpleasant deaths as Haggard deals

[31] Hugh Mulleneux Walmsley, of the Colonel Ottoman Imperial Army, *The Ruined Cities of Zululand*, i–ii (London: Chapman and Hall 1869). The work is dedicated to 'my brother, Captain Walmsley . . . Govt. Agent, Zulu Frontier, Natal. Founded on a manuscript Received from Him'.

[32] See Norman Etherington's article 'South African Origins of Rider Haggard's Early African Romances', *Notes and Queries*, 222 (Oct. 1977), 436–8.

to his native servants. The journey marks the same progress from natural to human antagonism, from animal to African attacks.

The men also get involved with an African 'tribe' (the Amatonga) which is divided by a cunning, opportunistic chief (Umhleswa) and a courageous deputy (Sgalam). In the Walmsley text the two roles are, interestingly, the reverse of the Haggard text: the bad chief supports the European men, because of the firearms he can obtain from them, while the good deputy is the one who opposes them. As in Haggard, the men are trapped by a vengeful female (Sgalam's wife), and are assisted by a beautiful nurse (though here she is Portuguese, not African). As in Haggard's work, the ruins are associated with a lost white civilization. But there are significant differences in the characterization of the ruins. When Hughes and Wyzinski reach the ruins, nature has already claimed them for herself:

Overshadowing the fallen blocks of stone, the date-tree and palmyra waved their fan-like leaves. Dense masses of powerful creepers crept up the ruins, rending the solid masonry; and the seeds of the trees dropping year by year had produced a rapid undergrowth, those which had once been valuable fruit-trees having degenerated into wild ones. Chaos had, in a word, re-appeared where once trade and prosperity, order and regularity reigned. (168)

When the men manage to chop their way inside a 'ruined chamber', they are met by a huge swarm of bats. Their response to the situation is dismay. 'The day-dream of my life realized. I stand among the ruins of the cities of old; but where they begin, or where they end I know not. The forest has re-asserted her old rights, torn from her by the hand of civilization' (170). After wandering around, 'lost . . . in conjectures on the past', the men conclude that 'it is impossible . . . for us to explore further these relics of the past. We can but tell of their existence' (173). Mystery here proves to be dispiriting, not romantically uplifting. Instead of Bryce's bleakness of landscape, luxuriance and natural fertility prevail. The ruins are both concealed and destroyed by them. It seems that in order for the ruins to effect their magic, they must be preserved in as close as possible a form as the original; an extinct environment is preferable to a live one whose own history usurps that of the ruins.

In striking contrast to *King Solomon's Mines*, the protagonists encounter the ruins well before the end of the book. The ruins thus prove a narrative as well as a subjective anti-climax. Haggard's protagonists encounter the ruins only at the end of the book in a truly climactic episode. While Walmsley's text concerns the interaction of present *nature* with the past civilization, Haggard's mines reveal a concern about the role of financial *economy* within both that civilization and the present. The difference between the thematic emphasis on nature and on the economy marks the difference between a text belonging to the immediate aftermath of Darwin's *Origin*, and one belonging to the era of late Victorian imperialism. For Walmsley, evolutionary competitiveness within nature translates as competitiveness between human society and nature. For Haggard, the forces of nature and evolutionism do not present an adversarial but a potentially cooperative relationship to his romantic imperialist agenda. What threatens that agenda is humanity in the form of racialized resistance, and a capitalism owned by the wrong class.

BUILDING ON THE BIBLE

Haggard's presentation of the mining site in *King Solomon's Mines* rests on a striking constellation of economic, racial, cultural, and sexual concerns. Complexities multiply when we consider the Hebraic elements alongside the Phoenician elements discussed above. For the titular owner of the mines is, after all, King Solomon: the Phoenician traders may have allegedly built the settlement and managed the mines, but as Haggard's title— and the Bible—emphasize, the mine's primary beneficiary is Solomon, just as it is Solomon's narrative which produces and contains this sub-narrative. When the trio of men reach the site of the mine they are greeted by three colossi, whose presence mystifies them until Quatermain recalls that
'Solomon went astray after strange gods, the names of three of whom I remembered—"Ashtoreth the goddess of the Zidonians, Chemosh the god of the Moabites, and Milcom the god of the children of Ammon"—and I suggested to my companions that the three figures before us might represent these false divinities'

(209). Sir Henry likes this suggestion and extends it: 'Ashtoreth of the Hebrews was the Astarte of the Phoenicians, who were the great traders of Solomon's time . . . afterwards was the Aphrodite of the Greeks . . . Perhaps these colossi were designed by some Phoenician official who managed the mines' (209).

In the biblical source it is Solomon's lust for 'strange women' that causes his deviation to false gods:

But king Solomon loved many strange women, together with the daughter of Pharoah, women of the Moabites, Ammonites, Edomites, Zidonians, and Hittites . . . Of the nations concerning which the Lord said unto the children of Israel, Ye shall not go in to them, neither shall they come in unto you: for surely they will turn away your heart after their gods: Solomon clave unto these in love . . . For it came to pass, when Solomon was old, that his wives turned away his heart after other gods . . . For Solomon went after Ashtoreth the goddess of the Zidonians, and after Milcom the abomination of the Ammonites . . . Then did Solomon build an high place for Chemosh (1 Kings, 11: 1–7)

The entrance to King Solomon's Mines is correspondingly marked by a colossal testament to Solomon's seduction by an Eastern pleasure principle: the horned feminine deity of Ashtoreth. This sets up the possibility of a connection between Solomon's pursuit of wealth and his sexual desire. If the latter involves him in religious, cultural, and racial betrayal through miscegenation, the same associations taint the former.

Biblical commentators of this period reinforce this cluster of associations. C. W. Emmet, in the 'Solomon' entry of the *Dictionary of the Bible* (1909), asserts that Solomon's fall 'is connected with his polygamy and foreign wives. He not only allowed them their own worship . . . but shared in it . . . This idolatry was, in fact, the natural syncretism resulting from his habitual foreign intercourse. Self-indulgence and the pride of wealth evidently played their part in his deterioration'.[33] Solomon's sexual and financial desires are identified, coded as excessive and inextricable from the degenerate experience of (Oriental) cultural hybridization. For this commentator, the Eastern influence on Solomon was political also:

He consolidated the kingdom, welding its disorganized tribal divisions together into a short-lived unity, *by the power of an Oriental*

[33] James Hastings, ed., *Dictionary of the Bible* (New York: Charles Scribner's Sons 1909), 870.

despotism . . . More than any other Jewish king, he realized the importance of foreign alliances, which were closely connected with his *commercial policy*. [Re his marriage to Pharoah's daughter]: Solomon was
able to control, and no doubt profited by, the caravan trade between
the Euphrates and the Nile . . . From Egypt . . . came horses and
chariots for Solomon's own use, and for the purposes of a Syrian trade.
(868–70) (emphases added)

The inevitable consequence of Orientalization is, it seems, the
socially unjust, theatrical misuse of acquired wealth. Emmet's
final judgement is a full-scale indictment of Solomon's achievements as political, economic, cultural, and sexual disasters:

The impression is given us of great wealth . . . But the gold was used
chiefly in unproductive forms of display, and probably but little was in
circulation among the people; he had a difficulty in paying Hiram. His
passion for buildings was extravagant . . . By his personal popularity
and extravagant display Solomon won a great 'name', and gave Israel
a position among the nations. His reign came to be idealized, but his
policy was clearly economically and socially unsound, and could only
lead to ruin. (869)

George A. Barton, author of the 'Israel' entry in the same
dictionary, shares this judgement and further links Solomon's
seduction by Eastern despotism and sexuality to his cultivation
of an Egyptian 'imperial' architecture. Barton, like Emmet,
again alleges the socio-economic costs of such achievements:

Solomon, born in the purple, determined to bring his kingdom into
line with the great powers of the world. He accordingly consummated
a marriage with the daughter of Pharoah, probably one of the Pharoahs
of the Tanite branch of the 21st century. This marriage brought him
into touch with the old civilization of Egypt. In order to equip his
capital with public buildings suitable to the estate of such an empire,
Solomon hired Phoenician architects, and constructed a palace for
himself one for the daughter of Pharoah, and a Temple of such
magnificence as the rustic Israelites had never seen . . . there is no
doubt that in the way of luxury they [these buildings] far surpassed
anything previously known in Israel. The whole pile was approached
through a hypostyle hall built on Egyptian models . . . These religious
innovations were looked upon with disfavour by many of Solomon's
contemporaries, and the buildings, although the boast of a later age,
were regarded with mingled feelings by those who were compelled to
pay the taxes by which they were erected . . . His method of living
was of course in accord with the magnificent buildings which he had

erected. To support this splendour the old system of taxation was inadequate, and a new method had to be devised. (393–417)

This commentary allows us to attach further significance to *King Solomon's Mines*'s encounter with the ancient mines and their sculptural paraphernalia. Earlier I pointed to the precariousness, for Haggard, of the ancient mineral-producing civilization. For commentators on the Great Zimbabwe this fragility issued from a threat that was internal—the existence of a potentially insurrectionary slave work force—and external—violent southern-migrating 'Bantu' peoples. Haggard's emphasis on Solomon's rule and his corruption introduces several additional elements to the fragility of ancient mining production. As we have seen, the Phoenicians represent for Haggard a maritime trading people whose own nomadic nature has been converted by the exigencies of this particular venture. The development of Solomon's mineral wealth has required settlement. The traders accordingly transmute into a managerial class who control the means of production. They are divided not only by class but also by race and (originally) culture from the Jewish power that owns production and is stationed overseas.

It does not require too much of a stretch of imagination to apply this scenario to the emergent South African mineral industries of Haggard's time: an international and/or overseas financial-capitalist class owning the mines, a nationally diverse class of managers, and a predominantly African workforce. What bothers Haggard, I think, is not only the political threat posed by an exploited, collective workforce, but also the disparate geographical, ethnic, and cultural bases of the managerial and the bourgeois, production-owning classes here. The latter, like Solomon, own the exploited land but live in another, and while providing nothing by their own labour own the 'stamp' impressed on the coins. Their sole, and blatant, concern is economic profit.

A corrective to this dispiriting scenario is invented within the pages of *King Solomon's Mines*. Sir Henry takes the place of the absentee and corrupted, profit-seeking Solomon, supplying active leadership, familial responsibility, and altruistic idealism, all of which entitle him to a more 'legitimate' ruling class relationship with the mines and their wealth. The colonial and trader Allan Quatermain occupies the managerial place of the

ancient Phoenicians and the present mine management. Captain
Good supplies the naval (sailing) power and also manual labour.
The trio of men together supplies the fantasy of a culturally,
nationally, and ethnically homogeneous ensemble whose divi-
sion of labour absorbs the mining workforce into itself. Labouring to acquire the treasure themselves, the trio have to re-enact
the uncomfortable underground movements of the original
miners. Labour becomes free rather than coerced, and unlike
Solomon, entitles the men to the wealth they gain.

The fantasy guiding the construction of Haggard's trio, in
their encounter with Great Zimbabwe/Solomon's Mines, is the
transformation of a multinational capitalist phenomenon into
an exclusively national one. The men also supply a corrective to
Solomon's 'Orientalized' sexuality and its racial, cultural,
and political co-ordinates. Utilitarianism replaces (feminine)
aestheticism; homosociality replaces heterosexuality; Anglo-
Saxonism replaces Jewish/Eastern (sexual and cultural) syncretism; a hierarchical 'fair' teamwork replaces 'unjust' Oriental
despotism; propriety replaces luxury, excess and transgression.
The association of mining with greed, racial and national diversity, and sexual corruption can now be confined to a single
chapter in an unfolding narrative of imperial legitimation. (That
this fantasy is undermined in a number of ways will be discussed
in the next chapter.)

CONCLUSION

Haggard's representation of a legitimate form of imperial
mineral wealth needs to be understood as a version of Adorno
and Horkheimer's 'dialectic of enlightenment'. The critique of
existing capitalist modes of production proceeds by the invention of a hybrid genre that synthesizes modalities of realism
and romance to the ultimate end of an authoritarian (and indeterminate) mystique. Haggard's 'proper' political economy
posits a mythic identity between ancient and (imaginary) contemporary imperial processes only to contradict that identity by
the accentuation of ancient 'inferiority'. Ultimately it is not the
contrary claims of scientific rationality and mythic irrationality,
factuality and invention, that is important here but their formal

equality and interchangeability in Haggard's discourse: their abstraction, that is, into an empty form, the contents of which are simply a question of style.

The legitimacy of imperial capitalism comes to depend not on the process of production but on the identity of the capitalists, a hybrid class of metropolitan and colonial nobility and trade, middle-aged and young; united in their nation (England) and their exclusion from existing centres of socio-economic power. If we can read off from this a number of national, racial, and sexual anxieties, we must be careful to acknowledge the political and economic components of these anxieties. For Haggard, the threat to imperial power and identity is certainly racial and sexual—but never abstracted from the labour relations of mining itself. The threat to the Zimbabwean mines of the past was from African slave labour and/or marauding 'Bantu' peoples, and also from the racial and national divisions between managerial and ruling classes. A racially homogeneous production unit would seem to be essential to ensure security of both production and accumulation. Also the on-site domination and responsibility of political leaders: no absentee King Solomon, corrupted by sexual desire to the excessive pursuit of wealth and loss of political integrity, but only a non-sexual imperial British stock is, in Haggard's view, entitled to power and profit.

2

Trading on Africa:
King Solomon's Mines (2)

HAGGARD'S imperial fiction genre projects an ideal British
subject composed of a cross-generational alliance of landed
gentry, colonial trader and naval officer. The romance also
projects an ideal African subject, a pastoral-military hybrid
people through which the British realize themselves as the
proper subjects of imperial narrative.[1] In this chapter I will
examine the politics of representation of the British and
Africans, and argue that they are governed by an instrumental
reasoning inextricable from imperial capitalism.[2] This is most
pronounced in Allan Quatermain, whose subjectivity as trader
both hides and reveals a capitalist logic of exchange value
throughout the narrative. African bodies literally contain
economic value for the British, which usually becomes evident
when the Africans meet their death and are reduced to an
abstracted monetary equivalent.[3] The African Kukuana are

[1] On pastoralism in Haggard's fiction, see Gail Low, ch. 2 'The Dominion of
Sons', *White Skins. Black Masks: Representation and Colonialism* (London:
Routledge 1996), 36–65. Useful general discussions of imperial and colonial con-
structions of primitivism are to be found in Nicholas Thomas, *Colonialism's
Culture: Anthropology, Travel and Government* (Cambridge: Polity Press 1994),
ch. 6 'The Primitivist and the Postcolonial', 170–95; Marianna Torgovnick, *Gone
Primitive: Savage Intellects, Modern Lives* (Chicago: University of Chicago Press
1990). Intelligent discussions of *King Solomon's Mines*'s romantic structure are Jeff
D. Bass, 'The Romance as Rhetorical Dissociation: The Purification of Imperialism
in *King Solomon's Mines*', *The Quarterly Journal of Speech*, 67 (1981), 259–69;
Richard F. Patteson, '*King Solomon's Mines*: Imperialism and Narrative Structure',
Journal of Narrative Technique, 8 (1978), 112–23.
[2] A related discussion of commodity logic in late Victorian culture is to be found
in Thomas Richards, *The Commodity Culture of Victorian England: Advertising
and Spectacle, 1851–1914* (London: Verso 1991).
[3] On the economic value of the biological body, see the social Darwinist and
eugenic writings of Karl Pearson, *National Life from the Standpoint of Science*
(London: Adam and Charles Black 1901). In Pearson, the discourses of mid-19th-
cent. political economy are rhetorically discredited: the analysis of the process of
capitalist production and accumulation, and the categories of class and class conflict, are to be replaced by a methodology appropriate to the late Victorian period,
one which situations the human body as 'capital' and replaces class with race.

also significant for what they reveal about British concepts of
political authority, opposition and justice, and the racial double
standard that consistently undercuts them.

PROPER ENGLISH GENTLEMEN

Haggard's model of British imperial authority involves more
than the fusion of metropolitan with colonial subjects; it
involves a fusion of generations and classes. Haggard's conjunction of a man of Quatermain's generation with two men of
the next generation suggests the invention of a family relationship and a reciprocity between two distinct moments of South
Africa's and imperial Britain's history.[4] To the newly emergent
generation of metropolitan-imperial capital is linked the 'old'
generation of settler-colonial mercantilism. Haggard's imagination foregrounds the concept of 'generation' by accentuating the
age of 25 rather than 21 as the age of individual majority. He
also intertwines his own biographical chronology with his trio
of British imperial protagonists, thereby reciprocally reinforcing
his own imperial authority along with his protagonists.

'Nearly 30 years ago' Allan Quatermain first encountered the
legend of King Solomon's Mines: in 1856, the birth year of
Haggard himself and the fictional Sir Henry. Allan Quatermain
is 55, making him 26 at the time of the younger men's birth and
the simultaneous transmission of the legend to his ears. It is only
when a man is of the age to symbolically assume patriarchal
status, to become self-reproducible, that he is equipped to take

---

[4] On the politics of generations and cross-generational alliances, see Anne
McClintock, *Imperial Leather: Race, Gender and Sexuality in the Colonial Contest*
(London: Routledge 1995), e.g. 241 on *King Solomon's Mines* as a 'family romance
of fathers, sons and brothers regenerating each other'. See also Low, *White Skins.
Black Masks.* This concern with cross-generational alliances is linked to a contempt
for the contemporary young generation, evident in e.g. James Cantlie's *Degeneration Amongst Londoners* (London: Field and Tuer, the Leadenhall Press 1885)
which alleges that: 'A democratic negativeness is what seems to be the aim and goal
of the rising generation', 47. Cantlie continues 'It is the *young* people now-a-days
who shape manners for their *elders* . . . The generation now passing away are
taking all the enthusiasm with them; it is the *old*, not the young people who are
enthusiastic. *They* spread our civilisation, made themselves rich and widened our
Empire, until now there seems not much more to do', 49–50. See Haggard's 'About
Fiction' for its attack on the culture of the schoolgirl (*The Contemporary Review*,
51, Feb. 1887), 172–80.

on the challenge of a legendary narrative and become author to his own narrative. Those like Sir Henry's younger brother who undertake such events before the age of 25 do not succeed. Although the trio and their age levels assume symbolic significance, they are not 'typical' representatives of their countries and eras. Sir Henry and Captain Good have a marginal and atypical relationship to the contemporary processes of British socio-economic development both in Britain and in South Africa. They are portrayed as victims rather than leaders of actual capitalist modernization; Sir Henry belongs to a rural England overtaken by urban production, while Captain Good's naval office is forcibly retired rather than receiving due recognition and promotion for its services to the Crown.

If in creating Sir Henry and Captain Good Haggard is criticizing the existing dispensation of metropolitan power, and substituting for it an idealized model of such power, a similar dynamic of criticism and imaginary correction is at work when Haggard constructs a harmonious, interdependent trio of colonial and metropolitan men. The reality of contemporary South African colonial and British metropolitan relations was far from harmonious, characterized as it was by frequent clashes of politico-economic interests and mutual mistrust.[5] Haggard's representation reconciles such divisions, arguing a complementarity of interests, values and qualities. In making Quatermain a colonial settler, Haggard also avoids the representational dilemmas that arise from metropolitan society. Elsewhere Haggard suggests that the activity of trade is worthy only of condemnation for its association with urbanism, profiteering and an international self-interest that acts against British national interest. 'Trade' in the metropolis signifies nothing other than industrial and financial capitalism as operated by the bourgeoisie. Thus *A Farmer's Year* sees Haggard inveighing against the way

Countries in China, Central Africa, anywhere, must be seized or hypothecated to provide 'new markets'—even 'at the cost of war'—for this is fashionable and imperialistic, and it is hoped, will bring profit

[5] See Hannah Arendt's far-ranging important discussion on imperialism as a political and economic phenomenon, in *The Origins of Totalitarianism* (1951; London: André Deutsch 1986), 123–302. She gives special attention to South Africa as the 'culture-bed' of British imperialism. Her discussion of 'Bantus' and 'Boers', 190–7, is however the least laudable of the section.

to the people with the most roles and influence, the traders and dwellers in the towns. (emphases added)[6]

Similarly, Haggard's 1916 'Land Settlement and Empire' interview equates trade with urbanity in the context of Australia: 'Take Australia, with nearly half its population living in the great cities! What are they living on? Really on the primary producers living on the land. *The others are middlemen, so to speak, traders,* and so forth' (emphases added).[7] By removing Quatermain's trading activities to South Africa Haggard bypasses such negative equations. Instead Quatermain's trading becomes part of a repertoire of labour activities—'trading, hunting, fighting, or mining' (11). He sells the fruits of his own mental or physical labour. Trading, now purged of its associations with bourgeois profiteering, is thus realigned with 'primary' production. However, Haggard retains—indeed, valorizes—certain metropolitan qualities in Quatermain, associated with the role of 'middleman'. Quatermain's trading involves the exercise of mediatory exchange rationality; he also serves as the fiction's narrator who mediates the romance.

Through Quatermain exclusionary definitions of 'gentleman' class are destabilized to allow the common reader to claim inclusion in such a class.[8] Quatermain's candour about his economic needs identifies him as one involved in 'honest labour'; his neediness contrasts with Sir Henry's ample inheritance. When the trio are offered 'white stones' by Ignosi should they assist him to wage war against his usurping uncle, Sir Henry declines: 'Wealth is good, and if it comes in our way we will take it; but a gentleman does not sell himself for wealth' (127). Allan Quatermain, in contrast, is prepared to sell his services: 'I am a trader, and have to make my living, so I accept your offer

[6] *A Farmer's Year* (1899; London: Longmans, Green and Co. 1906), p. xi. See Alun Howkins, 'Rider Haggard and Rural England: An Essay in Literature and History', in *The Imagined Past. History and Nostalgia*, ed. Christopher Shaw and Malcolm Chase (Manchester: Manchester University Press 1988), 81–94, for the argument that Haggard's 'attack on commerce is central to [his] view of the human male and his view of colonialism and civilisation' (83).

[7] 'Land Settlement and Empire. Interview with Sir Rider Haggard', *Lloyd's Weekly News* (26 Nov. 1916), 3.

[8] See Howkins, 'Haggard and Rural England', for a discussion of Allan Quatermain and the notion of a gentleman in Haggard's imperial fiction. Howkins argues that the notion 'is not a construction of birth or place . . . but of 'type', 85.

about those diamonds in case we should ever be in a position to avail ourselves of it' (127).

The 'gentleman' theme proved to be one of the more contentious aspects of Haggard's romances. The authors of both 'The Fall of Fiction' and a review in *The British Weekly* attack Haggard's dedication of *Allan Quatermain* to his son 'in the hope that . . . he, and many other boys whom I shall never know, may in the acts and thoughts of Allan Quatermain and his companions, as herein recorded, find something to help him and them to reach to what . . . I hold to be the highest rank whereto we can attain—the state and dignity of English gentlemen'.[9] Gavin Ogilvy believes that the fiction 'is more likely to make boys bloodthirsty blackguards' than gentlemen, and 'The Fall of Fiction' demurs that 'We had always supposed that a certain modesty and temperance of statement, a certain sobriety of intellectual tone, were among an English gentleman's typical traits. We had thought, too, that among the features notably absent from an English gentleman might be reckoned a gloating delight in details of carnage and horror and ferocity for their own ghastly sake' (325).

For Haggard it is indeed the issue of killing upon which the definition of 'gentleman' rests. The opening of *King Solomon's Mines* skilfully highlights these issues in a way that actively co-opts the reader. 'I, Allan Quatermain, of Durban, Natal, Gentleman, make oath and say—'he begins, and then self-interrupts that

Somehow it doesn't seem quite the right way to begin a book. And, besides, am I a gentleman? What is a gentleman? I don't quite know, and yet I have had to do with niggers—no, I'll scratch that word 'niggers' out, for I don't like it. I've known natives who *are*, and so you'll say, Harry, my boy, before you're done with this tale, and I have known mean whites with lots of money and fresh out from home, too, who *ain't*. Well, at any rate, I was born a gentleman, though I've been nothing but a poor travelling trader and hunter all my life, Whether I have remained so I know not, you must judge of that. Heaven knows I've tried. I've killed many men in my time, but I have never slain wantonly or stained my hand in innocent blood, only in self-defence (12–13).

[9] 'The Fall of Fiction', *Fortnightly Review*, 44 (1 Sept. 1888), 324–36; Gavin Ogilvy [J. M. Barrie], *The British Weekly. A Journal of Social and Christian Progress*, 2 (5 Aug. 1887), 218.

Rejecting 'official' legal modes of self-designation, Quatermain appears to relinquish the authority that goes with them, and with that, the confident claim to 'gentleman'. While inviting the reader to exercise free judgement about his own character—'Whether I have remained so I know not'—Quatermain at the same time retains full confidence in his powers to judge and define 'gentlemanliness' in Africans and other whites. In so doing he commands reader agreement: 'I've known natives who *are*, and so you'll say, Harry, my boy, before you're done with this tale. . . ' Both rhetorical tactics—that of confidently labelling others and of questioning his own label entitlement—invite reader trust and identification. Gentlemen are defined not through socio-economic class, race, or heredity but through moral behaviour that includes the use of 'polite' language—'native' rather than 'nigger'. This opening of the boundaries itself facilitates reader self-identification as a gentleman. This in place, the reader is stationed to support the book's ultimate definition of gentlemen as those who fight bravely and kill heroically for a just cause. Against Sir Henry's stipulation, traders can in fact prove to be gentlemen.

TRADE, EXCHANGE AND AN AFRICAN WAY OF DEATH

However determined Haggard is to present Quatermain's trading as oppositional and superior to capitalist processes of accumulation, he cannot avoid revealing an identity between the two. Quatermain's bartering is, in the end, indistinguishable from capitalism: the principle of direct exchange of goods/use-values upon which bartering is based develops here into a mediated abstraction, producing an instrumental and commodified account of human life. The climax of the novel—the trio's encounter with the treasure in the mines—argues, ostensibly, that human life and the pursuit of capital accumulation are based on incompatible value systems. Indeed, financial wealth is not merely 'valueless' and 'useless' when compared to the value of live bodies but is aligned with death.[10] Trapped in the cave, Quatermain opines

[10] On Haggard's view of human population or bodies as 'real' wealth, see his

There around us lay treasures enough to pay off a moderate national debt, or to build a fleet of ironclads, and yet we would gladly have bartered them all for the faintest chance of escape. Soon, doubtless, we should be glad to exchange them for a bit of food or a cup of water, and, after that, even for the privilege of a speedy close to our sufferings. Truly wealth, which men spend all their lives in acquiring, is a valueless thing at the last. (230–1)

Although Haggard does not acknowledge his debt, it is clear that he got the idea of this bread/gold bartering image from Olive Schreiner's *The Story of an African Farm*, one of the three books he singles out in his essay 'About Fiction' as being exceptionally fine.[11] The passage there runs 'bread is corruptible, gold is incorruptible; bread is light, gold is heavy; bread is common, gold is rare; but the hungry man will barter all your mines for one morsel of bread' (268). This passage occurs as part of Waldo's efforts to come to terms with the death of Lyndall. He rhetorically proceeds through various Christian and Transcendentalist approaches to mortality, in which the prospect of a 'gold' spiritual Lyndall is juxtaposed with her 'bread' or terrestrial form. However as the passage suggests the hungry Waldo is not consolable by this offer of gold. Schreiner's barter language articulates a psychic economy profoundly opposed to principles of exchange. Resistant to the Hereafter, this earthly soul not only cannot be 'bought' by such transcendental reasoning but considers it a theft: 'Give me back what I have lost, or give me nothing . . . Rob me of the thoughts, the feelings, the desires that are my life, and you have left nothing to take' (268).

In lifting the scene, Haggard appears to have transposed it from a figurative to a literal domain. His 'gold' is itself a phenomenal or material, not transcendental, substance; his 'bread' refers not to a beloved person but an object on which

---

Speech to the Canadian Club, March 1905: 'all the world is mad on trade, all the civilised world, at least, has got the idea that wealth is everything. I controvert that statement: I say that wealth is nothing. What is wealth without men and women to use it and spend it? . . . healthy men and women . . . these are the real wealth of the nation', *The Days of My Life* (London: Longmans, Green and Co 1926), ii. 271. Haggard was fond of this argument: it recurs in his 'Land Settlement and Empire' interview, in which he accompanies it with a reference to his own allegorical example of the mines scene in *King Solomon's Mines*, 3.

[11] *The Story of an African Farm* (1883; Harmondsworth: Penguin 1939). Haggard commends it in his 'About Fiction', 180.

depends physical survival itself. However the relationship between the two passages is actually more interesting and more complex.[12] Haggard performs a series of discursive and ideological alterations: for the three heroes, the opposition between bread and gold, physical nourishment and capital accumulation is ultimately broken down as the treasure takes on associations of food, something which prolongs rather than threatens their life.

At the same time, sexual romanticism—which features in the narrative of Captain Good's relationship with Foulata—undergoes the very transformation that Schreiner's narrative claims impossible. From being a threat to the survival of the imperial narrative and trio, Foulata's love is transmuted into a sublimated spiritual 'gold' which confirms their legitimacy. And at the same time, and through the very same actions, the surplus gold and diamond treasure is coded as both a transcendental symbol *and* a feminized signifier of illicit, excessive material desire. Haggard's theatrical presentation of this scene as a medieval tableau, a morality play in which the men learn that the greedy pursuit of wealth leads only to death, is then highly misleading. However, in one crucial way it is entirely accurate: the pursuit of material acquisition by British imperialists does indeed here lead to the death of black Africans. Foulata and Gagool both die in the mines. What is more, this is the culmination of a pattern followed throughout the fiction whereby white gain is equated with black death. Not for nothing is the Place of Death—the burial chamber of the African kings—situated in the entry to King Solomon's Mines.

The pattern commences with the self-sacrificial death of Khiva, who dies to save Captain Good from an enraged elephant. Umbopa remarks that Khiva 'died like a man' (55). Quatermain starts the next chapter with an account of the extraction of ivory. His account emphasizes the physical magnitude of the tusks and their implicit corresponding market value as ivory. The distress which Khiva's death has allegedly caused them is overtaken by a graphic calculation of the weight of the ivory which his death has enabled them to acquire:

[12] Robert Michalski reaches a similar conclusion that 'the apparent antagonism between the spiritual and the commercial which Haggard superficially professes breaks down', 'Divine Hunger: Culture and the Commodity in Rider Haggard's *She*', *Journal of Victorian Culture*, volume 1, number 1 (spring 1996), 88.

it took us two days to cut out the tusks and get them home and bury them carefully in the sand under a large tree . . . It was a wonderfully fine lot of ivory. I never saw a better, averaging as it did between forty and fifty pounds a tusk. The tusks of the great bull that killed poor Khiva scaled one hundred and seventy pounds the pair, as nearly as we could judge. As for Khiva himself, we buried what remained of him in an ant-bear hole, together with an assegai to protect himself with on his journey to a better world. (56)

Governing all of this is a somewhat rigged system of exchange. The Zulu Khiva exchanges his life for the posthumous accolade of masculinity ('he died like a man'), gained through the femininity of an entrousered Good. The trio trades in a servant for the wealth of ivory; to boot, there is the spiritual profit from the affirmation of the African servant's unswerving fidelity.

The next stage in this transaction between African death and British gain is more complicated, involving as it does the increased national stratification into British, Portuguese and 'Hottentot'. When they have crossed the desert, the men reach the mountains and spend a night there during which their 'Hottentot' servant Ventvogel dies from cold. The respective modes of death of these two servants are fitting to the different values ascribed to by Haggard to Zulu and 'Hottentot' peoples. Haggard's estimation of the 'Zulu' qualities of military prowess, fearlessness and selflessness is a high one. The relatively high value of these qualities is reflected in the high value of the ivory that Khiva's death commands. 'Hottentot' people, by contrast, rate much lower for Haggard in social and evolutionary terms: their worth to the imperialist quest here rests in their 'animal' qualities of olefactory skill. When they are desperate for water, it is Ventvogel who smells the pond at the top of the hills. After its discovery, his skills have no further utility for the trio, and he is free to be killed off.

Khiva's death increases the British stock by virtue of its bravery. Ventvogel's death comes about not through a feat of bravery but through physiological weakness. His value lies precisely in his physical inferiority to and instrumentalizability by the British, which he shares with the ancient Portuguese Dom.[13] Unlike the Dom, however, and unlike Khiva, he is not

---

[13] On the British disdain for Portuguese imperialism, see Dorothy Hammond and Alta Jablow, *The Africa that Never Was: Four Centuries of British Writing about Africa* (New York: Twayne 1970), 82.

deemed worthy of inclusion as a subject in a mutually beneficial exchange system. Ventvogel effectively replaces the slave who some time back found this dead Dom and transported the map to the young Silvestre, his descendant. In exchange for nursing the dying Silvestre, Quatermain was given the map; in exchange for the Dom's crucifix and pen, the British return a dead servant to the dead Portuguese and restore a symbolic European/African hierarchy.

The scene at the diamond mine is yet more complex in its exchange transactions, which take on the dynamics of a capitalism Haggard's novel attempts to disavow. The men arrive in time to witness the dying Foulata's declaration of love for Captain Good; their grief at her death is interrupted by their realization that they are trapped. The sequence of Quatermain's narration is important here: 'We turned and went, and as we did so I perceived by the unfinished wall across the passage the basket of food which poor Foulata had carried. I took it up, and brought it with me back to that accursed treasure chamber that was to be our grave. Then we went back and reverently bore in Foulata's corpse, laying it on the floor by the boxes of coin' (228). Foulata's remains become an essential component of the treasure chamber:

If ever it should be entered again by living man, which I do not think it will be, he will find a token of our presence in the open chests of jewels, the empty lamp, and the white bones of poor Foulata . . . Somehow, I seem to feel that the millions of pounds' worth of gems that lie in the three stone coffers will never shine round the neck of an earthly beauty. They and Foulata's bones will keep cold company till the end of all things. (236, 242)

Even dead Foulata continues to be an instrument of the British: she provides food. This service matters more than her death itself to the men, who take in her body only after taking in the food. This provision of food itself diminishes the opposition between life and wealth that the text claims; the men have some means of sustenance automatically or naturally supplied to them.

Foulata's death itself neatly exchanges an imperial threat (miscegenation) for an affirmation (symbolic; eternal devotion of a submissive Africa to her master). A similar exchange mechanism operates between the two women. Although Gagool's knowledge was necessary to get the men into the chamber, it has to be displaced by a force more positive to British imperialism. Gagool's eternal Evil gives way to Foulata's eternal Good, Hatred to Love. This scene is perhaps the most ideologically central to the book.[14] It is—especially in the deathly interchange between Gagool and Foulata—strikingly free of narrative plausibility, as is remarked by the 'Fall of Fiction' which singles out this scene for examination and condemnation. That Haggard should thus depart from any pretence at narrative consistency here itself underscores the scene's ideological significance: its composition is governed by overweening symbolic, not generic considerations. What it symbolizes, I argue, is the attempt to deny, in the very site of capital accumulation, any association with the dynamics of capitalism itself. Those dynamics surface through the very means of denial: the logic of barter-exchange; the juxtaposition of 'subsistence' with 'profit', of utility with surplus.

This process is best traced through comparison with the earlier scenes of instrumentalized African labour and death. Like Khiva, Foulata dies in the sacrificial act of protecting her 'masters' who have previously intervened to save her from sacrificial death by Kukuana ritual. Both deaths occur as a direct result of the Englishmen pursuing their appetites for material acquisition. In both instances, the burial of the dead takes place only after the British men have seen to their own profit. Quatermain records the preparation, burial, and calculation of the value of the ivory before he records the burial of Khiva. He spots and carries Foulata's food basket over before carrying over her bones. In both cases, too, the bodies of the Africans are rhetorically juxtaposed with the financial wealth their death is associated with.

However Khiva's death corresponds to use-value logic, while Foulata's belongs to the logic of capitalism. Khiva's death occurs through elephant hunting; the men's own labour produces the tusks. Quatermain's account stresses the sheer weight of the tusks. This suggests that their market value is measurable directly in proportion to their weight; in other words, that their

[14] Low argues a similar point: 'It is Gagool's critique of the treasure seekers which forces a crisis point in the story' (*White Skins. Black Masks*, 77).

economic value is an inherent property of their physical being rather than residing in the commodity value they command within capitalism. Whereas Khiva's financial value is equated with the ivory that he died in producing, as we have seen Quatermain mediates Foulata's financial value through the treasure —'the millions of pounds' worth of gems—and also through the value of the British men her food-basket saves.

Foulata's commodification links back to the associations of gold and diamonds with sexual economics. As I argued in the discussion of King Solomon's transcultural lustfulness, Haggard aligns an 'excessive' sexual desire with 'excessive' economic desire. The diamonds will not, as Quatermain suggests, form part of the sexualized capitalism whereby white men buy sex in exchange for gems and women exchange sex for financial security. Instead, the gems that the men receive enable Quatermain to purchase survival for himself and for his son. The treasure that the men take with them is identified with a principle of utility rather than greed, dynastic male self-preservation rather than heterosexual romance. The surplus treasure stands as an embodiment simultaneously of white culture's excessive material–sexual desire and of sublime black servitude.

Haggard's equations of diamonds and food are complex. The ancient Dom entered the treasure chamber 'and found the stones, and filled with stones the skin of a small goat, which the woman had with her to hold food' (220). The Dom, as we know, does not survive. His ideological values, it seems, have been skewed: he literally puts wealth in the place of food, ending up with neither: 'I saw the point of that sneer of hers about eating and drinking the diamonds now. Perhaps somebody had tried to serve the poor old Dom in the same way, when he abandoned the skin full of jewels' (228). In contrast the British trio go through a ritual dissociation of wealth from food only to end up with both (and in addition gain their metaphorical fusion). An ideological process of wealth naturalization enlists food imagery. The largest diamonds resemble 'pigeon-eggs'; when the men discover an escape route, Quatermain is struck with an idea:

The idea of diamonds was *nauseous*, seeing what they had entailed upon us; but, thought I, I may as well pocket a few in case we ever should get out of this ghastly hole . . . If it had not, from the habits of a lifetime, become a sort of second nature with me never to leave anything worth having behind, if there was the slightest chance of my being able to carry it away, I am sure I should not have bothered to fill my pockets. (emphasis added) (234; 235)

From being akin to food, and eliciting nauseous responses, the diamonds become associated with an instinct of self-preservation and end up a means of material sustenance. Yet the non-acquisitive inflection which Haggard gives to the men's wealth relies on the reasoning, semantics, and economic process of capitalism against which it is so theatrically set. The very co-existence of these two versions of economic value is possible only through the prior condition of an abstract notion of value through which they are both mediated. The differences between the men's 'pile' and the remaining huge treasure are quantitative not qualitative, despite Haggard's suggestions otherwise. That 'gold' and 'bread' can take on each other's symbolic meanings itself suggests that neither term has intrinsic meaning. That both terms rely on expression through women's bodies again suggests that Haggard's concept of intrinsically legitimate wealth relies on mechanics of mediation not inherent value. If the sexualization of gold/bread is supposed to provide a 'natural' alibi for capitalism, the conditions in which that sexualization occurs expose its ideological basis in capitalism.

AFRICAN OPPOSITION AS 'RESSENTIMENT'

The use of Africans to mediate fundamental ideological contradictions is a constant feature of this imperial narrative. This is most evident in the representation of Gagool, an African who must be instrumentalized for her scientific knowledge then killed as a potential obstacle to British imperial success.[15] Gagool embodies Haggard's disquiet at recent African anti-

[15] See McClintock, *Imperial Leather*, 245–6, for a discussion of Gagool as illustrative of 'mortal consequences for men of the power of female generation'. Several Anglo-American feminist critics have analysed Gagool as an example of Haggard's misogyny and/or fear of the British New Woman. These include Deirdre David, ch. 5 'Laboring for the Empire: Patriarchy and New Imperialism in Tennyson and H. Rider Haggard', *Rule Britannia: Women, Empire, and Victorian Writing*, (Ithaca: Cornell University Press 1995), 157–202.

British resistance, and his hostility to Zulu political structures in which a feminized class of *isanusis* mediate and complement the monarch's power. If Quatermain and company mythically repeat an ancient imperialism, Gagool presents the frightening prospect of a force which does not require repetition, rumoured to be the very same figure who witnessed ancient white civilization first hand, and 'learnt [her] art' from it.

Gagool affirms the historical priority of white civilization over black life in Africa; she testifies to the supremacy of its scientific and intellectual knowledge; she also, and significantly, affirms its acquisitiveness. She displays a supernatural ability when she turns to Quatermain's crew and tells them she knows that they came for 'a lost one' and for 'bright stones'. She also recognizes Umbopa as the lost heir to the throne. Given that she appears to be aware of the inevitability of the white master's victory it might seem odd, and certainly illogical, that Gagool should do her best to obstruct the British trio's progress. But this is precisely the point: to oppose the British, Haggard's text suggests, can only be unreasonable, caused by a constitutional malevolence of metaphysical proportions.[16] Indeed through Gagool Haggard provides a classic example of *ressentiment*. African resistance is delegitimized, rendered the opposite of a political action derived from principled and rigorous analysis.

Haggard's target is not only African political opposition but also, additionally, traditional structures of African governance. Ignosi considers that Gagool is 'the evil genius of the land . . . always it is she who has trained the witch-hunters, and made the land evil in the sight of the heavens above' (197–8). In the institution of *isanusis,* we witness senior women as office bearers of the kingdom rather than homemakers—a direct challenge to the 'natural' patriarchal order, as Haggard sees it, within both Britain and South Africa. Gagool and her *isanusis'* practices carry the additional threat of a critical power which can be used against the dominant power it is supposed to serve; the prospect of an instrumental reason in the wrong brains. This is portrayed

---

[16] Nietzsche formulated the concept of '*ressentiment*' in his *The Genealogy of Morals: An Attack*, trans. F. Golding (1887; New York: Doubleday 1956). On Nietzschean *ressentiment* as a feature of late 19th- and early 20th-cent. English fiction, see Fredric Jameson's discussion of Gissing and Conrad, *The Political Unconscious: Narrative as a Socially Symbolic Act* (London: Methuen 1981), 185–280.

for instance in the 'scheming' manipulation by Gagool of the famished population, when she takes advantage of their desperation and their 'fickleness' to turn them against their king and to install her own preferred monarch in his stead (101–2).

Such a situation echoes the nightmare scenario Haggard sketches of a metropolis rendered hungry and consequently susceptible to manipulation by socialism.[17] It also, of course, makes of genuine African succession disputes a mockery.[18] In both the *isanusis'* official power and their manipulation of that power to unofficial ends, they are placed in striking parallel with the actions of the British trio. If the men are compelled to intervene in the Kukuana succession dispute for reasons of their constitutive benevolence, Gagool is compelled through her constitutive malevolence. Gagool manipulates the masses to win support for her choice of Twala as king. Quatermain and company likewise manipulate the populace, through the device of an eclipse, to achieve backing for their campaign to instate Ignosi as king.

Gagool alone has the scientific knowledge to see through the men's eclipse ruse. Haggard effectively acknowledges and condones his trio's use of an instrumental reason, their capitalization on alleged African technological ignorance and willingness to ascribe supernatural status to the white men. This amounts to a double standard. For Gagool (and Africans) the possession and utilization of instrumental reasoning is by definition unethical, malicious, self-interested. For Quatermain and British subjects at large, the end is held to justify the means. Haggard's British imperialism needs a good Africa that by definition is instinctively pro-imperial, as is found in Foulata. But Haggard

---

[17] See Haggard's *The Poor and the Land. Being a Report on the Salvation Army Colonies in the US and at Hadleigh, England with the Scheme of National Land Settlement* (London: Longmans, Green and Co. 1905), p. xxxix: 'And if nothing is done what then? Every winter a clamour and a crisis with wild threats and violence, appeased for the hour by ever-increasing inroads on the rates and other public funds. Then when the next winter comes the same desperate, ominous shapes of Misery and Want, and in their hands the Swords of Socialism'.

[18] For a reading of the novel as reflecting Ndebele succession disputes, see Tim Couzens, who argues that Umbopa is Kanda-Kuruman, and Twala is Lobengula ('Literature and Ideology: The Patterson Embassy to Lobengula 1878 and *King Solomon's Mines*', University of London Institute of Commonwealth Studies, Collected Seminar Papers 5, 1977). McClintock reads the novel as reflecting the Zulu succession crisis between Cetshwayo (Twala) and Mbulazi (*Imperial Leather*, 249).

also, apparently, needs affirmation of white imperialism as an inescapable and metaphysical force that predates and succeeds black Africa. Gagool provides this cognition. Arguably, this exposes imperialism as an ideological process; its mythical pretensions are belied by the very fact that it needs a Gagool to testify to, and validate, its origin.

This argument, however, overlooks the effects of placing such validation in the mouth of a hostile, demonized interlocutor. This allows the reader both to absorb and disavow what Gagool testifies to; her metaphysical malevolence compromises her reliability as witness, her allegations of the trio's materialism serve to deflect the truth of that charge. Gagool does not recognize any difference between the white men in front of her and the white men of antiquity, the acquisitive Jews and Phoenicians. Yet while Haggard affirms a mythical transcultural, ahistorical imperial subjectivity, to which Gagool testifies, he also sets in place a strict racial and national differentiation so that the British trio embody an exclusively British and contemporary imperialism, idealized, *sui generis*, free of acquisitive taint.

NOBLE SAVAGERY AND ONTOLOGICAL DOOM

Haggard makes heavy use of Africans as testifiers. Gagool's testifying, as we have seen, endows the trio with the aura of a generalized white antiquity and simultaneously the sanctity of an English modernity. Through Umbopa/Ignosi's testifying, the English reader can enjoy the performance of 'poetic' metaphysical fatalism at a safe remove.[19] The author of 'The Fall of Fiction' takes exception to this rhetorical invention:

From Bulwer in his feebler moods Mr Haggard appears to catch his trick of spurious philosophizing. This is for the most part merely tiresome, but sometimes rises to the ridiculous by being put into ludicrously incongruous mouths. An African savage thus moralizes: 'Out of the dark we come, into the dark we go. Like a storm-driven bird at night we fly out of the No-where. . . .' Our dusky brother seems to have been studying Carlyle and Mr Bailey's *Festus*. (335)

[19] See Wendy Katz, ch. 4 'An Intelligible Order: Haggard's Fatalism', *Rider Haggard and the Fiction of Empire: A Critical Study of British Imperial Fiction*, (Cambridge: Cambridge University Press 1987), 84–107.

The Spectator makes a similar complaint:

Sometimes Mr Haggard is, we think, a little too audacious, as when he makes Ignosi burst out into almost the same language as that with which the priest of the Saxon gods answered the invitation of Paullinus:—'Like a storm-driven bird at night we fly out of nowhere; for a moment our wing are seen in the light,' etc. Perhaps Alexander Smith and *Edwin of Deira* are better read and appreciated among the Zulus than we think.[20]

The contemporary parodists of Haggard likewise enjoyed the bathos of his metaphysical interludes. A late twentieth-century critic, however, takes them very seriously. For Alan Sandison, 'Haggard is deeply moved and perturbed by the implication of current evolutionary theory'.[21] Haggard grapples with evolutionism's challenge to providential order, but cannot affirm any such order. Sandison argues that Haggard thus portrays 'the subservience of all races, creeds and opinions to process and flux, and . . . evoke[s] with compassion the community of all creation in a vast, ungoverned movement the genesis of which is as enigmatic as the end is obscure and troubling' (41–2). More specifically, Haggard's *King Solomon's Mines* is said to 'repudiate without fuss the whole arrogant notion of the white man's burden . . . it is Haggard's presentation of [the Zulu/ Kukuana] as being under the same doom as the Europeans and sensitively aware of the fact that results in the remarkable degree of identification of native and European spiritual life' (31).

Sandison is rare among Haggard critics, past and present, in taking Haggard's ontological anxiety seriously. But his conclusions fall wide of the mark. For all their racism, the commentators from 'The Fall of Fiction' and *The Spectator* have a point: Haggard's way of issuing these ontological sentiments is contrived. As with the equally forced diamond mine encounter of Foulata and Gagool, such awkwardness indicates ideological intensity. Rather than relativize, as Sandison asserts, such rhetorical strategy works to entrench British imperial power over Africans. It converts a social and political condition into an abstraction, one which disguises British agency in dispossessing Africans and simultaneously projects Haggard's own

[20] *The Spectator*, 58 (7 Nov. 1885), 1473.
[21] Alan Sandison, *The Wheel of Empire* (London: Macmillan 1967), 37.

experience of politico-economic dispossession by an urban bourgeoisie.

These dynamics are clearest in the contrasting rhetoric of Sir Henry and Umbopa. As the men prepare for their trek across the desert Sir Henry argues a discourse of heroic quest and human empowerment, conditioned on a Christian providentialism.[22] Quatermain translates for Umbopa, whose reply discourse is radically different, emphasizing not human power but human weakness, fatality, transience and lack of control over that fleeting life as the condition for heroic venture:

'Great words, my father,' answered the Zulu (I always called him a Zulu, though he was not really one), 'great swelling words fit to fill the mouth of a man. Thou art right, my father Incubu. Listen! what is Life? It is a feather, it is the seed of the grass, blown hither and thither, sometimes multiplying itself and dying in the act, sometimes carried away into the heavens. But if the seed be good and heavy it may perchance travel a little way on the road it wills. It is well to try and journey one's road and to fight with the air. Man must die. At the worst he can but die a little sooner. (59)

In the dialogue between the men up to this point, Quatermain's translation has been confined to Umbopa's 'Zulu' so that Sir Henry can understand Umbopa; as he states, 'Umbopa understood English, though he rarely spoke it' (58). Sir Henry's move from a personal discourse about his brother to a metaphysically general topic suddenly seems to necessitate Quatermain's translation into Zulu. This is another example of Haggard overriding his own narrative conventions in order to articulate an important ideological point. Haggard wants to convey that not Sir Henry's language so much as his sentiments are alien to Umbopa, who now takes on the burden of Zulu representativeness. Sir Henry's confident discourse of human agency and divine providence are encoded as the exclusive property of English men and unavailable to Zulu people. Umbopa's own discourse from this point is, correspondingly, coded as exclusively Zulu.

Quatermain characterizes Umbopa's speech as 'one of those strange bursts of rhetorical eloquence which Zulus sometimes indulge in, and which to my mind, full as they are of vain

[22] See Katz, ch. 3 'Some Talk of Alexander: The Imperial Hero', *Rider Haggard and the Fiction of Empire*, 58–83.

repetitions, show that the race is by no means devoid of poetic instinct and of intellectual power' (59). Zulu poetry and intellect resides in the ability to express a nihilistic conviction of human ontology through a variety of metaphors: 'Like a storm-driven bird at night we fly out of the Nowhere; for a moment our wings are seen in the light of the fire, and, lo! we are gone again into the Nowhere. Life is nothing. Life is all. It is the hand with which we hold off Death. It is the glow-worm that shines in the night-time and is black in the morning; it is the white breath of the oxen in winters' (60).

By the end of Umbopa's 'burst' even the residual notion of heroic agency evident in the first instalment of his speech has vanished. 'Life' consists of a series of random aesthetic figures. Only Zulus are privy to this ontological insight, according to Umbopa; white men's knowledge is confined to technologies of science: 'Tell me, O white men, who are wise, who know the secrets of the world, and the world of stars, and the world that lies above and around the stars; who flash their words from afar without a voice; tell me, white men, the secret of our life . . . Ye cannot answer; ye know not. Listen, I will answer' (59). Haggard here projects his gentry class's demotion within contemporary capitalism. Attributing a metaphysical 'lifeworld' to Zulu culture is a strategy of containment that enables Haggard to articulate and disavow his own metropolitan condition. To this extent, Sandison is accurate. Where he presents this as Haggard's non-racist identification with Zulu people as all subject to existential flux, however, I read this identification as a form of instrumentalization.

If this African subject here serves as mouthpiece and deflection of Haggard's metropolitan pessimism, he also serves to deflect British imperial and colonial responsibility for the demise of the Zulu kingdom. As I have argued, Umbopa's sentiments are explicitly juxtaposed against Sir Henry's, so that the universal terms used by both are belied by the racial and national specificity given to their respective speech-acts. The Zulu speak of human mortality and powerlessness; by implication, only to the Zulu do such negative qualities apply. Not the British but metaphysical law has generated such a condition for them; a political, knowable situation is turned into an aesthetic and incomprehensible experience.

Ultimately, Haggard's discourses here entrench racial and national differences as absolute. For the English, as we have seen, the metaphysical discourse signals a confident trust in a human agency supported by divine providence. For the Zulu, Haggard presents an authoritarian ideology of blind occultism, total submission to an allegedly indeterminable process. That Haggard chooses in this scene to label Umbopa as an actual 'Zulu', rather than as a fictional Kukuana, is no accident. It reveals the extent to which the metaphysical postulations presented here are deeply implicated in factual, political, South African realities, the realities of the British invasion of Zululand and the bloody aftermath.

AFRICAN PASTORAL

When Quatermain introduces us to the African pastoral kingdom of Kukuanaland his description of the landscape is far from being the neutral document it pretends to be.[23] Every geographical feature he selects is ideologically loaded:

To the left stretched a vast expanse of rich, undulating veldt or grass land, on which we could just make out countless herds of game or cattle, at that distance we could not tell which. This expanse appeared to be ringed in by a wall of distant mountains. To the right the country was more or less mountainous, that is, solitary hills stood up from its level, with stretches of cultivated lands between, amongst which we could distinctly see groups of dome-shaped huts. (88)

The paradise that is Kukuanaland—filled with fertile, cultivated land, an infinite supply of 'cattle or game'—is carefully and insistently framed by mountains, on its left side, and is itself filled with 'solitary hills'. These features sum up the twin economic ingredients of Haggard's dream African society: agriculture and warfare. The mountains inside Kukuanaland are, as the British trio goes on to discover, as natural fortresses.[24]

[23] Several critics have discussed the gender dynamics of Haggard's African landscape. These include Rebecca Stott, 'The Dark Continent: Africa as Female Body in Haggard's Adventure Fiction', *Feminist Review*, 32 (summer 1989), 69–89; David Bunn, 'Embodying Africa: Woman and Romance in Colonial Fiction', *English in Africa*, volume 15, number 1 (May 1988), 1–28; McClintock, ch. 1 'The Lay of the Land: Genealogies of Imperialism', *Imperial Leather*, 21–74.

[24] Under Ignosi's generalship, the Greys range themselves on the crescent formation of hills which, in the civil war, enables them to defeat Twala's troops.

Warfare, of a defensive kind, is characterized as a central, recurring feature of Kukuana life. They are periodically subjected to invasion from peoples of the mysterious North, as Infadoos explains: 'now and again warriors sweep down upon us in clouds from a land we know not, and we slay them' (101).

It has been the crucial Haggardian 25 years—a generation—since the last war of defence, which was followed 'just after' by the civil war in which Twala seized power illegally from his brother. In this sense, the civil war in which the British trio consequently participates carries the sanction of biological cycle: time for a new generation of warriors to constitute themselves as such. The society's cultural self-reproduction through warfare is, of course, simultaneously a form of physical self-destruction. This is a 'natural' economy, as fantasized by Haggard, in which the Kukuana are culturally and biologically pre-programmed to a cycle of demographic self-regulation. Their numbers do not expand but remain fixed, through the balancing of warfare's mortality rate against sexual reproduction.[25]

Such a fantasy cycle proceeds through a strategy of naturalization to disavow the political dynamics of war in general, and African invasion by aliens such as the British in particular. This determination to render warfare an essential ingredient conjoins an equally intense concern to attribute an agrarian pastoralism to Kukuana society. This produces an apparent contradiction: if a cyclical warmaking ensures social renewal, it also threatens it. The 'natural' pursuit of self-defence and bloodlust by the Kukuana jeopardizes their physical and political ecology, introducing famine and a crisis in government. During the last 'great war' against invaders, 'no man could sow or reap'; as a consequence, 'a famine came upon the land, and the people murmured because of the famine, and looked round like a starved lion for something to rend' (101). This provides Gagool with her opportunity to turn the people against the king and crown Twala in his place.

As I have already argued, Haggard's representation of common people as susceptible through hunger to political

[25] After the conclusion of Ignosi's war, Infadoos comments that 'The Kukuana people can only be kept cool by letting the blood flow sometimes. Many were killed indeed, but the women were left, and others would soon grow up to take the places of the fallen. After this the land would be quiet for a while', 197.

manipulation echoes his fears of a British populace driven into the hands of socialist agitators through a hunger brought on by urban capitalism and corollary decline in agricultural employment and production. The difference is that Haggard presents the British situation as dysfunctional, the result of the triumph by an unnatural system over a natural system. However the famine situation Haggard invents in Kukuanaland is one he condones as the product of a 'natural' predisposition to militarism. His reformist energies for Kukuana society are limited to the elimination of the institution of the female *isanusis* with their power to allocate death. Kukuana life (like that of the Zulu Khiva and the 'Hottentot' Ventvogel) proves utterly dispensable within Haggard's imperial ideology.[26] African death is sanctioned provided that its cause is 'natural', as occurs in defensive warfare, rather than 'unnatural', including a death incurred through the decree of senior ranked women. Haggard's commitment to the military economy of the Kukuana derives from his veneration of Zulu militarism, from which he borrows much. But more important to my discussion is what Haggard does not borrow; the differences between Zulu and Kukuana land and society.[27]

The key to their difference is geography. The Kukuana are, as Quatermain's opening vista records, as segregated from the south as they are open to the north from which they have descended. Unlike the Zulu the Kukuana are emphasized as agricultural producers who inhabit a land of which 'in beauty,

[26] See *Punch*, 17 Jan. 1892, 28: 'Mr Punch's Prize Novels. No XI The Book of Kookarie. Chapter I. "I am not a brave man, but nobody ever was a surer shot with an Express longbow, no one ever killed more Africans men and elephants than I have in my time. But I do love blood. I love it in regular rivers all over the place; with gashes and slashes and lopped heads and arms and legs rolling about everywhere. Black blood is the best variety; I mean the blood of black men because nobody really cares twopence about them and you can massacre several thousands of them in half-a-dozen lines and offend no single soul. And, after all, I am not certain that black men have any souls, so that makes things safe all round, as someone says in the *Bab Ballads*".'

[27] See McClintock, *Imperial Leather*, and Gail Low, *White Skins. Black Masks*, for interpretations which view Haggard in this novel as reflecting recent events and ideologies of Zululand in an unmediated way, so that, for example, to McClintock the novel reveals 'the attempted reconstruction of the Zulu nation through control of female reproductive and labor power', 240. See Laura Chrisman, 'Gendering Imperial Culture', in *Cultural Readings of Imperialism: Edward Said and the Gravity of History*, ed. K. Ansell-Pearson, B. Parry, and J. Squires (London: Lawrence and Wishart 1997) for a critique of this Zulu literalism, 290–304.

in natural wealth, and in climate I have never seen its like'
(103). By geographically separating the Kukuana from South
Africa, Haggard is able to invent a risk-free model of Zulu
history and society. Haggard and other ideologues of the British
empire saw Zulu society as an 'imperialist' force that pursued
political expansionism through military means. This perception
justified British invasion in 1879 of Zululand, causing the
Anglo-Zulu War and subsequent civil war of 1880–4. Over
this period Zululand, geographically adjacent to Natal, lost
sovereignty over most of its terrain and within Natal Zulu
'reserves' were established as a source of cheap colonial wage
labour. Haggard's fantasy provides a very different scenario.
The Kukuana are culturally static, preserved in an ahistorical
timewarp, speaking a medieval version of Zulu (93). Where the
Zulu, especially under Shaka, are part of history, the Kukuana
are removed from it; where the Zulu kingdom incorporated a
range of peoples, the Kukuana are ethnically homogeneous.

Most important of all, where the Zulu are connected to white
South Africa, the Kukuana are isolated from it. The militaristic
Zulu are perceived as a possible threat to settler colonialism;
Kukuana society retains Zulu militarism but confines its expression to defence against invading North Africans. The Zulu are
subjected systematically to structures and forces of capitalist
modernization; Haggard's fantasy of the Kukuana preserves
them from this process. The fantasy synthesizes idealized traits
both of the 'imperial' war-making Zulu and settler-colonial
agrarian production. As a socio-economic ideal Kukuana provides what Haggard cannot have in the metropolis: a pseudo-
medieval, self-sufficient society of yeomen farmers who also
double as warrior noblemen.[28] As regards Haggard's racial and

---

[28] See e.g. Haggard's *A Farmer's Year* (1899; London: Longmans, Green and Co.
1906); also his 'Introductory Address' as chairman of a conference on 'the Garden
City in relation to Agriculture', in which he stresses the importance of the reconsti-
tution of the feudal 'yeoman class' through his advocacy of a state provision of
smallholdings (Thomas Adams, *Garden City and Agriculture: How to Solve the
Problem of Rural Depopulation*; London: Garden City Press 1905), 1–11. There is
a latent instrumentalism and authoritarianism in this discourse: the system of
yeomanry is recommended not for the benefit of redundant farm workers so much
as for the symbolic benefit to Haggard's mythology of the English 'race' and nation,
and there is almost a suggestion that if such yeomen are not voluntarily forthcoming, they should be made to come forth. See Howkins for a discussion of
Haggard's rural English activities and ideologies ('Haggard and Rural England'),
89–92. This strain of coercion underlying a discourse of rural regeneration is found

cultural values, what the representation of Kukuana promotes is an ideology of separatism: segregation of African and white society.

Simple though such segregationism is in principle, its mediation through Allan Quatermain is not. The burden of affirming absolute, hierarchical racial and cultural separatism falls exclusively to Haggard's African characters, reported through Quatermain, whose own views, in contrast, evade responsibility for the racism they imply. Foulata's dying affirmation is 'that I am glad to die because I know that he cannot cumber his life with such as me, for the sun cannot mate with the darkness, nor the white with the black' (226–7). Quatermain converts this statement into a question; pondering her death, he opines:

The poor creature was no ordinary native girl, but a person of great, I had almost said stately, beauty, and of considerable refinement of mind. But no amount of beauty or refinement could have made an entanglement between Good and herself a desirable occurrence; for, as she herself put it, 'Can the sun mate with the darkness, or the white with the black? (241)

A similar response occurs earlier, when Twala offers 'Would ye have wives from among our people, white men? If so, choose the fairest here'; Quatermain relates:

As the prospect did not seem to be without attractions to Good . . . I,

elsewhere in Haggard. He not only supported General William Booth's Salvation Army scheme of colonization, but conducted a study-tour of the colonies established in the United States and England, and wrote a book-length report which was to become a government Blue Book (*The Poor and the Land. Being a Report on the Salvation Army Colonies in the U.S. and at Hadleigh, England with the Scheme of National Land Settlement*, London: Longmans, Green and Co. 1905). Booth's colonization plan was: '*Forward them* [the degenerate poor] from the City to the Country, and there continuing the process of regeneration, and *then pouring them forth* on to the virgin soils that await their coming in other lands *keeping hold of them with a strong government*, and yet making them free men and women; and so laying the foundation, per chance, of another Empire to swell to vast proportions in later times' (emphases added). Booth's statement is from his *In Darkest England and the Way Out* (1890) quoted in Gareth Stedman-Jones, *Outcast London: A Study in the Relationship between Classes in Victorian Society* (Harmondsworth: Peregrine Books 1984), 311. Particularly relevant to issues of the ideology of ruralism and urban degeneration are ch. 6 'Casual Labour and Rural Immigration: The Theory of Urban Degeneration', 127–51, and ch. 16 'From "Demoralisation" to "Degeneration": The Threat of Outcast London', 281–314. See also Jeffrey Weeks's ch. 7 'The Population Question in the Early Twentieth Century', *Sex, Politics and Society: The Regulation of Sexuality since 1800* (London: Longman 1981), 122–40.

being elderly and wise, and foreseeing the endless complications that anything of the sort would involve (for women bring trouble as surely as the night follows the day), put in a hasty answer: 'Thanks, O king, but we white men wed only with white women like ourselves. Your maidens are fair, but they are not for us!' The king laughed. 'It is well. In our land there is a proverb which says, "Woman's eyes are always bright, whatever the colour" . . . but perhaps these things are not so in the stars. In a land where men are white all things are possible.' (144)

Quatermain's strictures against miscegenation are presented with Foulata's own authority, contingent rather than absolute; an open-ended question. To Twala Quatermain presents his apprehensions as primarily concerned with heterosexual activity in general; he gives these a racial explanation for strategic not ideological reasons. In both instances, Haggard rhetorically juxtaposes the personal opinion of an older man with the racially generalized and generalizing conclusions of an African representative. Haggard insinuates that it is Africans, not whites, who think in primarily hierarchical terms; any use by a white of a racist language of black inferiority then becomes a strategic accommodation to the established categories of African thought and culture.

Haggard's manipulation of African 'objectivity' and white 'subjectivity' to promote his racially hierarchical segregationism takes a striking turn at the book's conclusion. When the newly crowned Ignosi gets upset at the news of the trio's imminent departure, Quatermain appeals to him 'tell us, when thou didst wander in Zululand, and among the white men in Natal, did not thine heart turn to the land thy mother told thee of, they native land, where thou didst see the light, and play when thou wast little, the land where thy place was? . . . Then thus does our heart turn to our land and to our own place'. This achieves the desired recognition from Ignosi: 'I do perceive that thy words are, now as ever, wise and full of reason, Macumazahn; that which flies in the air loves not to run along the ground; *the white man loves not to live on the level of the black*' (245; emphases added).

MYSTIFICATION OF AUTHORITY

Ignosi prohibits Western development in his kingdom. His declaration upholds the discourses of an African anti-capitalist pastoralism and corollary racial segregationism which are so fundamental to Haggard's version of imperial fantasy.[29] However Ignosi's rejection of Westernization as a cultural and economic system is accompanied by his endorsement of particular white individuals, who are to be granted unlimited access to his country:

No other white man shall cross the mountains . . . I will see no traders with their guns and rum. My people shall fight with the spear, and drink water, like their forefathers before them. I will have no praying-men to put fear of death into men's hearts, to stir them up against the king, and make a path for the white men who follow to run on . . . None shall ever come for the shining stones; no, not an army, for if they come I will send a regiment and fill up the pit . . . so that none can come even to that door of which ye speak . . . But for ye three, Incubu, Macumazahn, and Bougwan, the path is always open. (245–6)

Beneath this simple policy of exceptionalism lies another fundamental component of Haggard's imperialism: the notion of a mystically authoritative subject.[30] Ignosi's mystical authority is dialectically linked to the construction of the British trio's authority. There is a crucial difference: the African's authority derives from his office as monarch, while the trio is seen to transcend categories of official rank. Ignosi's military leaders venerate Quatermain's powers of calculation and strategy. Quatermain follows up his advice with the rider to the

[29] See Brian Street, *The Savage in Literature: Representations of 'Primitive' Society in English Fiction 1858–1920* (London: Routledge and Kegan Paul 1975), 123, for an argument that the land is already effectively a colony of Britain. See also Low, *White Skins. Black Masks*, 81–3. She observes that Umbopa's critique resembles 'the comments of the Mpondomise chief, Mhlonto, on the increased white settlement in African frontiers in 1880' (82). Low concludes by suggesting that 'in the contemporary historical world of segregationist politics and African locations, the 'separation' that Ignosi seems to be advocating only leads to a denial of the effects of the white presence, not to their diminishing' (83).

[30] On the interracial friendships of the book Low comments that 'such bonds of affection which exist across racial and cultural groups are always singular relations between individual men. Because they are not communal they do not violate the *colonial* identity of the male subject predicated on cultural boundaries' (*White Skins. Black Masks*, 61).

reader that 'the real decision as to our course lay with Ignosi, who, since he had been recognized as rightful king, could exercise the almost unbounded rights of sovereignty, including, of course, the final decision on matters of generalship' (171–2).

The trio facilitates the crowning of the rightful king whose almost unbounded power is to be even further increased by the elimination of the office of *isanusis* with their powers of witch-hunting. All then that stands between king Ignosi and tyranny is his innate, categorical 'goodness', rhetorically established by his denunciation of Evil. This quality, Haggard suggests, is as mysteriously inherent to the legitimate king as it is to the individual Ignosi; the man and the role are naturally elided in their essential nobility. Through their 'natural' authority, the British trio assumes powers normally reserved for African monarchs. Ignosi removes the capacity to impose death without trial; yet, simultaneously grants the trio the power of death. In effect, the British imperialists unofficially assume the power that has been taken away from the African *isanusis*. Not only do they become law-makers but also actually absorb the transcendental status of law itself.

The dynamic between Ignosi and the trio is another example of Haggard's ideological mechanics of exchange, mediated here through the abstract quality of noble authority. Both the trio and Ignosi claim their patrimony—treasure and monarchy respectively. Each party mediates the other's access to that patrimony. Nobility serves as a natural and non-racialized quality— but it operates in ways that are strictly racially differentiated and serve to uphold racist hierarchy and segregationism. African noble authority then is defined as the adherence to, and embodiment of, the natural endowments of a collective culture and social structure. British nobility and authority, by contrast, are defined as and through the individual ability to transcend received social structures, to depart from culture mores, to be flexible and to recognize the natural nobility of African others.

Both versions derive from and perpetuate a mystifying, authoritarian ideology. As with Haggard's deployment of metaphysical discourses, so too with these representations of natural authority. African authority emerges through submission to a cultural heritage of ontological fatalism, political absolutism, and fixity of rank. British authority, through the opposite: an active not passive stance towards providence; heroic individual action and instrumental reason, not collective culture and external social rank.

CONCLUSION

Careful analysis of Haggard's imperial narrative reveals that the fantasy of a self-contained British mining ecosystem is undercut by the dependency of the British on African labour. This dependency has economic expression through the use of live and dead Africans to produce and measure British economic wealth. Africans mediate notions of British imperial subjectivity in its political, cultural and intellectual as well as its economic forms. It is only by the critical analytical tools taken from political economy—in particular, the notions of instrumental rationality, exchange value and mediation—that the dynamics of Haggard's imperial subject-formation can come to light. The same goes for categories of analysis derived from political thought: the dynamics of British and African representation here can only be grasped through the comparative exploration of concepts of political leadership, monarchy, resistance and social collectivity. At the same time, only by exploring the conjunction of metropolitan with South African historical and ideological concerns can the critic assess Haggard's invention of a fictional African people as an ideological strategy of containment. Political economy and history supply the foundations for critical analysis here, but they need to be seen as interdependent with categories of race and gender. Race and gender alone cannot account for the form these representations take—but Haggard's representation of African and British subjects is, like his representation of imperial mining capitalism itself, fundamentally racialized and gendered, governed by normative, hierarchical and anxious notions of racial and sexual identity.

3

The British Conquest of Zululand:
Haggard's Politics and Ideology

IN British constructions of African peoples, the Zulu people hold an important place.[1] This intense ideological investment derives from the historical interactions of Britain and Zululand.[2] Zululand was one of the last African kingdoms to be conquered by the British. For the annexing British colonial administration, as for the British metropolis, Zululand up until 1879 was distinguished not only by its autonomy but also by its highly developed political structure.[3] The state was headed by the king, and the main apparatus of state power was its military system, in which all men served from puberty until they were given permission to marry and establish a homestead. The foundations for this structure were laid by the early nineteenth-century Zulu king Shaka, who during the period known as the *Mfecane* conquered and incorporated a huge number of peoples

[1] See Christine Bolt, *Victorian Attitudes to Race* (London: Routledge Kegan Paul 1971), 144–5, for documentation of British admiration of the military prowess of the Zulu, Masai, and Ndebele, and the influence of social darwinism on such estimation. See also Dorothy Hammond and Alta Jablow, *The Africa that Never Was: Four Centuries of British Writing about Africa* (New York: Twayne 1970), esp. 111–12, on British constructions of the Zulu. The writers suggest that 'admiration for the Zulus seemed almost mandatory for the novelists of empire', 112.

[2] The heritage of this contradictory ideology can today be seen in the Zulu nationalism of the Inkatha movement and its ambiguous relationship to the South African state. For insights into the process of colonial reconstructions of ethnic 'tradition' see Terence Ranger, 'The Invention of Tradition in Colonial Africa', in *The Invention of Tradition*, ed. Eric Hobsbawm and Terence Ranger (Cambridge: Cambridge University Press 1983), 211–63. See also Hosea Jaffe, 'The Present as Colonialised Past', in *A History of Africa* (London: Zed Books 1985), 8–10.

[3] For a sensitive and meticulously detailed account of the invasion and civil war, see Jeff Guy, *The Destruction of the Zulu Kingdom: The Civil War in Zululand. 1879–1884* (London: Longman 1979). See also Shula Marks and Richard Rathbone, eds., *Industrialisation and Social Change in South Africa: African Class Formation, Culture, and Consciousness 1870–1930* (London: Longman 1982). On early 20th-cent. Zulu history see Shula Marks, *The Ambiguities of Dependence in South Africa: Class, Nation, and the State in Twentieth Century Natal* (London: Johns Hopkins University Press 1986).

into the emergent nation.[4] Shaka is a constant motif in late nineteenth-century imperialist and colonialist discourses, in which
he is popularly known as a 'black Napoleon', an imperialist
avant la lettre.

In late Victorian writings, the origins of the Zulu 'empire'
feature as much as the end of its empire, and these two moments
of its trajectory are frequently inextricable. The evident identification with the Zulu reveals many anxieties and fantasies
concerning concepts of political power. Thus the early nineteenth-century expansionism of Shaka functions frequently
as analogue and precursor of British imperialism. And the
eventual destruction of Zululand accordingly both affirms and
threatens British notions of imperial supremacy; the reminder
that powerful, seemingly invincible, empires can fall, is not
necessarily reassuring. The more the Zulu feature as exemplars
of militarism and African political authority the more they seem
to elicit British ambivalence. Associated with intense physical
power, the Zulu become metropolitan emblems of 'primitive'
vitality. This is fetishized as the antidote to a capitalist
modernity that experiences itself as reificatory. At the same
time, this African vitality is reviled as a savage threat to
civilization.

The above constructions find perhaps their fullest, and
certainly their most contradictory, expression in the writings of
Rider Haggard. Jeff Guy, a modern historian of the Zulu
nation, accords Haggard a central place in the popular history
of English representations of the Zulu: earlier Victorian images
by Bishop Colenso and Disraeli were intensified and superseded
by 'the grotesque imagination of Rider Haggard who become

---

[4] Established accounts of the *Mfecane* include *Economy and Society in
Pre-Industrial South Africa,* ed. Shula Marks and Antony Atmore (London:
Longman 1980), particularly the editors' Introd., 1–43. See also John Omer-
Cooper, 'Aspects of Political Change in the Nineteenth-century *Mfecane*', *African
Societies in Southern Africa,* ed. Leonard Thompson (London: Heinemann 1969),
207–29. Recent South African historiography has intensely debated the interpreta-
tion of the *Mfecane* and Shaka's role within it. See e.g. the differences between
Julian Cobbing in his 'Jettisoning the *Mfecane* (with Perestroika)', University of the
Witwatersrand African Studies Institute Seminar paper (1988), and Carolyn
Hamilton, 'The Character and Objects of Chaka: A Re-consideration of the Making
of Shaka as *Mfecane* "motor"', University of the Witwatersrand African Studies
Institute Seminar paper (1991). The importance of the *Mfecane* period to 20th-
century African writers will be addressed in my chapters 7 and 8, on Sol Plaatje's
Mhudi (1930; London: Heinemann 1982).

the great popular writer of his time by showing the Zulu "as they were, in all their superstitious madness and bloodstained grandeur", and who successfully confused in his readers' minds campfire anecdotes about the rise of Shaka with the later history of the kingdom'.[5] Haggard saw his Zulu writing as a particularly important aspect of his oeuvre. Not only did he single out the 'pure Zulu story' *Nada the Lily* as his best book, he regarded it as a valuable chronicle of 'a dying people' and a contribution to Zulu self-knowledge as well as to English knowledge of the Zulu. He expressed the hope that 'hundreds of years hence the highly educated descendants of the Zulu race may read it and learn there something of the spirit of their own savage ancestors'.[6]

Nada, written during 1889–90 shortly after the British South African annexation of Zululand, may be Haggard's most extended fictional articulation of Zuluness, but it was not his first. It needs to be seen as the culmination of a process of ideological construction that began in 1876, before the invasion of Zululand in 1879, and the subsequent civil war and annexation. The start of Haggard's discursive relationship with the Zulu was also the start of his writing career itself. His very first piece

[5] Jeff Guy, *Destruction of the Zulu Kingdom*, p. xx. His quotation is from Haggard's 'Dedication' of his *Child of Storm* (London: Cassell 1912), p. vi. Substantial discussions of Haggard's fictional and non-fictional representations of the Zulu and his relations with Shepstone can be found in Gail Low, ch. 2 'The Dominion of Sons', 36–65, and ch. 3 'Mimesis of Savagery', 66–103, *White Skins. Black Masks: Representation and Colonialism* (London: Routledge 1996); Anne McClintock, ch. 6 'The White Family of Man', 232–57, *Imperial Leather: Race, Gender and Sexuality in the Colonial Contest* (London: Routledge 1995); Carolyn Hamilton, 'Theophilus Shepstone and the Making of Rider Haggard's Shaka', University of Cape Town Centre for African Studies Seminar paper (1995); Terence Ranger, 'The Rural African Voice in Zimbabwe Rhodesia: archaism and tradition', *Social Analysis*, 4 (Sept. 1980), 100–15.

[6] H. Rider Haggard, *The Days of My Life*, (London: Longmans, Green and Co. 1926), 16; i. *Nada the Lily* (London: Longmans, Green and Co. 1892). Many of Haggard's romances feature Zulus, usually in the form of the lone assistant 'Umslopogaas'. Three tales, however, feature Zulu society in full, addressing other periods of 19th-cent. Zulu history, including the 1856 battle between the brothers Cetshwayo and Mbelazi: *Marie* (London: Cassell 1911*)*, *Child of Storm* (London: Cassell 1912), and *Finished* (London: Macdonald and Co. 1917). Although these texts merit examination (the contrast between the eponymous heroines of *Marie* and *Child of Storm*, white and black respectively, is interesting from the point of view of Haggard's engagement with 'the feminine'), they add little to the understanding of Haggard's relation to the Zulu that is provided by *Nada*. They also feature Allan Quatermain as their central protagonist, and cannot therefore claim the exclusive 'Zulu-ness' of *Nada*.

of writing, a journalistic account of 'A Zulu War-Dance', was written in May 1876, after a trip which he had made as a young colonial administrator to the Natal location of a 'chief Pagadi', 'a powerful chief who had fled from the Zulus in the early days of the colony, and had ever since dwelt loyally and peacefully here . . . beneath the protection of the Crown'.[7]

This was followed by his major book-length commentary on South African current affairs, *Cetywayo and His White Neighbours. Or, Remarks on Recent Events in Zululand, Natal, and the Transvaal*, first published in 1881, when Haggard had returned to England.[8] By the time of publication, the Zulu king Cetshwayo was still alive and his future was up in the air. In 1888, Haggard published a second edition of *Cetywayo*, with a new preface. By this time, British South Africa had formally annexed Zululand and Cetshwayo was dead. Haggard's writing thus spans the whole troubled decade of the conquest of Zululand, each publication marking a significant point in the process of domination. These historical points create differences of ideological emphasis and confusion: such differences are the concern of this chapter. *Nada* differs from Haggard's earlier Zulu texts not only by virtue of its historical location but also by its genre: unlike the other texts it is a piece of fiction, a historical romance with a strong fantasy sub-plot, set during the reign of Shaka. Haggard's shift to the medium of fiction needs interpretation as an attempt to resolve his contradictions, which were those of settler-colonial and metropolitan British society as a whole. This chapter will analyse what is at stake in Haggard's eventual resort to fictionality by offering an account of colonial and metropolitan Zulu representations through the period of British conquest.

---

[7] First published in *Gentleman's Magazine*, 243 (July 1877), 94–107. The edition used here was published as an appendix in Haggard's *Cetywayo and His White Neighbours: Or, Remarks on Recent Events in Zululand, Natal, and the Transvaal* (London: Trübner and Co. 1882), 278–94. Except when I am referring to Haggard's own text, I will use the modern spelling for African names throughout: Cetshwayo ('Cetywayo' in Haggard); Shaka (Chaka, in Haggard); Dingane (Dingaan, in Haggard).

[8] Haggard, as above. The second edition, with a new introduction, will also be used in this chapter (London: Trübner and Co. 1888). Hamilton, 'Theophilus Shepstone', 20, remarks that *Cetywayo* 'was widely read and informed a host of important opinion makers, men like Lord Carnarvon, Lord Randolph Churchill, and Haggard's old associate from the annexation days, Marshall Clarke. The reprinted section alone sold over thirty thousand copies'.

COLONIAL REALITIES, METROPOLITAN FANTASIES:
HAGGARD BEFORE THE ANGLO-ZULU WAR

Haggard's personal professional experience in South Africa as a
minor administrator in Natal and the Transvaal had little direct
connection with Zululand.[9] His first-hand experience of the
Zulu was limited to those who lived in Natal 'locations'. It
would however be erroneous to assume that the Natal and
Transvaal administrations within which Haggard worked were
irrelevant to the Zululand Zulus. The three officials with whom
Haggard was most involved, Sir Henry Bulwer the Lieutenant-
Governor of Natal, Theophilus Shepstone Natal's Secretary for
Native Affairs, and Melmoth Osborn the Colonial Secretary of
the Transvaal were in fact to dominate the colonial establish-
ment's participation in Zululand from 1879 to 1887.

One might assume, as Haggard's biographer Morton Cohen
does, that Haggard's attachment to these colonial officials gave
him a clearly colonial, as opposed to metropolitan-imperial,
perspective on Zuluness.[10] But this assumption is inaccurate.
Haggard's relations with these men were confined to their
Transvaal and Natal activities. It does not follow that Haggard
unequivocally supported their Zululand activities and ideological explanations, which operated only after he had left their
employ; nor did he necessarily share their material motivations.
Unlike Cohen, I want to argue the importance of seeing
Haggard's construction of Zuluness and the Zulu nation as a
compound of settler-colonial and metropolitan positions. These
positions are themselves contradictory, as will I hope become
clear in the ensuing discussion. The structure of 'A Zulu War-
Dance' exhibits the tensions between them. This piece is
valuable as a record of pre-Zulu-War ideology. It is also
valuable because Haggard's aim was not the serious analysis of
his *Cetywayo* but rather an informative entertainment for the
'highly-civilized reader' who dwells 'amid tamer scenes' (282).

[9] This biographical material is taken from Morton Cohen, *Rider Haggard: His
Life and Work* (London: Macmillan 1960).

[10] Ibid. 72: 'Haggard wrote boldly and bluntly from the point of view of an
English colonial and made no effort whatever to conceal his opinions of the Boers.'
This is also the view taken by Gail Low and Anne McClintock. See Hannah
Arendt's discussion of the distinction between the 'imperial factor', that is, the
British home government, and the colonial administration, *The Origins of
Totalitarianism* (1951; London: André Deutsch 1986), 132–4.

The result is a relatively uninhibited discourse in which the anxieties which inform the later works are given free reign. The dance of the title is particularly interesting as an enactment of, and commentary on, the fraught relationship of aesthetic representation to factual militarism. This relationship rests on the peculiar dynamics of fantasy and Zuluness, fiction and history, which later constitute the divided structure of *Nada the Lily*. Haggard's decision to make Pagadi's colonial reservation the primary focus of his 'Zulu War-Dance' allows him to bring in the autonomous kingdom of neighbouring Zululand as a foil to the colonized community. Zululand features as a pure and imaginary site of Zuluness, exposing the inferior reality of Pagadi's subjugated site. Haggard centralizes two aspects of Zulu society: the war-dance collective and the chief himself.

Before his narrative describes these two it offers us an icon of noble savagery, a young 'finely-built warrior arrayed in the full panoply of savage war' (287). This scene strikingly departs from descriptive mode to give a prescriptive commentary on the impact of white colonialism. Thus Haggard concludes his account of the warrior:

As he stood before us with lifted weapon and outstretched shield, his plume bending to the breeze, and his savage aspect made more savage still by the graceful, statuesque pose, the dilated eye and warlike mould of the set features, as he stood there, an emblem and a type of the times and the things which are passing away, his feet resting on ground which he held on sufferance, and his hands grasping weapons impotent as a child's toy against those of the white man,—he who was the rightful lord of all,—what reflections did he not induce, what a moral did he not teach! (287)

At the very moment when Haggard affirms the supremacy of white authority the referent becomes ambiguous: 'he who was the rightful lord of all' can denote the Zulu as well as the 'white man'.[11] This suggests an anxiety about the stability of that white power: the lament for the Zulu's passing as the result of an inevitable historical process makes thinkable the possibility that white domination too may pass. To compound this ideological

---

[11] See Low, *White Skins. Black Masks*, 50–62, for a discussion of the voyeuristic positioning of Haggard's white male narrators in relating African males. Low sees this as 'the Orientalist gaze', 'both a disciplining and narcissistic eye/I. Its gaze which lingers on the physical surfaces of the black man's body is in this case also homoerotic'.

fragility, the warrior's function as epitome of savagery is undermined by his role as an aesthetic anachronism.

Haggard portrays the war-dance as a metonymic chain.[12] The
dancers undergo constant metamorphosis, sliding from one
animal form to another. Their cry is now 'the snorting of a
troop of buffaloes, now the shriek of the eagle as he seizes his
prey, anon the terrible cry of the "nightprowler", the lion, and
now—more thrilling than all—the piercing wail of a woman'
(290). The dance deconstructs gender as well as animal identities. 'Whatever the cry', Haggard asserts, 'the cadence rises and
falls in perfect time and unanimity; no two mix with one
another so as to mar the effect of each' (290). He finally
observes that 'Wild as seems the confusion, through it all, even
in the moments of highest excitement, some sort of rough order
is maintained; more, it would seem, by mutual sounds than by
word of command or sense of discipline' (291).

The multiple metamorphoses are totally synchronized, the
men absolutely united through an intuitive bonding that does
not require external command nor even a 'sense of discipline'.
The warriors thus become an autonomous, self-regulating force.
This then is an image of de-individuation that contrasts sharply
with the individual, objectified positioning of the narrating
British onlooker. The war-dancing men condense two attributes
essential to Haggard's future Zulu representations. They are
essential also to the contents and operations of his fantasy mode
itself. Savage wildness on one hand and extreme discipline on
the other; a strictly policed free-flow, operating within established spatial, temporal, and cultural limits.

However, after all the excitement of this war simulation in
which the men repeatedly mime 'killing and being killed',
Haggard seems compelled to downgrade it:

Imposing as was this old-time war-dance, it is not difficult to imagine
the heights to which its savage grandeur must have swelled when it
was held—as was the custom at each new year—at the kraal of
Cetywayo, King of the Zulus. Then 30,000 warriors took part in it,
and a tragic interest was added to the fierce spectacle by the slaughter
of many men. It was, in fact, a great political opportunity for getting
rid of the 'irreconcilable' element from council and field. Then, in the

---

[12] The metonymic chain is a standard feature of fantastic literature. See
Rosemary Jackson, *Fantasy: The Literature of Subversion* (London: Methuen
1981).

moment of wildest enthusiasm, the witch-finder darted forward and lightly touched with a switch some doomed man. (292–3)

In the place of the old chief Pagadi, loyal to the British government and resident in Natal, Haggard evokes the spectre of an autonomous Zulu king, resident in his own Zululand. This is a king who attempts absolute social unity by command, and uses the dance as his medium. The dance does not, as in Pagadi's reserve, merely simulate death but instead provides its actual occasion. Pagadi's colonial version retrospectively ceases to be a satisfying representation of war and becomes instead an unsatisfying compensatory aesthetic alternative. In rendering the dance both expression and sublimation of Zulu murderousness, Haggard reveals himself to be ambivalent towards both Natal colonialism and Zulu autonomy. His discourse here also suggests ambivalence towards the aesthetic sphere itself: he both establishes and disputes its adequacy to its object.

Haggard presents the warrior collective as the autonomous and self-regulating centre of Zuluness, which requires no external control or leadership. Yet he also wants to position the chief as the centre of the community; its leader, source and cultural representative: 'this system of chieftainship and its attendant law is, to all the social bearings of South African native life, what the tree is to its branches . . . dependent on it are all the native's customs, all his keen ideas of right and justice; in it lies embodied his history of the past, and from it springs his hope for the future' (293). The old chief of the Natal reserve has an organic foundational relationship to his community. This differs considerably from Zulu monarch Cetshwayo's relationship with his subjects. The king's need to eliminate 'irreconcilable' elements reveals his authority to be far from consensual. His power aspires towards autarchy; his leadership is potentially antagonistic towards his people. The differences between Pagadi and Cetshwayo here illustrate some differences between 'colonial' and 'metropolitan' models of political power. The colonial model recognizes Theophilus Shepstone as a fellow leader. He can be identified with a certain self-conception of colonial authority, that which wants to regard itself as wholly representative of its (alien) populace, paternalistically ruling by consent.[13]

[13] But see Low, *White Skins. Black Masks*, 74–5, for a contrasting perspective,

The royal Cetshwayo, in contrast, engages a fantasy of absolute, despotic control that does not recognize as legitimate any colonial element just as it excludes any internal opposition. Such a model is fundamentally incompatible with the colonial political model of Pagadi and Shepstone. The very autonomy and absolutism associated here with the Zulu king's rule make him a stronger candidate for British metropolitan fantasy and imperial identification than the tame Pagadi.

THE ANGLO-ZULU WAR AND SETTLEMENT: IDEOLOGIES AND PRACTICES

For the neighbouring British colony of Natal, Zululand's autonomous existence was politically and economically undesirable.[14] Natal was a poor, underinvested colony, whose white farming populace saw control over Zululand as the solution to their difficulties: it would provide an abundance of land and a cheap source of wage labour. For a while, Zululand was also contrary to metropolitan British interests. In 1875 the British government had launched a 'Confederation Scheme' whose aim was the establishment of 'a strong, united, white-dominated southern Africa' that would facilitate British capitalist development of the region. Zululand impeded such a plan. Accordingly the new High Commissioner appointed to supervise confederation, Sir Bartle Frere, launched an aggressive campaign for expansion into Zululand. In December 1878, he sent the king Cetshwayo an ultimatum that contained demands he knew to be impossible.

On 11 January 1879, British troops under Lord Chelmsford arrived to enforce the terms of the ultimatum. Instead of the expected easy military victory they encountered a powerfully

which reads this notion of absolute, despotic rule as a specifically colonial rather than metropolitan fantasy; it is a notion of Shepstone's which instates him in the role of absolute Zulu monarch. Hamilton in 'Theophilus Shepstone' concurs, seeing Shepstone's rule as imitating (his conception of) Shaka's. McClintock (*Imperial Leather*, 251) sees Shepstone's colonial fantasy of power over the Zulu as a divine paternal one: 'Shepstone manipulated the invented traditions of fathers and kings, mimicking allegiance to certain customs of Zulu chieftainship, while retaining for himself the superior status of father . . . Shepstone drew on an ideology of divine fatherhood as preordained and natural, the founding source of all authority'.

[14] My information is drawn from Guy's *Destruction of the Zulu Kingdom*.

united Zulu force which destroyed their headquarter column at
Isandlwana eleven days later. In fact, the Zulu proved to be
militarily unbeatable. It was established that the Zulu would
disarm if they could hold on to their land. As a consequence, the
British metropolitan government abandoned its plans for direct
annexation. This was a crucial *volte-face*. From now on British
home interests in Zululand were to be directly at odds with
colonial Natal's interests; Natal continued to desire direct
annexation of the African kingdom. Theophilus Shepstone, the
colony's Secretary of Native Affairs, Haggard's former employ-
er, and the dedicatee of *Nada* was centrally involved in Natal's
operations.

Sir Garnet Wolseley devised a post-invasion settlement that
removed Cetshwayo from office and divided Zululand into
thirteen chiefdoms, each ruled by an appointed chief. According
to Jeff Guy, this notorious settlement, which 'excluded from
authority men of status and power in the country, the representatives of the old Zulu order' inaugurated the real period of the
destruction of the Zulu kingdom, through a civil war which
lasted until 1884 (239). Most of the chiefs appointed under the
settlement were unable to exercise power. But four had strong
connections with the colonial trading world. Two of them in
particular, Hamu and Zibhebhu began to appropriate land and
terrorize the populace of northern Zululand. These chiefs soon
gained the support of the colonial officials, who saw them as
useful assistants in the project of destabilizing Zululand with
the aim of achieving Natalian control. Meanwhile the victims of
those chiefs' oppression joined a movement of the Usuthu,
supporters of Cetshwayo's royal house. When the opposition of
colonial officials became clear, they directed their campaign for
the restoration of Cetshwayo at metropolitan Britain. The home
government had abandoned interest in annexation of Zululand
in 1879 and now had a purely strategic interest in the land
whose geographical position between the Transvaal and the sea
made it a potential impediment to Boer expansionism. It was
therefore now in the interests of the British home administration
to facilitate a strong and unified Zululand, which Cetshwayo's
restoration could provide.

From initially opposing the Zulu king, then, Britain had
moved radically to official support for his restoration. Formerly

in favour of Natal's annexation schemes, Britain now wished to keep Zululand in a state of relative autonomy. This of course was anathema to the officials of Natal. Lord Henry Bulwer, Natal's Lieutenant Governor, was responsible for preparing a report on the settlement. Knowing that the home government would not agree to direct annexation, Bulwer proposed a compromise settlement: the partition of the country into three parts, the southern part to be under direct British rule (the Reserve), a northern part to be under the colonial ally Zibhebhu, and the middle part to be under the Zulu king Cetshwayo. This scheme was put into action and on 29 January 1883 Shepstone reinstated Cetshwayo as king. Violence immediately broke out. The attack by Zibhebhu on the Usuthu at Ulundi in July 1883 'virtually annihilated the leaders of the old political order, and drove the king into hiding'; this marks, according to Guy, the real end of the Zulu kingdom (242).

Cetshwayo died in October under suspicious circumstances. After his death, there was a deadlock. The Usuthu continued to fight against Zibhebhu and formed an alliance with the Boers to do so. By late 1884, the colonial ally Zibhebhu had been defeated. The royalist Usuthu were now forced to sign a concession that granted the Boers a large portion of land. They petitioned the British Government for aid, which was denied them; the government adhered to its policy of non-involvement. But in October 1885 the Boers claimed so much land for their New Republic that London issued a warning, feeling its own interests threatened. The Boers took their revenge on the Usuthu who again petitioned for aid, and this time Bulwer recommended British action. His successor Sir Arthur Havelock opened negotiations with the Boers and the country was effectively divided between them, with a small area remaining to the Zulu outside the New Republic and the British Reserve. In June 1887, this area also was absorbed into the Reserve and the creation of British Zululand was announced. The process of capitalization now began in earnest, and Guy remarks that 'by 1894 Zululand was . . . one of the chief sources of the native labour supply on the Rand' (239).

Surrounding and informing these events is a mass of colonial and imperial ideology that is important in providing the context for Haggard's ideological project. Profound epistemological and

political problems present themselves here: the need to characterize Zulu society and its place in South Africa proves to be as
difficult as it is vital for Haggard's contemporaries. They are
often eager to assess the Zulu kingdom's historical trajectory
and frequently feature the early nineteenth-century ruler Shaka
in their pre-settlement discourses. The colonial Shepstone for
example constructs the Zulu military system as one that had
'served a bloody purpose in the time of Shaka, but was now a
dangerous anachronism'. Sir Bartle Frere, the High Commissioner appointed to supervise the original confederation
scheme, alleges that Cetshwayo 'was trying to reconstruct the
brutalizing system of Chaka'. These examples suggest how
Shaka's rule could represent the original and now outdated condition of Zulu life; it marks the point at which traditional
Zuluness began.

But post-war settlement ideologies rudely challenge such
associations by conjuring up the era preceding Shaka as the
truly original scene of African cultures and politics. The essence
of Zuluness becomes fractured by this recourse to pre-*Mfecane*
ethnicity. For example Wolseley, in charge of the devising the
settlement, claims:

In the redistribution of territory which I have now made, I have given
a place to the representatives of these subjugated people [the 'tribes' of
the 'Ndwandwe, the Umtetwa, and the Zungu,' who occupied the land
before Shaka's 'conquest'], who, though to a large extent amalga-
mated, after this relapse of time, with the Zulus, are I am assured,
mindful of their ancient and independent origin, and proud of their
distinct traditions. (71)

Pre-settlement accounts of the current relationship between
the Zulu king and his people are no less conflicted. Zulu society
is presented as a seamless totality, a cohesive and dangerously
well-organized and united people. Shepstone casts the Zulu
society as an 'engine constructed and used to generate power'
(47).[15] The technological modernity of this image conflicts
interestingly with his suggestion that the military system is an
anachronism. In this scenario, the king is embodiment and

---

[15] It is so ubiquitous as to make examples redundant. For an example from the
renowned 19th-cent. South African historian George McCall Theal, see *History of
South Africa from 1795 to 1872* (4th edn.; London: Allen and Unwin Ltd 1915), i.
438, 'the army became a vast machine'.

custodian of the Zulu people. Sir Bartle Frere casts the king as the modernizing head of a nascent nationalist resistance movement: Africans in general felt 'that the time was come for them all to join the flood of new ideas and ways which threatened to sweep away the idle, sensuous elysium of Kaffirdom' (48).

Other representations contest this united proto-nationalist characterization of the Zulu kingdom. The same Shepstone leads officials to believe that Zulu society is essentially disunified, full of internal political divisions. This version sees the king as cruel oppressor of his people. The very same Frere claims that his plans would 'free the Zulu people from the tyranny of a bloody despot' (49). The king serves then as both the representative of, and the tyrant over, 'Africans'. The colonial Frere to justify annexation plans uses this distinction between the Zulu people and the king. However, the same distinction is also used to opposite ends, to justify the decision *not* to annex the land but instead to remove the king and subdivide it, as occurred in Wolseley's settlement. This line of reasoning maintains that the war had been against the king and that the Zulu people therefore could retain their land. The king however had to be deposed, to 'maintain the fiction that it was Cetshwayo's excesses which had persuaded Britain to invade the kingdom' (61).

Some influential historians have seen the disastrous settlement designed by Wolseley as an example of Machievellian scheming, designed to achieve the breakdown which the invasion had failed to secure.[16] Jeff Guy however contends that the arrangement was simply the result of ignorance and expediency. Wolseley's ideological defence, which presents the land as being returned to its traditional, decentred, pre-*Mfecane* condition, constitutes a problem for the analysis of colonial discourse and action. Notably Guy contradicts himself on this point. After claiming that Wolseley's settlement was the fault of his ignorance of Zulu history and polity, he goes on to claim that such speech was disingenuous rhetoric designed 'to make the settlement more palatable' and persuade the British public of the value of the war (78).

[16] The editors of *The Oxford History of South Africa*, vol. ii (Oxford: Oxford University Press 1971), Leonard Thompson and Monica Wilson, argue that 'no more astute device could have been found for setting Zulu against Zulu and thus consummating the military victory without further cost or responsibility', p. ii.

If the premises of Wolseley's own settlement ideology are difficult to ascertain, the same can be said of other colonial and metropolitan responses to the settlement. Accompanying the face-saving, ignorant and Machievellian dynamics outlined above, there was also an ideological strain of humanitarianism together with the belief in the Zulu kingdom as an autonomous society. This strain suggests that unfortunate though the decentralization policy had been, at least the principle of *Zulu* rather than colonial ownership and political control had been honoured. There is even a hint of this strain in the discourse of Lord Bulwer, Natal's Lieutenant Governor, who was appointed to report on the settlement and draw up an alternative. Bulwer originally approved the settlement 'in that it avoided annexation and therefore left the land in the possession of those people for whose welfare the war had been fought' (134).

The failure of the settlement saw both convergence and increased antagonism between the discourses of imperial England and colonial Natal. Britain moved away from the politics of decentralized chieftain rule of Zululand, and moved towards support for a central, paramount government, while Natal intensified its own demands for a rigorous authoritarian government. In this there was a confluence. Bulwer's statement that 'paramount and supreme authority, which is an essential condition of the Government of any native race' was necessary articulates the drift of both colonial and imperial ideologies. But there the identity ends. The British home government saw the Zulu king himself as the desirable form of this supreme authority. The Natal settlers of course preferred such authority to be white and settler.

The colonial Shepstone argues in a language of 'responsibility'; Britain and Natal 'cannot rid ourselves of the responsibilities which the results of the war, and which the frank acceptance of those results by the Zulu people have placed upon us' (81). He advocates the extension of white authority (221). Metropolitan Britain in contrast abstained from direct involvement, as was consistent with its post-war ideology of relative autonomy for Zululand. In effect, this meant a refusal to extend assistance to those victims of the mess it had partly created through its invasion and the civil war that followed from the settlement.

Against the brute fact of that final annexation and Zululand's absorption into South African capitalism, then, stands a welter of discursive confusions at each stage of the messy process leading up to that capitalization. As I have pointed out, the historian Jeff Guy himself offers contradictory interpretations of the administrators, seeing both an informed purpose and un-intended ignorance at work in their destructive policies. Contra-dictions abound: the High Commissioner Bartle Frere alleges both that Cetshwayo is an unpopular despot and the head of a popular nationalist movement. Sir Garnet Wolseley asserts that the inhabitants of Zululand still adhere to the diverse authorities and customs of the era that preceded Shaka—an 'organic' model of traditions reminiscent of Haggard's model for chief Pagadi. This contradicts Bulwer's notion that Zulus follow a 'might is right' doctrine and accept whoever conquers them as their proper authority—which corresponds to Haggard's alternative Cetshwayo model.

These discourses suggest a situation that at times polarizes colonial and metropolitan administrations to reveal striking con-flicts of interest. These discourses also suggest how slippery the relation between reason and rationalization can become. The colonial administration can align a language of 'authority', 'security', and 'responsibility' with a policy of brutal political and economic domination. Meanwhile the home British govern-ment is portrayed by its advocates (and those who appeal to it, like the Usuthu) as a guarantor of humanitarianism and 'justice'. It utilizes alternative notions of benign and respectful non-inter-ference to advance an equally inhumane irresponsibility and strategic uninterest. All these contradictions indicate that it is necessary to acknowledge the material contexts and interests of those involved in promoting ideologies of colonialism.

If due recognition needs to be given to the material differences of these interest groups, such recognition must also be given to the way in which their discourses frequently blur the boundary between reason and fantasy, instrumentality and irrationality. There is no point in attempting to ascertain whether Shepstone, for example, was 'really' a schemer or basically the victim of his own delusions. Much more important is the fact that this kind of indeterminacy can prevail as con-sistently and pervasively it does.

AFTER THE WAR: HAGGARD'S ANALYSIS

I have discussed how in the years before the Zulu War the autonomous kingdom of Zululand functioned for Haggard as a pure space of African 'noble savagery', in contrast to the tame Natal reserve of chief Pagadi. The war, the ensuing destruction of the Zulu kingdom and the formal annexation of Zululand by Natal bring these functions to an end. Haggard's consequent confusion makes its way into the pages of his *Cetywayo* to produce a highly oxymoronic discourse in which the settler-colonial perspectives of Shepstone constantly collide and combine with metropolitan perspectives.[17]

Haggard's *Cetywayo* discussion moves swiftly to Cetshwayo's coronation in 1872 and the origins of the invasion. He rejects one of the colonial justifications for the invasion, that Cetshwayo was too bloody a ruler in home policy and had violated his coronation agreement to govern his subjects in a more humanitarian fashion.[18] Instead Haggard argues that:

> The Government of Natal had no right to dictate the terms to a Zulu king on which he was to hold his throne. The Zulu nation was an independent nation, and had never been conquered or annexed by Natal. If the Government of that colony was able by friendly negotiations to put a stop to Zulu slaughter, it was a matter for congratulation on humanitarian grounds; but it is difficult to follow the argument that because it was not able . . . to do so . . . England was justified in making war on the Zulus. (10)

Haggard's defence of the king's sovereignty *vis-à-vis* his own subjects reveals a strong investment in the notion that a Zulu ruler must of necessity be tyrannical in order to qualify as authentic. The condition and essence of Zulu monarchy is despotism.

Haggard's own initial attempt to justify the invasion rests on

---

[17] Low sees Haggard's *Cetywayo* as directly reflective of a settler-colonial ideology, 'a colonial plan to bring traditional self-sufficient African communities into a wage-labour economy based on the development of Natal for white settlers' (*White Skins. Black Masks*, 70).

[18] The four conditions of this coronation agreement ('that the indiscriminate shedding of blood should cease; that no Zulu should be condemned without open trial; that no Zulu's life be taken without previous knowledge and consent of the king; that for minor crimes the loss of property should be substituted for death', *Cetywayo* 9) are the conditions to which Umbopa agrees, in *King Solomon's Mines*, when he begins his reign over the Kukuanas.

the Shepstone/Frere line of the dangerous nature of Zulu blood-lust:

Sir Bartle Frere declared war upon the Zulu because he was afraid, and had good reason to be afraid, that, if he did not, Cetywayo would before long sweep either the Transvaal or Natal; whilst, on the other hand, the Zulus fought us because our policy was too philanthropic to allow them to fight anybody else. (17)

Both halves of the sentence seem designed to soften the fact of a conflict between British and Zulu interests. In the first half, Cetshwayo is presented as a threat to the two adjacent colonies, not to British power as such. The sentence's second half presents a Zulu driven to aggression against the British by default.

When he develops this argument the paradoxes become glaring. Haggard tries to account for antagonism between the Zulu and British powers via the route of Zulu devotion to, and respect for, British power. He describes how Cetshwayo's army had been so insistent upon a spear-washing exercise that the king, forced to choose a target, settled on the Swazis of Swazi-land, who 'are themselves Zulus' and who had refused to recognize Cetshwayo's sovereignty.[19] But the pro-British Cetshwayo wanted permission for attack from the Natal Government. Haggard observes that 'the Governor of Natal could not in decency sanction . . . a war of extermination against the Swazis' and laments the obligations of such a civil code. Had the proposed war gone ahead 'the Zulu spears would have been washed, and there would have been no Zulu War. As it is, Englishmen have been killed instead of Swazis' (20–1).

The Zulu then attempted to target the Boers of the Transvaal as an outlet for their irrepressible bloodlust, but were thwarted by the annexation of that state by the British. As the Transvaal was now British property, Cetshwayo—again, acting in pro-British mode—did not want to attack it (23).[20] Haggard's leap from this demonstration of Zulu loyalty to Zulu turning on their own 'mother' seems impossible but a certain logic permits it. Had the British been less civil—that is, more like the Zulu—the disjuncture would not have been necessary. What

---

[19] As the Swazi battle that Haggard recommends here failed to materialize, he supplied a fictional version in *Nada*.

[20] This story of Cetshwayo's refusal to fight the British Transvaal is repeated in the dedication of *Nada*.

was needed was for the British/Zulu 'identity' to have been more privileged. This implies that Zulu bloodlust would have been satisfied with only one war. This however directly contradicts Haggard's contention of the irrepressible and perpetual nature of Zulu power. Haggard's ideology of the Zulu thus seems fundamentally divided. He is driven to see the Zulu and Cetshwayo as categorically impelled to colonial expansionism and war, regardless of the nationality of their neighbours. Just as powerful is his need to view the British and the Zulu as fundamentally in affinity with one another.

Haggard's discourse purveys the fantasy of Zulu as possessors of unbeatable military prowess. In pursuing this fantasy Haggard claims that what we saw in the war was only a small sample of Cetshwayo's military strength: 'the reason he [Cetshwayo] has himself given for this [less than totally aggressive] conduct is that he did not wish to irritate the white man; *that he had not made the war, and was only anxious to defend his country*' (29; emphases added). Had he wanted it to, Cetshwayo's mighty army could have demolished the British colonies, Haggard contends. To allege the purely defensive nature of Cetshwayo's actions in the war with the British might have struck Haggard as a rather major indictment of the British invasion itself. Indeed such an allegation demolishes the entire justification for the invasion as a response to Zulu expansionism. But Haggard is so bound up in establishing one aspect of Zulu/imperial power that he does not notice how much it defeats his other line of argument.

Somewhat later, Haggard presents us with yet another verdict on the Zulu performance in the war. No longer the defensive force which (because of its pro-British feelings) refrained from deploying its full power, the Zulu now become an army which used its power to the full and were fairly defeated: 'It cannot be too clearly understood, that, when the Zulus laid down their arms they did so, hoping and believing that they would be taken over by the English Government, which, *having been fairly beaten by it*, they now looked on as their head or king' (38; emphasis added). Causality and responsibility effectively vanish from this fraught scenario.[21] Haggard's Zulus and

---

[21] This inability enter into structural relations of interaction and causality is a feature of (in Lacanian parlance) 'imaginary' as opposed to 'symbolic' discourse. See

British are established as abstract protagonists both isolated from and (ideally) identical to each other; they are not able to form an interactive relation in which certain actions cause others. They both represent the abstraction of active military force, but this is a force that in this context, it seems, must be passive and merely reactive. The attempt to provide an explanation for the 'war' by working backwards first from one end (the Zulu) and then the other (the British) falters, then; there appears to be no centre point at which these explanations can meet. All that remains is the fact of a disjuncture, and the fact of the post-war settlement that leaves Zululand in fragments.

Haggard terms this settlement 'an abomination and a disgrace to England' (42). Haggard's analysis of settlement continues its oxymoronic pattern: colonial and metropolitan perspectives impossibly conjoin and cancel each other out. His position initially resembles Shepstonian colonialism. Like Shepstone, he argues for the institution in Zululand of a hut tax and white magistrates to administer it. Like the colonial administrator Bulwer he presents the argument that the Zulus follow a 'might is right' politics which involves submission to, and desire for, government by their victorious British foe; it also involves preference for a centralized authoritative government rather than a subdivided set of chieftainships. These proposals are completely consistent with a politics that aims for Zululand's eventual annexation and total control by settler colonials. But at the same time, and equally, Haggard's discourse articulates a humanitarianism very similar to that found in the *anti*-colonial writing of, for example, Florence Dixie.[22]

One needs to take seriously the vehemence of his disgust at the possibility that the settlement may have intended to weaken Zulu power and the fabric of its society: 'Such a settlement as

Homi Bhabha, 'The Other Question', *Screen*, volume 24, number 6 (Nov.–Dec. 1983), 18–36.

[22] Florence Douglas (better known as Florence Dixie), A *Defence of Zululand and Its King* (London: Chatto and Windus 1882). She was a rather unfortunate addition to the Zulu cause—see Guy's references to her. But her book appears to have influenced Haggard more than he is prepared to admit. Hamilton makes a similar observation on Haggard's critique of the pro-Zulu monarchy Colensos, in *Cetywayo*: 'Haggard's rhetoric echoed that of the war-mongering officials seeking to "liberate" the country from the tyranny of the Zulu kings. But Haggard's criticism of Colenso was contradictory, for elsewhere, Haggard makes practically the same judgement as Colenso' ('Theophilus Shepstone', 13).

this could only have one object and one result, neither of which is at all creditable to the English people. The Zulus were parcelled out among thirteen chiefs, in order that their strength might be kept down by internecine war and mutual distrust and jealousy' and the intensity of the exclamation 'Did we owe nothing to this people whose kingdom we had broken up, and whom we had been shooting down by thousands? They may well ask, as they do continually, what they have done that we should treat them as we and are doing?' (39, 38). Haggard's charge that the home government has caused more bloodshed than ever there was in Cetshwayo's day is a replica of Florence Dixie's anti-colonial line, and may even be lifted from her.[23]

Haggard's commentary here was written when the question of Cetshwayo's restoration was still an open one. A pro-colonialist might seize this opportunity to argue unequivocally against any restoration. Haggard does indeed state that 'the large majority of the Natalians consider that his restoration would be an act of suicidal folly, and their opinion is certainly entitled to great weight, since they are after all the people principally concerned' (46). But he goes on to reveal an imperial, metropolitan fantasy affinity with the king. Haggard is insistent that to reinstate the king 'is to restore the status quo as it was before the war . . . a Zulu king must either be allowed to rule in his own fashion or not at all' (47). Affirming the necessity of Cetshwayo's (imperial) autonomy, Haggard again evokes the sentiment of mutual supportiveness between the metropolitan British and the Zulu. Cetshwayo, if restored, would 'prove a staunch ally' to Britain (48).[24] But the war itself has shattered the permanency of such a bond: 'But supposing him re-established on the throne, how long would it be before a revolution, or the hand of the assassin, to say nothing of the ordinary chances of nature, put an end to him, and how do we know that his successor in power would share his views?' (48).[25]

[23] Douglas, *Defence of Zululand*, 124.

[24] See ibid. 101, where Douglas argues that Cetshwayo 'has learnt from his mistakes' and would now be an ally to Britain.

[25] There is no space here to discuss Haggard's attitudes towards Zulus in his chapter on Natal, nor his attitudes towards other 'natives' in the chapters on the Transvaal. On Natal Zulus, he evinces an ambivalent desire for a Zulu non-contaminated by 'civilization', while contrasting their 'nobility' favourably against the 'weak', pacific, industrious Sotho.

In other words, the war itself is to be blamed; it is responsible for the destruction of the stable condition of 'alliance' between Zulu and British. This is hardly the argument one would expect from an ideologue of settler colonialism in Natal. Throughout this discourse there is a strain which laments the war, and manifests (however vaguely) a conservative desire for prelapsarianism, identifiable as the pre-war state of Zululand's autonomy, Cetshwayo's sovereignty, and the alleged goodwill between England and Zululand. As I have suggested a complex set of identifications and fantasies are at work here whereby the image of the militarist, autarkic and expansionist Zulu constitutes an ideal for British constructions of its own empire. Britain's fantasies of itself seem vitally dependent upon its fantasies of its Zulu counterpart; the loss of that Zulu potency jeopardizes Haggard's imperial selving, even as it affirms it.

Haggard proceeds to propose that Zululand be made into a British protectorate. Thus it would take the form, as Bechuanaland did, of semi-autonomous control and accountability to the British Crown itself rather than to South African colonial states. Such a proposal reads in this light as an attempt to restore to Zululand something—if only the illusion—of its former strength and autonomy. This is a contentious interpretation. It is also, importantly, only part of the story. For Haggard's language and arguments, as have already been pointed out, also support pro-settler readings. Ultimately Haggard's contradictory and ambiguous projections about Zululand and Zulu kings manifest a desire for a fundamentally impossible fusion of colonial and imperial narratives: the establishment of a space of Zuluness which conflates the colonial tameness of Pagadi in 'War-Dance' with the imperial wildness of Cetshwayo, i.e. of a land which is simultaneously under colonial dominion *and* autonomous. It is to be sealed off from white habitation, and from history itself. It is to function as a kind of pacific pugnacity; to signify a savage militarism and aggressive aggrandizing energy, without actually threatening, or coming into contact with, surrounding white power. This is remarkably similar, as we have already seen, to the condition of Kukuanaland at the end of *King Solomon's Mines*, forever closed off from white settlers, having the qualities both of African 'authenticity' and of white surrogacy.

By 1888, the date of Haggard's updated preface to *Cetywayo*, the whole conflict is over, the king is dead, and Natal has annexed Zululand. One might expect this situation to resolve Haggard's ambivalence but it only seems to intensify it. His attitude towards Cetshwayo is fraught; he now condemns him for violating his restoration promises, then condemns rather the government for believing that the king would adhere to them: 'a savage king, finding himself in his own country, but shorn of a third of his territories and more than half of his royal prerogative' is not to be blamed for 'doing those things that a Zulu so placed is accustomed to do' (p. xix). Cetshwayo is both a 'savage potentate' aggressively combative, and a victim of his white advisers, egged on by them to 'acts of folly' (rather than acts of aggression).

This double strategy of both upholding and belittling Zulu nobility is echoed in the way Haggard wavers between blaming the Zulu Usuthu for their misfortunes, and holding the British government responsible. Through the Usuthu's decision to ally with the Boers, Haggard claims, 'a large portion of their tribal inheritance was alienated for ever', and 'had it not been for the interference of the English government the Boers by this time would have had not a third or a half but all of Zululand, and in a very few years the Zulu people would have utterly ceased to be' (p. xlii). Immediately he undercuts himself: 'Of course this argument cannot be pushed too far against the Usutus, for it is the English Government that is really responsible for the partition of Zululand, as it is responsible for every Zulu life that has been lost since the restoration of Cetywayo' (p. xliii). Volatile to the last, his final conclusion switches again: 'But when all is said and done, Dinizulu and his advisers are still directly to blame for the partition of Zululand' (pp. xliii–xliv).

Unable to determine the source and cause of the problem, Haggard gives up on corporate governmental bodies of either the Zulu or the British, and exits from the sphere of political and social interactions altogether. He resorts to the notion of the period's whole history as generated entirely through individuals, singling out 'Sir Henry Bulwer and Mr Osborn, who, in the face of official callousness and discouragement, opposition, intrigue, and anarchy, for several years continually strove to save the Zulu people from destruction' (p. xlv). He makes further retreat into an individualism which jettisons public political action altogether: 'The history of the country for good and evil has to a very large degree been shaped by the policy and actions of individuals rather than by that of the Home Government' (p. xlv).

On the other hand, Haggard downgrades the legitimacy (and the desperation) of Zulu political activity as expressed in the Usuthu alliance with the Boers by resorting to a fairly uncharacteristic discourse of 'savage mentality'. The alliance was motivated by the short-term gratification of revenge, for which the Zulu were prepared to jeopardize their long-term future:

Savages are like children endowed with the strength and intellect (as opposed to the intelligence) of men. They long to attain the object of the moment with the passionate longing of a child for a new toy. Their *intellect* may warn them of the dangers in the path . . . but their *intelligence* is over-ruled by their desire. (p. xliii)

All of this suggests that Haggard has abandoned the public sphere and regressed to a severely infantile condition to reconstruct the Zulu. History consists of a heap of fragments that do not cohere into a narrative. The only explanations are to be found in the actions of individuals and the motivation of 'revenge'. As revenge is an action that is essentially reactive, it is therefore of only limited utility in explaining historical dynamics.

CONCLUSION

The analyst of colonial and metropolitan ideologies of empire encounters a striking range of representations during the decade of British conquest over Zululand. One thing unites these representations: the discursive dominance of *political* categories. Notions of Zulu national political sovereignty, royal absolutism, forms of military organization, appear to exercise both settler and metropolitan imaginations rather more than general notions of racial otherness and inferiority. That the discourses of the Zulu do not render them part of a racial generality should sound a cautionary note for a colonial discourse analysis premised on the assumption that blackness has a fixed meaning beyond historical and regional conditions, or the assumption that the notion of 'race' alone explains the dynamic of African representations.

The predominance of political emphasis in the representations of the Zulu also has implications for the analysis of British colonial and metropolitan imperial subjectivity during this period. It suggests that generalizations that cut across these two to posit a 'white' or 'British' psyche are of limited intellectual value; the factors that shape metropolitan and colonial anxieties, needs and priorities can be different and even in contradiction. We can see from both spheres just how unstable British political identities could be. Representations of the Zulu reveal considerable enthusiasm for fantasies of non-democratic or absolutist royal rule, supported by a culture of militarism; these fantasies, clearly, tell us something about the kinds of political administration some ideologues would have liked to see operating within Britain too. 'If only the British would behave more like the Zulu' appears to be one leitmotif of Haggard. That so much political self-conception can appear to revolve around African identification, or involve a frantic desire (in Haggard's case) to fantasize a confluence of interests between a black 'imperial' and white imperial people— this should alert us to the complexity of the relations between political fantasy and domination at this time.

4
The Fictions of Zulu History:
Nada the Lily

In the last chapter, we saw the variability of metropolitan and colonial ideologies of the Zulu throughout the fraught period of the Anglo-Zulu War. Haggard's non-fictional writings of the Zulu during this time are significant for a number of reasons. Their contradictory logic reveals an intense fantasy of a harmonious relationship between British and Zulu. It is unwilling to recognize the fact of an armed political conflict between the two and the fact of British responsibility for the eventual destruction of the Zulu nation with its sovereign king. Haggard's serious attempts to analyse the situation reveal him to be torn. He views the war and subsequent destruction of the Zulu nation as inevitable—tragic fate—and at the same time sees this situation as entirely avoidable, if only the right people had been in charge of government decisions or history itself. His turn to historical fiction in the form of *Nada the Lily* needs to be seen as an attempt to chronicle the Zulu people in a way that removes the British from implication in the death of the Zulu kingdom.[1] *Nada* rewrites the Zulus as victims, not agents, of history. Haggard's portrayal of Shaka and Dingane's political activities is one that minimizes their militancy and sovereignty. At same time, Haggard celebrates a version of Zulu militarism but in the safe, consumable form of non-historical subplot.

This may seem a relatively uncomplicated and obvious ideological agenda. But it is complicated by Haggard's confusions regarding his function as exonerator. From the opening of the book's Dedication, it is clear that Haggard is on the defensive, and this defensiveness is directed as much against white metropolitans and colonials as it is against Zulus, and the process of history itself. He wants to defend Theophilus Shepstone against the malevolent misinterpretations of his Transvaal actions given

---

[1] *Nada the Lily* (London: Longmans, Green and Co. 1892). The edition used throughout this chapter is that of 1949 (London: Macdonald and Co.).

by 'enemies' who 'have borne false witness against you on this matter'. Shepstone's motivations have been misunderstood, and those responsible remain unnamed. At stake is a radical contest of interpretative authority: who is and should be empowered to interpret the present and the past of Southern Africa.

Shepstone has been judged wrongly, but for Haggard the real problem is that Shepstone has been judged at all: Shepstone should be in charge of interpretation, not its object. What endows Shepstone with this interpretative, and political, authority? For Haggard, the Zulu people themselves. Shepstone has earned authority through his accumulated intimate experience and knowledge of the Zulu:

I have written a book that tells of men and matters of which you know the most of any who still look upon the light . . . If you knew not Chaka, you and he have seen the same suns shine; you knew his brother Panda and his captains . . . You have seen the circle of the witch-doctors and the unconquerable Zulu *impis* rushing to war; you have crowned their kings and shared their counsels, and with your son's blood you have expiated a statesman's error and a general's fault.

He has also earned his authority through being 'recognized' by the Zulu as their master, their father: 'they gave you the Bayeté, the royal salute, declaring by the mouth of their Council that in you dwelt the spirit of Chaka'.

I want to isolate a number of issues from this, all of which are keys to the dynamics of Haggard's imperial fiction of the Zulu. One is the way in which for Haggard, cultural, moral, and political authority is directly proportionate to (perceived) material centrality: the more sidelined one is from material power, the more authority one accrues, and especially so if in addition to being sidelined one is injured by that central power. Thus whatever Shepstone's actual centrality in the destruction of Zululand (about which Haggard may have been ignorant), his role for Haggard must be one who has been marginalized and victimized by the 'real' wielders of power and by malevolent ideologues (for instance, pro-Zulu liberals from the metropole and the colonies; state officials whose opinions differed from Shepstone's, as well as Zulus themselves who criticized Shepstone).

Another key issue is the source of Shepstone's perceived authority: Haggard sees this as deriving equally from Shepstone's knowledge of the Zulu and from his symbolic status *as* Zulu. In other words, this is both an epistemological and an ontological authority. They have their political corollaries in modalities that Haggard conceived respectively as colonial and imperial. The former situates the colonial as a mediator, advisor, kingmaker; one who has an organic and residential relationship with those he advises. The latter situates the imperial as supreme despot, not one who 'knows' but one who 'is' the king.

Finally, the dynamics of Haggard's Dedication are important for what they indicate about Haggard's notion of his own authority to intervene in Zulu history, provide the proper and authentic interpretation of its rulers and events.[2] His authority derives from his filial relationship with Shepstone. Haggard declares to Shepstone that when he (Shepstone) has died, 'Only your name will not be forgotten; as it was heard in life so it shall be heard in story, and I pray that, however humbly, mine may pass down with it'. Shepstone's posterity will be ensured, in part, by Haggard's writing; Haggard's posterity, in turn, by his association with the Shepstone he has given to posterity.

Haggard's authority to write about the Zulu derives then from Shepstone's knowledge of them. Haggard's authority also stems from the fact that he (Haggard) like the Zulus recognizes Shepstone as supreme Zulu king. If Shepstone is 'father' of the Zulus, and Haggard addresses him as father, then by association Haggard too in being 'son' is also automatically Zulu. The equations become most absurd, and revealing, in the final Zulu 'royal salute' and praise-song which Haggard gives 'to which, now that its kings are gone and the "People of Heaven" are no more a nation, with Her Majesty you are alone entitled'. The Zulu is given in the main text, with an English translation as footnote. The praise song firmly situates Shepstone as a father who:

> Nursed us from of old!
> You who overshadowed all peoples and took charge of them,

[2] See Gail Low, *White Skins. Black Masks: Representation and Colonialism* (London: Routledge 1996), 84–90, for a discussion of *Nada* and Haggard's appropriatory narrative politics of storytelling.

And ended by mastering the Boers with your single strength!
Help of the fatherless when in trouble!

From this welter of dedicatory confusion some conclusions
can be drawn. Haggard's *Nada* project takes as its starting point
the notion that he and Shepstone are somehow the true heirs of
the Zulu; in Shepstone alone does authentic Zuluness reside
now that the Zulu nation is dead. This whole book becomes,
clearly, an exercise in self-legitimation and vindication, to be
achieved through donning the garb of Zulu history, speech and
identity. But exactly who the legitimation is to be demonstrated
to, and the vindication directed against, remains unclear.

ZULU POLITICAL HISTORY: DELEGITIMATION AND MYSTIQUE

Haggard's project to reconstruct Zulu history has a number of
strands, all of which involve discrediting Zulu political achievements and exonerating the white colonial power from any
part in the decline and loss of national autonomy. Haggard's
representation of history as made by Shaka and his successor
Dingane is a crucial element in his delegitimation process; so too
is his invention and manipulation of the kingmaker Mopo and
Shaka's fictitious son Umslopogaas.[3]

From Haggard's prefatory comments, one would expect him
to produce a Shaka of imperial proportions:

The Zulu military organization, perhaps the most wonderful in its way
that the world has seen, is already a thing of the past . . . It was Chaka
who invented that organization, building it up from the smallest begin-
nings. When he appeared, at the commencement of this century, it was
as the ruler of a single small tribe; when he fell, in the year 1828,
beneath the assegais of his brothers, Umhlangana and Dingaan, and of
his servant, Mopo . . . all south-eastern Africa was at his feet, and it is
said that in his march to power he had slaughtered more than a
million human beings. An attempt has been made in these pages to set
out the true character of this colossal genius and most evil man,—a
Napoleon and a Tiberius in one. (11–12)

---

[3] Haggard probably got his inspiration for Mopo from the account of Shaka's
death given by Fynn in John Bird, ed., *Annals of Natal 1495–1845* (Cape Town: C.
Strüik 1865) in which 'Umbopo' (Mbopha, whose names Haggard expressly
modifies to Mopo) plays a prominent part and even temporarily assumes power
afterwards.

Instead Haggard gives us a Shaka who is essentially reactive not proactive.[4] Metaphysical rather than political, standing outside of history rather than producing it, he emerges not as a great military or political leader, nor as a mysterious and incomprehensible genius but as a fighting machine motivated primarily by childhood grievance and a desire for revenge.[5] Haggard's portrayal of Dingane could not contrast more: he is a weak-willed schemer, motivated by lust and greed, who engineers a Boer massacre.

Haggard's portrayal of Shaka is strikingly unlike that of F. B. Fynney, the 'late Zulu border agent' Haggard cites as a friend and primary source of historical information.[6] The colonial Fynney is more interested in Shaka's 'character' than in his metaphysical significance.[7] For Fynney, far from being a mass

[4] Carolyn Hamilton, 'Theophilus Shepstone and the Making of Rider Haggard's Shaka', University of Cape Town Centre for African Studies Seminar paper (1995), pursues a very different interpretation of Haggard's Shaka in *Nada the Lily*. She sees this Shaka as 'both a bloodthirsty tyrant and as a noble and able leader' (16), 'a fully ambiguous figure in relation to power and sovereignty' (18); her argument hinges on the tenet that the novel 'explores the way in which the Shepstone system sought to reach into a Zulu world to discover the principles by which it might best establish its authority' (16). This is an accurate summary of Haggard's earlier, non-fictional representations of Shaka, but I am arguing that by the time Haggard came to write *Nada the Lily* his representational priorities and ideological values had shifted.

[5] For two contrasting modern African literary representations of Shaka, see Thomas Mofolo, *Chaka*, trans. Daniel P. Kunene (1925; London: Heinemann 1981); Mazisi Kunene, *Emperor Shaka the Great: A Zulu Epic*, trans. the author (London: Heinemann 1986). The former presents an early Christian analysis of Shaka. The latter presents a modern Zulu nationalist position, celebratory rather than condemnatory. See Donald Burness, *Shaka: King of the Zulus in African Literature* (Washington, DC: Three Continents Press 1976), for a comprehensive account of modern literary representations of Shaka. The sensationalism of Haggard's historiography is maintained in e.g. E. A. Ritter, *Shaka Zulu: The Rise of the Zulu Empire* (New York: Putnam 1957) and Peter Becker, *Rule of Fear: The Life and Times of Dingane, King of the Zulu* (London: Longman 1964).

[6] Haggard cites F. B. Fynney, 'late border Agent' for Natal, whose *Zululand and the Zulus* (1880; Pretoria: the State Library 1967) was a source for *Nada*. Haggard lists his other sources as being John Bird; David Leslie, *Among the Zulus and Amatongas* (Glasgow: printed for private circulation 1875); Bishop Henry Callaway, *The Religious System of the Amazulu* (Springvale: J. A. Blair 1869).

[7] A contrasting, metaphysically orientated contemporary account of Shaka can be found in Revd. W. C. Holden, *The Past and Future of the Kaffir Races. In Three Parts: I. Their History. II. Their Manners and Customs. III. The means needful for their Preservation and Improvement* (London: Publ. for the Author 1866). Lacking Fynney's concerns with Shaka's political stature and character, Holden tries to assign Shaka a place within God's trajectory, but attempts to recuperate what are to him Shaka's mass-murders (which, for Fynney, constitute instead the laudable

exterminator, Shaka was instead a generous, compassionate and
widely adored nation-builder:

After destroying the head of a tribe, Tyaka [Shaka] showed great consideration for the people, supplying them liberally with cattle; and,
whilst dreaded, he as said to have a liberal hand, and to be a bene-
factor to those with small kraals, so that each day found him adding
numbers of fresh subjects to his already large following, and thus
increasing his power. It may be a matter of wonder that such a man
could gain esteem; but he did and was literally worshipped. He did all
he could to reassure those whom he had conquered. (7)

Fynney enumerates other of Shaka's good points, most significantly: 'He was also a staunch friend of the white man, and I am
of opinion that he would have been a friend to civilizing
influences, for he had a great mind' (11–12). Fynney does allow
his Shaka an expressly negative quality: 'Tyaka appears never to
have forgotten a grudge. Makedama was killed for having
refused him and his mother to remain in the tribe during the
time of the quarrel with Senzangakona [Shaka's father]' (11).
For Fynney, Shaka's capriciousness is another dominant
feature; he cites an anecdote about Shaka making a bet with his
councillors 'about the strength of a certain tribe—that "their
bodies would fill a certain donga" . . . The tribe was butchered,
but did not fill the donga, and Tyaka lost his bet' (11). Shaka's
character is concluded to be an 'enigma', driven by totally
unpredictable changes of mood (9).
    Fynney alternates between two Shakas. The first is one whose
greatness consists of military and political achievements, which
are huge in scale but uncomplicatedly laudable. The second
consists of a Shaka whose greatness is signalled by his

project of nation-building) prove problematic. He tries turning Shaka into both the
guilty victim of God's vengeance against offending South African heathens, and also
His instrument. The extermination of heathen savages by an equally savage king
was the precondition for this new white Christian era whose industry will cause the
'fertile valleys' to 'yield their ample stores', 42. This is a Christianity aligned with
colonial principles of commercial and industrial progress. Yet Holden's conclusion,
that the heathens' death was a necessary part of the divine scheme, receives a subsequent check a few pages on. Comparing the reign of Terror in France with Shaka's
regime, he now sees fit to deplore the loss of human life: 'on these altars of "reason"
and savageism the hecatomb of human beings was offered', 44. Both reigns illustrate
the wretchedness of humanity that necessarily results from Godlessness. Ultimately,
these governments seem to confound or defy Holden's providential scheme: the
more they elicit assertions of their divine use-value, the more they testify to their
irreducibility to that scheme.

Burckhardtian incomprehensibility and tyrannical irrationality.[8] The first, rationally and politically accessible Shaka corresponds to his alleged compatibility or proleptic identity with white 'civilization', while the second Shaka corresponds with his function as the epitome of savage otherness. Haggard's novel does not maintain these correspondences. If for Fynney Shaka's achievements as a nation- or empire-builder need to be affirmed as a basis for white colonial self-affirmation, for Haggard the opposite applies; white colonial and imperial identity seems contingent on the dissociation of Shaka from active and enduring empire-building. Haggard omits allusions to Shaka's technical military innovations that he had himself outlined admiringly in *Cetywayo*. Haggard also reduces any reference to the actual battles and conquests to an occasional throwaway remark or casual description. Missing too is any description of Shaka's popularity with his subjects, so enthusiastically affirmed by his source Fynney.

Haggard dissociates Shaka from not only the military/ political sphere, but also from the public sphere in general. Haggard's portrait instead draws on the domestic and characterological aspects of Fynney's account. But the Shaka who emerges has little in common with the unpredictable and incomprehensible Shaka of Fynney's domestic descriptions. Haggard's Shaka is, by contrast, very comprehensible, once one has grasped the rather limited conception of absolutist power that underlies his representation. It is an absolutism that is onto- logical rather than political, and predetermined. Thus when we first meet Shaka, a boy in flight from his tribe, accompanied by his mother, he is already fixed into his essence as an isolated individual, fully aware of his destiny as a supreme power, which he prophesies. His capacity for violence is also fully formed.

The portrait of Shaka as a monarch is dominated by a sequence of three acts: his killing off of his *isanusis*, arranged by Mopo; his matricide (and simultaneous destruction of Mopo's residence), which provides the occasion for a new 'smelling-out' of general enemies; his execution of the Langeni tribe in the Tatiyana ravine. Despite its appearance as an arbitrary series of

---

[8] See Georg Lukács's important analysis of Burckhardtianism in late 19th-cent. historical fiction, *The Historical Novel*, trans. Hannah and Stanley Mitchell (Harmondsworth: Penguin 1976).

sensational excesses, the sequence is in fact a steady and logical progression. In the targets and provocations of Shaka's violence, the sequence shifts in temporality: it moves from the present (contemporary *isanusi* trouble), to the recent past (the time of his son's birth and the treacherous preservation of his son by his own mother), to his own youth (the time of the Langeni people's slighting of him). This is simultaneously a move from a social class (the *isanusis*) to a domestic unit (his own and Mopo's family) to a tribe (the Langeni).

The first slaughter, significantly the only one done in concert with Mopo, is caused by an internecine clash of professional classes: the *isanusis* (diviners) have taken to smelling-out Shaka's *impis* (military commanders), their rivals in power.[9] Shaka's measure is depicted as an expedient to which he is driven to prevent the decimation of the military. Prompted by social necessity rather than choice, the massacre is produced by the aggressive activities of others. Mopo, not Shaka, is the originator of the plot. All that Shaka does, in effect, is to authorize it. The second act, the matricide, signals a shift from a conflict which only indirectly concerns Shaka (his military leaders are under threat, not himself) to one which directly concerns him, the preservation of his son by his and Mopo's family. Again, violent though his act is, it is fundamentally reactive, a response to a betrayal of him by those whom he trusted. The final act, the massacre of the Langeni, is again a reactive gesture. Shaka had promised to kill one person for every drop of milk he was denied; he now fulfils this. The massacre is hardly the capricious gesture that it is in Fynney; it is inevitable.

Shaka's actions, then, are literally anachronistic in origin; as time progresses, he regresses. He is far from being the figure who lays the social and military foundations for the future; he hardly has the capacity for being responsive to the present. Shaka's actions seem impelled by an ideology that demands absolute self-identity and autonomy. His murder of his mother quite literally renders him self-sufficient: having removed him-

---

[9] For a discussion of typical British literary representations of *isanusi* power, see Brian Street, *The Savage in English Literature: Representations of 'Primitive' Society in English Fiction 1858–1920* (London: Routledge and Kegan Paul 1975), esp. ch. 6 ' "Primitive" Politics in Popular Literature', 129–53, and ch. 7 ' "Primitive" Religion in Popular Literature', 154–84.

self from the lineage of the future by killing all progeny, he now effectively removes himself from his past lineage. The Langeni episode finally squares his present with his past self, rendering him self-consistent as well as self-sufficient. This unity is no sooner achieved than it is lost. The dying curse of Baleka during the Langeni massacre, that Shaka will now be incapable of proper sleep, gives him such bad dreams that he moves his residence to escape them.

Haggard associates Shaka with the forces of tragic fate; rather than being a major agent of history Shaka is turned into its victim, doomed to be overtaken by the forces of nature in the form of Mopo (as his nemesis) and by the white peoples whose advent he prophesies and supports. Fynney's assertion that Shaka 'was a friend to the white man', who would have been 'open to civilizing influences' is echoed through the way Haggard has Shaka promise part of his land to the English under King George, as the reader is casually informed. For Haggard, the political legitimacy of eventual white power over Zululand involves Shaka's theoretical endorsement; he is not seen as adversarial towards white imperial expansionism (unlike Dingane and Cetshwayo) nor (as in Fynney's writing) as its mirror and precursor.

Haggard turns Shaka's 'imperial' impulses into mere fictional potentiality, in the form of his imaginary son Umslopogaas. This is a particularly ironic aspect of Haggard's ideological project, because it involves a 'rescue' dynamic. Haggard presents a Shaka determined to eliminate his own family line. Umslopogaas is saved from destruction against Shaka's will and without his knowledge; in him lives on the 'authentic' martial, expansionist spirit of his father. As a later section will analyse, Umslopogaas's is the ideal articulation of Zuluness in which perpetual aggressive warfare is symbolic only, practised within geographically confined limits with ghost troops. It contains no aspirations towards material nation- or empire-building and only targets the black Africans who have provoked it. Simultaneously Haggard negates the 'Shakan' elements of his actual historical successors, Dingane, Mpande, and Cetshwayo, portraying them as inferior or deviant versions of Zulu power. Shaka's legacy is thus to be found not in the Zulu nation which survived him and which eventually culminated in open political conflict with the British, but instead in an imaginary son who chooses a nomadic life of individual autonomy and hidden identity rather than claiming his historical throne. By inventing this Shakan offspring and genealogy Haggard can 'rescue' Shaka from himself: despite his best efforts to destroy his line it lives on in Umslopogaas and Haggard alone is responsible for preserving an authentic Zulu historical imperial legacy!

In the second half of Haggard's novel, Dingane comes to power. He replaces Shaka's murderousness towards the family unit, and antagonism towards heterosexuality, by excessive heterosexual lechery. The reign of Dingane is also distinguished by the advent of the Boers as heralds of white colonialism, and Dingane's political resistance that takes the form of a massacre of the Boers. These two qualities—his sexual and his political desires—are crucially interconnected in Haggard's representation. Dingane's susceptibility to sexual greed is presented as evidence of his moral and political weakness, and also as part of the inevitable force of nature, one which equally determines Umslopogaas's fate. Both men are victim of their attraction to Nada who thus causes their downfall: their competing claims lead to a conflict that culminates in Dingane's death and Umslopogaas's renunciation of any desire to pursue his 'rightful' position as king of the Zulu nation. Nada additionally generates conflict between Umslopogaas and his jealous first wife Zinita who consequently betrays him to the king. Women, and heterosexuality, are thus stationed as the cause of the Zulu nation's fall.

Through his emphasis on the fatal destructiveness of heterosexuality, and femininity, Haggard diminishes the importance of white colonialism as a contributory factor in the decline of the Zulu nation. And by associating Dingane's lechery with his political motivations, Haggard effectively diminishes the force of Dingane's anti-colonial resistance. Femininity, fatality, and race are brought together in the supernatural song that Mopo hears after the massacre of his Langeni people:

The song was of the making of Things, and of the beginning and the end of Peoples. It told of how the black folk grew, and of how the white folk should eat them up, and wherefore they were and wherefore they should cease to be. It told of Evil and of Good, and Woman and of Man, and of how these war against each other, and why it is that they war, and what are the ends of the struggle. It told also of the people of the Zulu, and it spoke of a place of a Little Hand where they should conquer, and of a place where a White Hand should prevail against them, and how they shall melt away beneath the shadow of the White Hand and be forgotten, passing to a land where things do not die, but live on forever, the Good with the Good, the Evil with the Evil. (167)

In this Manichaean scheme, conflict between Woman and Man is as primary and inevitable as the conflict between Evil and Good, and black and white peoples. Sexual difference, it seems, leads necessarily to sexual conflict. But while the end of black/white conflict is explicit (the triumph of whiteness), the end result of sexual struggle is not. The passage, like the novel as a whole, appears to suggest a fundamental connection between sexual and colonial struggles; at the same time, the precise nature of that connection is deliberately mysterious. In practice, sexuality in the novel serves as a means of diverting attention from racial and political concerns, and of exonerating white colonialism.

Haggard's desire to give metaphysical sanction to white power takes a different form when he portrays Dingane's massacre of the Boers which Dingane undertakes, he claims, to free the land from 'white wizards'. The most directly political and rational act of the novel (and the only one, apart from the assassination of Shaka, to have real historical substance) Haggard renders as something meaningless that defies comprehension. On concluding his description of the massacre, Mopo exclaims to his addressee:

Say, my father, why does the Umkulunkulu who sits in the Heavens above allow such things to be done on the earth beneath? I have heard the preaching of the white men, and they say that they know all about Him—that His names are Power and Mercy and Love. Why, then, does He suffer these things to be done—Why does He suffer such men as Chaka and Dingaan to torment the people of the earth, and in the end pay them but one death for all the thousands that they have given to others? Because of the wickedness of the peoples, you say; but no, no, that cannot be, for do not the guiltless go with the guilty—ay, do not the innocent children perish by the hundred? . . . You know many things, but of these you do not know: you cannot tell us what we were an hour before birth, nor what we shall be an hour after death, nor why we were born, nor why we die. (216)

The contrast between the narrative response to the massacre of African Langeni people, and that of the Boers, could not be sharper. The Langeni episode elicits an explanation of the pre-ordained nature of white colonialism and genocide of black people. The Boer episode constitutes a rhetorical outrage to divine order itself.

NEOCOLONIAL AGENTS AND AFRICAN PROXIES

Mopo is the ideological centre of the novel, and Haggard stations him as the secret spring of Zulu history. It is Mopo who, as Shaka's right-hand man, suggests and devises Shaka's grand *isanusi* slaughter; it is Mopo's sister who gives birth to the son of Shaka who gets saved from infanticide, and Mopo who raises the son Umslopogaas under the pretence that the boy is his own. It is Mopo's daughter Nada who is the eponymous heroine of the book, Mopo's home 'tribe' which is 'butchered' to fill the ravine, and Mopo's mother who has caused the grievance for which the tribe dies (his father is Makedama, following Fynney's anecdote). It is Mopo who heads the conspiracy to assassinate Shaka; Mopo who puts Mpande on the throne by arranging the alliance with the Boers, Mopo who kills Dingane off in Swaziland; and finally, Mopo whose first person narration of the whole tale to an anonymous white traveller constitutes the book and whose immediate death on completing the tale marks the end of the book.

Mopo is a proxy of white colonial Victorian values; on the other hand, he represents a generalized traditional 'African' populace, its culture, values, and opposition to the 'oppression' it suffers from Zulu monarchy. His proxy status is explicit through the intertextuality of his speech to Dingane when he affirms the inevitability of white power and revenge for the massacre of Retief. His speech is lifted from one of Theophilus Shepstone or more precisely from Haggard's own dedication of *Nada* to Shepstone.[10] Mopo is then positioned as both the 'real' power and determinant of nineteenth-century Zulu history, and

[10] 'Thou canst not kill these white men, for they are not of one race, but of many races, and the sea is their home; they rise out of the black water. Destroy those that are here, and others shall come to avenge them, more and more and more! Now thou hast smitten in thy hour; in theirs they shall smite in turn', 215.

as its victim. His stationing as the power behind the throne corresponds with the self-appointed role of late nineteenth-century colonial and British agents like Shepstone, adopting advisory roles within Zulu society. Haggard in the 1888 edition of *Cetywayo* deplores the deleterious effects of Cetshwayo's white 'advisers' on his policies. He states that Cetshwayo might instead have paid attention to his rightful advisers, 'Sir Henry Bulwer, Mr Osborn and Mr Fynn'.[11]

In the case of the white advisers it is, for Haggard, a relatively simple matter of replacing the wrong ones with the right ones. But the distinction becomes rather more openly arbitrary when Haggard makes an African character the bearer of this colonial role. The subjectivism of the boundary separating legitimate advice from illegitimate scheming becomes glaring. Intellectual power associated with this advisory, custodial role keeps sliding into self-serving manipulation and 'plotting'. This is suggested, inadvertently, when Mopo arranges for the death of Shaka's *isanusis*. The *isanusis* are seen as motivated by the desire to expand their own power at the expense of the *indunas,* their rivals; they use or abuse their 'smelling-out' powers to eliminate the military. Mopo employs a moral argument against the *isanusis* to calm Shaka's unease about destroying them. The *isanusis* are not true officials because they abuse their office by turning it to political rather than its authentic spiritual ends. Yet this distinction between legitimate and illegitimate power breaks down through the very context in which it occurs. Mopo describes himself as sharing the *isanusis'* 'magic, one who had the seeing eye and the hearing ear' (63). All that distinguishes him from them is that his interests here happen to coincide with those of the king (who is anxious to stop his military from being eliminated).

Mopo's argument only underscores his own interest in this situation; he is as motivated by self-preservation and political gain as those against whom he schemes. Haggard departed from his sources in making Mopo serve Shaka as an *izinyanga,* or spiritual doctor. In the sources, Mopo is identified as an *induna,* a military chief. It is significant that when Dingane takes over

[11] *Cetywayo and His White Neighbours. Or, Remarks on Recent Events in Zululand, Natal, and the Transvaal* (2nd edn.; London: Trübner and Co. 1888), p. xxx.

from Shaka as Zulu king, Mopo's official capacity reverts to the military *induna* of the sources. What this suggests is that Haggard's political vision sees two legitimate models of power for colonialism to pursue: the role of spiritual guidance to an African king associated with military force rather than 'guile'; or, in the case of a devious and weakwilled African monarch, the role of military office.

Mopo's identification with, and promotion of, white Victorian cultural and political norms is clearest is in the ideologies of the family and of individualism which run throughout *Nada* and generate its narrative plot. But Haggard also supplies a contradictory counter-affirmation of African polygamy and tribal collectivity. When Mopo senses that Shaka is turning against him, he takes the precaution of sending Umslopogaas, Nada, and Nada's mother (his wife) Macropha out of the country, to preserve them from the threat of Shakan violence. To preserve them is also to preserve and uphold his nuclear family unit. This unit is associated with the operations of natural law. Haggard confirms natural law as mysteriously omnipotent when he allows romantic love to form between Nada and Umslopogaas who are raised as sister and brother and ignorant of their actual kinship as cousins. Observing Nada's romantic grief at the loss of Umslopogaas Mopo 'marvelled that the voice of nature should speak so truly in her, telling her that which was lawful, even when it seemed to be most unlawful' (86). The best vindication of the 'natural' laws of familial bonding, it seems, is achieved through their apparent violation.

This ideological affirmation of the nuclear family is short-lived. After removing his family from danger Mopo returns to his kraal, only to find it reduced to ashes. Not only is it destroyed: also destroyed are, we hear, all of his *other* wives and children (who have never featured in the text and remain an undifferentiated mass). And it is the destruction of *these* families which prompts Mopo to seek revenge against Shaka, which itself propels the novel's plot. At precisely the point when the ideological supremacy of the family as a unit is affirmed, that ideological focus splits into two incompatible models of the nuclear and the polygamous, both of which are supposed to function as pretexts for narrative action. Haggard's attempt to make Mopo simultaneously the representative of white Victorian and traditional African family structures thus breaks down into incoherence. Exactly the same incoherence emerges with Shaka's massacre of Mopo's people the Langeni. Mopo's history is that of the gifted individual. He was expelled from the Langeni as a boy, rejected by his father and the *izinyanga* to whom he was apprenticed (occasioned by envy of his exceptional gifts). His exile, exceptionality, and non-identification with his people are the preconditions for his narrative centrality and his political achievement in Shaka's court. But when the Langeni is destroyed, Mopo abruptly shifts into the ideological mode of the 'tribal'.

The strains and contradictions in Mopo's representation show the failure of Haggard's ideology. If *Nada* constitutes an attempt to erase the presence and theme of white colonialism, its historical, political responsibility for Southern African destruction, then this same white colonialism is exposed through the political and familial machinations of Mopo, whose role as a proxy for Victorian colonial values continually conflicts with his role as injured African everyman. In a similar vein, the attempt to displace colonial responsibility for the decline of the Zulu house by the mechanism of an inevitable terminal heterosexuality—triggered by Nada the lily herself—fails. For Nada like Mopo is revealed as a colonial proxy: her fatally attractive beauty derives from her extraordinary light skin, her whiteness. In other words, through the figure of Nada Haggard inadvertently suggests the destructive role performed by white settler colonials who disrupt as Nada does herself the rhythms and structures of traditional community life. Heterosexual romance of a nuclear kind is far from being the 'natural' force Haggard wants to portray it as: it is betrayed as openly ideological, imposed, alien, and destructive.

ZULUNESS AS FANTASY: IMPERIAL COMMODIFICATION AND CANNIBALISM

Haggard's preface declares the purely imaginary status of his wolf-kingdom episodes: 'the wilder and more romantic incidents of this story . . . the author can only say that they seem to

him of a sort that might well have been mythically connected
with the names of those heroes'. These episodes—in which the
(invented) son of Shaka, Umslopogaas, and his friend Galazi
rule over a pack of wolves—have received the highest praise
among critics of the novel.[12] This is a fantasy of an exclusively
homosocial society, ruled by two young men, dedicated to
militarist and expansionist principles, and removed from the
cycle of sexual reproduction.

In the wolf society we find all the components of Zulu fantasy
outlined in Haggard's early 'Zulu War-Dance': animal metamorphosis, literalization, equivocation, and strict spatial,
temporal, and political limits to the movement and scope of the
kingdom's activity.[13] Haggard establishes the status of the
wolves as a completely ambiguous one, equally naturalistic and
supernatural, animal and human. They remain fixed in number,
unable to reproduce themselves or to die naturally—they can
only die by the hands of men. They have an infinite appetite, but
they can only go hunting in the places where they originally (as
cannibal humans) fed their appetite, and they can only operate
at night. Like the actions of the main plot characters, then,
theirs are primarily reactive responses to pre-established conditions. If we take them to be ghosts, their punishment (an endless life of endless hunger) has a Dante-esque correspondence to
their crime of cannibalism.

While the wolves are anthropomorphized, the youths who
rule them are bestialized. When Umslopogaas first goes running
with the pack 'it came into the heart of Umslopogaas, that he,
too, was a wolf. They rushed madly, yet his feet were swift as
the swiftest; no wolf could outstrip him, and in him was but one
desire—the desire of prey' (129). The youths can be both essentially differentiated from their subjects and identified with them.
Both their humanity and their ability to 'pass' as wolves assure
their particular authority. The wolves can only recognize them
as rulers if they wear their wolf furs; when Umslopogaas forgets
to, he finds himself subject to wolf aggression. Their public wolf
status, then, depends on their clothing. Their psychology also

---

[12] See Haggard's description of the responses of Andrew Lang, Rudyard Kipling
(who got the idea for *The Jungle Books* from this section), and Charles Longman,
in his chapter on *Nada* in *The Days of My Life* (London: Longmans, Green and Co.
1926), ii. 1–38.

[13] 'A Zulu War-Dance', *Gentleman's Magazine*, 243 (July 1877), 94–107.

depends upon the company they keep. It is only when running with the wolves that Umslopogaas takes on their 'appetite' for prey. These rulers rule by assuming a certain identity with their subjects, but retain autonomy. The boys can enjoy ravening with the wolves, but are not held responsible for it; they are merely echoing and serving their subjects. As self-determining 'brothers', the youths are not held accountable to their subjects and need not, during the daytime, even be associated with it. As rulers, Umslopogaas and Galazi are confined to the pre-established territories of the wolves/ghosts. Within these limits they pursue guerrilla warfare which for the most part has no motive other than murderousness itself: 'For ever they ravaged through the land at night, and, falling on those they hated, they ate them up, till their name and the name of the ghost-wolves became terrible in the ears of men, and the land was swept clean' (138).

The language of 'sweeping clean', and 'eating up', echoes Haggard's description of Cetshwayo's Zulu monarchy, in *Cetywayo*. Indeed this fantasy section foregrounds the 'imperialistic' aggression that Haggard's non-fiction characterizes as essential to Zulu government in general and Shaka's reign in particular. But in his fictionalized account of the historical Zulu under Shaka and Dingane, such territorial aggression is minimized to a few passing allusions. It is only in these imaginary scenes, with invented not historical Zulu personages, that Haggard fully indulges his fantasies of murderousness as the core of Zulu royal governing policy. However these youthful rulers destroy without taking over the power structures of their conquered communities. Instead they retire to their invisible home in Ghost Mountain. In this way, Haggard articulates the paradoxical fantasy of Zulu despotism, colonial expansionism without physical conquest.

To get to this position of Zulu–wolf symbiosis, with its imaginary non-expanding expansionism, Haggard gives the youth Galazi like the youth Umslopogaas a family narrative of Zulu dispossession and migration. In Galazi's narrative all the elements of Haggard's Zulu fantasy receive their most extreme, unadulterated articulations, familial, political, and sexual. Galazi's grandfather was a younger brother of Shaka's father Senzangacona. Through his departure and subsequent rule,

Haggard can indulge his yearning for homicidal inter-African conflict and unbridled racialized tyranny:

But he quarrelled with Senzangacona, and became a wanderer. With certain of the people of the Umtetwa he wandered into Swaziland, and sojourned with the Halakazi tribe in their great caves; and the end of it was that he killed the chief of the tribe and took his place. After he was dead, my father ruled in his place; but there was a great party in the tribe that hated his rule because he was of the Zulu race, and it would have set up a chief of the old Swazi blood in his place. Still, they could not do this, for my father's hand was heavy on the people. (107)

The father decides to exterminate 'twenty of the headmen, with their wives and children, because he knew that they plotted against him. But the headmen learned what was to come, and they prevailed upon a wife of my father, a woman of their own blood, to poison him' (107). Notably, it is a woman who is the agent of 'betrayal'; women, here as throughout *Nada*, are associated with familial, ethnic, and tribal loyalties. The dying father requests that Galazi avenge him, and the boy promises to 'stamp out the men of the tribe of Halakazi, every one of them, except those of my own blood, and bring their women to slavery and their children to bonds' (108). He eventually succeeds in this plan. Initially Galazi kills the treacherous wife and stepmother as he leaves for exile and refuses the offer of a home with an old man in Zulu country because 'I wished to be a chief myself, even if I lived alone' (109).

As with the young Shaka and Mopo, envious patriarchs drive Galazi into exile. But Shaka and Mopo leave for exile in the company of a supportive female; in contrast, Galazi's support network and social bonding are exclusively male. In Galazi's story, the homosociality, like the brutality of Zulu conquest over the Swazi, is pushed to a simple extreme. The eventual genocide of the Swazi here provides Haggard with a fantasy corrective to 'bad' history. As we saw in the last chapter throughout his historical discussion in *Cetywayo* is Haggard's lament that the Zulu had been prevented from washing their spears with the blood of the Swazis: if that had been permitted, then the Zulu War might not have occurred.[14] Zulu venting of

[14] See *Cetywayo*, 20–1.

their bloodlust against the worthy black opponents of the Swazi would have satisfied all parties.

Following the template of his father's brutal colonialism, Galazi takes over the kingdom by killing off the king and queen wolves. He rules alone as king, until Umslopogaas's arrival; their joint rule suggests a version of political absolutism and sovereignty that is identical with material social powerlessness. ('I wished to be a chief myself, even if I lived alone'). In these two young men, and their wolf-kingdom, Haggard tries to siphon off the 'spirit' of Zulu political prowess and martial supremacy away from its material manifestations in its kings Shaka and Dingane (and Cetshwayo). A pure Zuluness is reserved for Umslopogaas and Galazi. In these fictional and dispossessed characters, Zuluness can be reconstructed as an aesthetic fixture and British regenerative resource.

In this reconstruction of Zuluness as an imaginary regenerative resource what is most revealing is Haggard's obsession with the practices of 'eating up', as a literal and metaphorical process.[15] The themes of hunger and consumption run throughout the novel. The narrator 'Zweete' (Mopo) tells his unnamed white addressee that 'the white men gather themselves together even now against U'Cetywayo, as vultures gather round a dying ox' (26). This is scene setting; the narration of the novel occurs 'during the winter before the Zulu War' (17). The imagery of vultures of course has the double effect of casting the Zulu people as victims rather than political agents, and of removing responsibility for the destruction of the Zulu kingdom from the white men who are stationed as parasites poised to consume a creature already in terminal condition. White men are not agents any more than Zulus are here, but they are consumers of black bodies.

The imagery gives away more than its ostensible ideological agenda. Haggard's decision to render the ghost-wolves former cannibals is the most heightened expression of his consumption fantasies.[16] Under the youths' rule, the wolf-ghosts roam,

[15] Haggard's obsession with consumption metaphors is evident throughout his 'About Fiction', in which he characterises his metropolitan readership as possessing an 'enormous appetite' and 'are prepared, like a diseased ostrich, to swallow stones, and even carrion, rather than not get their fill of novelties', *The Contemporary Review*, 51 (Feb. 1887), 173.

[16] Robert Michalski, 'Divine Hunger: Culture and the Commodity in Rider

'eating' people up. Haggard here takes a Zulu idiom ('eating up' as a phrase for killing), gives it a literal significance, and then deploys it as a metaphor again. The more he attempts to render the imperial spirit of Zuluness as one which equates killing with consuming, with a literal foundation in cannibalism, the more Haggard underscores the fundamentally and murderous cannibalistic impulses at work in his own imperial fiction here.

The Zulu throughout the novel and most particularly in the wolf-kingdom episodes are subjected to a multiple form of cannibalistic appropriation and consumption. I want to argue that ultimately Haggard has an interest in casting the Zulu as a dead carcass—only if seen to be dead can they be safely eaten—while at the same time paradoxically he wants to recuperate something of their 'live' spirit, because only if this spirit is alive can it animate the degenerate spirit of the British body that consumes it. In other words, by 'eating up' the bodies of brave Zulu warriors, the enervated British soldier body can ingest and be revived by the spirit, culture and potency of the Zulu.[17] As we saw in *King Solomon's Mines*, African death for Haggard is associated with food; the murdered body of Foulata protectively carries the breadbasket which the men take away before coming back to bury her body. These associations are taken to an extreme in *Nada*. There is a principle of bartering and mediation at work in the earlier novel, linked to an economics of exchange: in exchange for providing the men's food the body of Foulata is buried with the treasure, endowed with its tribute and symbolic value. But in *Nada* no such 'exchange' compensation operates; the emphasis falls entirely on a one-sided economics of consumption.[18] The body of the African

Haggard's *She*', *Journal of Victorian Culture*, volume 1, number 1 (spring 1996), 76–97, suggests of cannibalism in Haggard's *She* that 'Haggard . . . employed cannibalism as a trope with which to figure economic and cultural relations. The discourse surrounding cannibalism brings into play issues of economic scarcity and abundance, the differences between need and desire, the specifically cultural aspects of various forms of consumption, issues concerning the consumption of culture itself' (83). See Patrick Brantlinger's discussion of the 'reverse cannibalism' dynamics of imperial Gothic, *Rule of Darkness: British Literature and Imperialism, 1830–1914* (Ithaca: Cornell University Press 1988), 246–7.

[17] Michalski ('Divine Hunger', 92) notes that 'some literary critics of the late nineteenth century considered a transfusion of 'savage' blood a necessary antidote to cultural decadence'.

[18] Michalski (ibid. 85) remarks that 'cannibalism is a form of exchange which

Zulu itself is to be consumed, not the food which that body carries. The only 'compensation' or trade-off is Haggard's production of the Zulu as a commodity in the form of the book itself; they are 'eternalized' as an object of metropolitan consumption.

CONCLUSION

Nada the Lily is an important document of British imperial fiction and ideology, particularly because of its glaring contradictions and incoherence. This is a fantasy by Haggard of the Zulu but at same time, a fantasy of the imperial British *as* Zulus. And as such it reveals, inadvertently, just what the British have done to the Zulus, both literally and through the production of this fiction: eaten them up, pursuing a form of self-regeneration through instrumentalization or consumption of the Zulu body. The more Haggard tries to escape British historical responsibility for the demise of the Zulu kingdom, the more he shows it up through his deployment of neo-colonial proxies and fatal sexuality as alibis. The more he aspires to 'preserve' 'authentic' Zulu culture against its loss through modernization, the more he shows his conception of Zuluness to be a highly modern, colonial and metropolitan fiction. The same mechanisms used to defend and preserve Zuluness—the fictionalized slots of the wolf-kingdom—expose such Zuluness as precisely a fictional fantasy. The more Haggard claims to act against the logic of industrial capitalism, the more he reveals his book to be implicated in capitalist principles of consumerism. What emerges—apart from contradictions—is an interesting form of imperial nihilism. *Nada* is a book in which nothing can be affirmed, not even ambivalently. The morality and legitimacy of white power, so confidently articulated in *King Solomon's Mines,* is absent here.

resists all mediation: the cannibal directly appropriates and consumes the body of another'.

5
Colonialism Demystified:
Trooper Peter Halket of Mashonaland

HAGGARD'S legitimation of mineral wealth acquisition relies, as we have seen, on a 'bread/gold' opposition he appropriates from Olive Schreiner's *Story of an African Farm*. Schreiner's 1897 novella *Trooper Peter Halket of Mashonaland* in turn engages with the mystique of colonial capitalism effected by Haggard's earlier romance.[1] The impetus for *King Solomon's Mines* came not only from South African mining developments but also the archaeological investigations of the more northern land of 'Monomotapa'. These investigations and Haggard together helped perpetuate the fantasy of Great Zimbabwe as the setting for the biblical land of Ophir, ancient site of gold. Schreiner's *Trooper Peter* takes as its target the bloody culmination of this fantasy: the invention of Rhodesia by Cecil Rhodes and his British South African Company.[2] The pursuit of

[1] Schreiner, *Trooper Peter Halket of Mashonaland* (London: T. Fisher Unwin 1897). The edition used here is that of the 1974 reprint, introduced by Marion Friedmann (Johannesburg: A. D. Donker). *Trooper Peter* was republished by A. D. Donker in 1992 with an introduction by Sally-Ann Murray, 9–25. See the review essay by Carolyn Burdett, 'Olive Schreiner Revisited', *English in Africa. 21st birthday issue. 'Revisions',* volume 21, numbers 1 and 2 (July 1994), 221–32. The best current biography of Schreiner is by Ruth First and Ann Scott, *Olive Schreiner: A Biography* (London: Women's Press 1989). For the contexts of *Trooper Peter* see ch. 4 'England 1881–1889', 108–88; ch. 5 'South Africa 1890–1894', 189–214; ch. 6 'The Boer War and Union', 215–64. For Schreiner's correspondence of the 1890s, the recent edition of Richard Rive, *Olive Schreiner: Letters. Volume 1. 1871–1899* (Oxford: Oxford University Press 1988) is the one used here. Joyce Avrech Berkman gives an intelligent discussion of Schreiner's social-political thought in *The Healing Imagination of Olive Schreiner: Beyond South African Colonialism* (Amherst: University of Massachusetts Press 1989).

[2] My information is drawn from Apollon Davidson, *Cecil Rhodes and His Time*, trans. Christopher English (USSR: Progress Publishers 1988). For Rhodes's own speeches, see 'Vindex', *Cecil Rhodes: His Political Life and Speeches, 1881–1900* (London: Chapman and Hall 1900). On Rhodesian ideology see Richard Faber, *The Vision and the Need: Late Victorian Imperialist Aims* (London: Faber and Faber 1966). For historical analysis see Colin Newbury, 'Out of the Pit: The Capital Accumulation of Cecil Rhodes', *Journal of Imperial and Commonwealth History*, volume 10, number 1 (Oct. 1981), 25–43; Rob Turrell, 'Rhodes, de Beers, and

(very small) gold mines fuelled a violent expropriation of Mashonaland and Matabeleland, which met with one of the largest African resistance movements, the *Chimurengas* of 1893–4 and 1896–7.[3]

The fictional projects of Schreiner and Haggard share more than geography; both are concerned with the material and subjective operations of imperial capitalism, with the dynamics of land settlement and cultivation, and the representation of Britishness within the metropolis and in the Southern African colonies. But there the similarities end. *Trooper Peter* is a fictional critique of British imperialism; *King Solomon's Mines*, a legitimation. *Trooper Peter* has been conveniently ignored by critics and literary historians who have identified Conrad's *Heart of Darkness* (1899) as the origin of serious Western literary critique of empire.[4] What Schreiner offers, two years

Monopoly', *Journal of Imperial and Commonwealth History*, volume 10, number 3 (May 1982), 311–42. See also I. R. Phimister's excellent 'The Making of Colonial Zimbabwe: Speculation and Violence 1890–1902', University of Cape Town Centre for African Studies Seminar paper (1982).

[3] For an authoritative (and now much debated) account of the 1896 *Chimurenga*, see Terence Ranger, *Revolt in Southern Rhodesia 1896–97* (London: Heinemann 1967). For contemporary British accounts of the uprising, see Sir Edwin Alfred Harvey Alderson, *With Mounted Infantry and the Mashonaland Field Force, 1896* (London: Methuen 1898); Lt Col Herbert C. O. Plumer, *An Irregular in Matabeleland* (London: Paul, Trench and Trübner 1897). Contemporary British fictional accounts of the 1896 uprising include Bertram Mitford, *John Ames, Native Commissioner; a Romance of the Matabele Rising* (London: F. V. White 1900). See Stanlake Samkange, *On Trial for My Country* (London: Heinemann 1966) and *Year of the Uprising* (London: Heinemann 1978) for a fictionalized account of Rhodes and the uprising from a modern Zimbabwean perspective.

[4] Two critics to compare positively Schreiner's novella with Conrad's are Sally Ledger, *The New Woman: Fiction and Feminism at the Fin de Siècle* (Manchester: Manchester University Press 1997), 86–90, and Simon Lewis, 'The Violence of the Canons: A Comparison between Conrad's *Heart of Darkness* and Schreiner's *Trooper Peter Halket of Mashonaland*', paper delivered at 'Conrad and Post-coloniality: "Heart of Darkness" Centenary Conference', Universities of Potchefstroom and Cape Town, March–April 1998. For critical responses to *Trooper Peter* in particular and Schreiner's fictional politics in general, see Stephen Gray, 'The Trooper at the Hanging Tree', 198–208; Isabel Hofmeyr, 'South African Liberalism and the Novel' 154–7; Peter Wilhelm, '*Peter Halket*, Rhodes and Colonialism', 208–12, all in *Olive Schreiner*, ed. Cherry Clayton (Johannesburg: A. D. Donker 1983). See also Rodney Davenport, 'Olive Schreiner and South African Politics', 93–107; Alan Paton, '*Trooper Peter Halket of Mashonaland*', 30–3; Arthur Ravenscroft, 'Literature and Politics: Two Zimbabwean Novels', 46–57, all in *Olive Schreiner and After: Essays in Honour of Guy Butler*, ed. M. van Wyk Smith and D. MacLennan (Cape Town: David Philip 1983). See also the discussion of *Trooper Peter* in Gerald Monsman, 'Olive Schreiner: Literature and the Politics

before Conrad, is more extensive in its exploration of metropolitan and colonial populations and administrations to include
women's agency (both African and English); working-class
experience, military and economic expressions of power.[5] Not
only scope but also ideology distinguish Schreiner's from
Conrad's project. For *Trooper Peter* foregrounds the conceptual
possibility of an active opposition to imperialism, featuring
Africans and white subjects who embrace the alternative value-
system of radical Christianity. As in *Heart of Darkness*,
imperial theme and aesthetic innovation go hand in hand. Those
few critics who acknowledge *Trooper Peter's* existence tend
mostly to dismiss the book as a crude propaganda exercise, their
aesthetic distaste somehow intensified by the recognition of
Schreiner's use of a fascinatingly wide range of literary modes
to effect her 'political propaganda'.[6] I want to argue against
this view and suggest that the novella is a piece of formal
experimentation and a sophisticated interrogation of the very

of Power', *Texas Studies in Literature and Language*, volume 30, number 4 (winter
1988), 583–610. For a socialist fictional critique of late 19th-cent. economic
imperialism see William Morris, *News From Nowhere. or an epoch of rest*, ed.
James Redmond (1891; London: Routledge and Kegan Paul 1970), 79–82.

[5] The dating of the composition of *Trooper Peter* is an unresolved question. It
was published in January 1897. According to Ruth First and Ann Scott, the work
was written in January 1896; Schreiner refers to it in a letter to a friend dated 9
January. Yet the Rive edition of Schreiner's letters dates this same letter as August
1896 (288). In an unpublished letter to her publisher T. Fisher Unwin, dated 28
September 1896, Schreiner alludes to the novella: 'Further, I have a story, somewhat
of the nature of an allegory, dealing with Rhodes and the problems in Rhodesia,
more especially with the treatment of the natives. I have it only in rough draft now,
but think it will be from 20 to 30 pages in length' (Unpublished manuscripts,
property of Harry Ransom Humanities Research Center, University of Texas at
Austin). In the light of this, the August date seems more likely; Schreiner would
probably not keep a text in 'rough draft' for eight months (especially one concerned
with an urgent political problem), and would probably begin publication negotiations (as this letter goes on to do) shortly after composition.

[6] These critics include Ridley Beeton, *Olive Schreiner: A Short Guide to her
Writings* (Cape Town: Timmins 1974); Vineta Colby, *A Singular Anomaly* (New
York: New York University Press 1970); Nadine Gordimer, in her foreword to the
1989 edition of First and Scott's *Biography* and reprinted as 'Afterword: The
Prison-House of Colonialism', in *An Olive Schreiner Reader: Writings on Women
and South Africa*, ed. Carol Barash (London: Pandora Press 1987), 221–7. See also
the readers' reports on the manuscript. These were less than favourable: 'This is
halfway between a tract and a novel . . . All that is good in the book is the actual
description of the sufferings of the "niggers" ', comments reader number one. 'A
great style gone to pieces is a sorry sight' comments reader number two.
Unpublished manuscripts, property of Harry Ransom Humanities Research Center,
University of Texas at Austin.

concepts of 'rhetoric' and 'propaganda' which these critics consider Schreiner to have overused.

Schreiner is best known today for *Story of an African Farm*, *From Man to Man*, and *Woman and Labour*.[7] Schreiner is mostly approached in Europe and the USA as a feminist writer; in South Africa she is largely known for her contribution to a South African literary culture.[8] But Schreiner herself considered *Trooper Peter*, with its emphasis on imperialism, one of her most important texts.[9] Absolute necessity drove her to its composition; the personal and professional costs of this political intervention were high. Her publishers feared a libel case.[10] As

---

[7] *The Story of an African Farm* (London: Chapman and Hall 1883); *From Man to Man; or Perhaps Only. . .* (London: T. Fisher Unwin 1926); *Woman and Labour* (London: T. Fisher Unwin 1911). The edition of *Woman and Labour* used here is London: Virago 1978. In *Woman and Labour* materialist evolutionism plus anti-historical transcendentalism form the basis of Schreiner's analysis of women's oppression and her arguments for liberation. See Friedrich Engels, *The Origin of the Family, Private Property and the State*, introd. E. B. Leacock, trans. Alec West (1884; New York: International Publishers 1975) for a contrasting materialist account of the evolution of the sexual divisions of labour.

[8] Representative Anglo-American feminist criticism of Schreiner's sexual politics includes: Sandra Gilbert and Susan Gubar, *No Man's Land: The Place of the Woman Writer in the Twentieth Century*, ii. *Sexchanges* (London: Yale University Press 1989), 47–82; Anne McClintock, ch. 7 'Olive Schreiner, the Limits of Colonial Feminism', *Imperial Leather: Race, Gender and Sexuality in the Colonial Contest* (London: Routledge 1995), 258–95; Elaine Showalter, *A Literature of Their Own* (London: Virago 1978); Liz Stanley, 'Olive Schreiner: New Women, Free Women, All Women', in *Feminist Theorists: Three Centuries of Women's Intellectual Traditions*, ed. Dale Spender (London: The Women's Press 1983), 229–43. Feminist criticism of a more European critical orientation includes Rachel Blau DuPlessis, 'The Rupture of Story and *The Story of an African Farm*', *Writing Beyond the Ending: Narrative Strategies of Twentieth-Century Women Writers* (Bloomington: Indiana University Press 1985), 20–30; Gerd Bjørhovde, *Rebellious Structures: Women Writers and the Crisis of the Novel, 1880–1900* (Oslo: Norwegian University Press 1987). For criticism that locates her writing within an emergent discourse of South African nationality and literature, see J. M. Coetzee, ch. 3 'Farm Novel and Plassroman', *White Writing: On the Culture of Letters in South Africa* (London: Yale University Press 1988), 63–81; Stephen Gray, 'Schreiner and the Novel Tradition', in *Southern African Literature. An Introduction* (London: Rex Collings 1979), 133–59; Graham Pechey, '*The Story of an African Farm*: Colonial History and the Discontinuous Text', *Critical Arts*, volume 3, number 1 (1983), 65–78; Itala Vivan, ed., *The Flawed Diamond. Essays on Olive Schreiner* (Coventry: Dangaroo Press 1991).

[9] See Schreiner's letter to her brother William Schreiner, 29 June 1898 (Rive, *Letters*, i. 332–3).

[10] See the description in First and Scott, *Biography*, 226–31, and Schreiner's letter to William Schreiner of above, for descriptions of the high emotional costs of composition. The publisher's fear of libel is clear in the correspondence with T. Fisher Unwin of Schreiner and her husband Samuel Cronwright-Schreiner,

an intervention, it was linked to a pragmatic political end: it was an appeal to the English people and government, in the hope of mobilizing protest against Cecil Rhodes's British South Africa Company. Ultimately, she hoped to help remove the Company's Royal Charter, through publicizing the atrocities perpetrated in the conquest of Mashonaland and Matabeleland.[11] The book's dedicatee was Sir George Grey: 'A great good man . . . once governor of the Cape Colony, who, during his rule in South Africa, bound to himself the Dutchmen, Englishmen, and Natives he governed, by an uncorruptible justice and a broad humanity; and who is remembered among us to-day as representing the noblest attributes of an Imperial Rule'.[12] From this and the primarily English target constituency of the novella, one might assume that Schreiner's project is confined to a mid-Victorian, paternalist liberalism. But by the mid-1890s this established ideology was itself disintegrating, internally divided over issues of imperial policy and shifting towards a statal–collective formation.[13] In other words, neither the English nor

unpublished, dating from September 1896 to August 1897 (unpublished manuscripts, property of Harry Ransom Humanities Research Center, University of Texas at Austin). The Schreiners' correspondence with T. Fisher Unwin reveals their intense concern that the book be a widely affordable, well-distributed, and well-translated text; their desire for its political impact is evident.

[11] John X. Merriman attempted, unsuccessfully, on 12 May 1896 to have the Charter revoked, in a speech to the Cape parliament. See Rive, *Letters*, i. 275.

[12] *Trooper Peter*, 9. Sir George Grey was from 1854 to 1862 the Governor of the Cape Colony and High Commissioner for South Africa. For a biography of George Grey, see J. Rutherford, *Sir George Grey: A Study in Colonial Government* (London: Cassell 1961). Schreiner's construction of Grey, in these texts, as the epitome of English justice and humanitarianism, may be based less on her knowledge of the details of his administration's policies than on her need to give historical and empirical foundation to her belief in the possibility of a contemporary social/political opposition to Rhodesianism. Elsewhere, in her non-fiction and correspondence, Schreiner evinces enthusiasm for Grey, along with other mid-Victorian South African politicians and administrators such as Saul Solomon. See her letters to W. T. Stead (Oct. 1896; Rive, *Letters*, i. 292–3); to Grey himself (4 Feb. 4 1897; Rive, *Letters*, i. 300–1); to Alfred Milner (10 July 1899; Rive, *Letters*, i. 368); to Havelock Ellis (30 Sept. 1899; Rive, 384). See also Schreiner in 'The Englishman', *Thoughts on South Africa*, (London: T. Fisher Unwin 1923), 364, and (with Samuel Cronwright-Schreiner) *The Political Situation* (London: T. Fisher Unwin 1896), 87.

[13] For an account of the crisis of British political structures and identities of this period, see Mary Langan and Bill Schwarz, eds., *Crises in the British State 1880–1930* (London: Hutchinson and Co. 1985), especially Stuart Hall and Bill Schwarz, ch. 1 'State and Society, 1880–1930', 7–32, and David Sutton, ch. 3 'Liberalism, State Collectivism and the Social Relations of Citizenship', 63–79. John Hobson exemplifies the 'new' English liberalism of the late 19th- and early 20th- cents. See

South African strands of liberalism was at this time readily reducible to a single, identifiable belief system or practice.[14] Schreiner's appeal to this liberal register in her dedication needs then to be seen as an element in a complex and at times contradictory rhetorical strategy.

This chapter sets out to analyse Schreiner's critical reformulation of colonial expansionism. Its key representatives in *Trooper Peter* are (apart from the Company itself) Cecil Rhodes, and the eponymous Peter, who stand at opposite ends of the Company power structure as its head and as footsoldier respectively. Schreiner's exploration of Rhodes is a graphic display of 'imperialism as a representational dilemma'. The indeterminacies of Schreiner's scheme here signal uncertainty about the origin of Rhodesian economic monopoly: is it an individual (Rhodes), a structure (capitalism), a negligent government or an irresponsible people? Schreiner's representation of Peter—the most acclaimed component of the book—not only serves as a radical exposé of the social and sexual violence of Rhodes's project but also constitutes a serious intervention in contemporary psychological debates concerning rationality and the unconscious within imperial culture.

WHOSE COMPANY: MONOPOLY CAPITALISM UNDER SCRUTINY

By the time of *Trooper Peter*'s composition, there was considerable opposition to the triumph of the rule of monopolies;

Hobson's *Imperialism: A Study*, (London: J. Nisbet and Co. 1902). See also Michael Freeden, ed., *J. A. Hobson: A Reader* (London: Unwin Hyman 1988). There are significant differences between Hobson's and Schreiner's anti-imperialism, but Schreiner's analysis of the Boer War influenced John Hobson whose *The War in South Africa: Its Causes and Effects* (London: J. Nisbet and Co. 1900) includes an interview with Schreiner. Bernard Porter, *Critics of Empire: British Radical Attitudes to Colonialism in Africa 1895–1914* (London: Macmillan 1968) offers an intelligent and informative discussion, in ch. 3 'Liberals and the Empire', 56–94; see also his ch. 7 'Hobson's '*Imperialism: A Study*', 207–38.

[14] For the traditions of liberalism in the Cape Colony, see Stanley Trapido, ' "The Friends of the Natives": Merchants, Peasants and the Political and Ideological Structure of Liberalism in the Cape, 1854–1910', in *Economy and Society in Pre-Industrial South Africa*, ed. Shula Marks and Anthony Atmore (London: Longman 1980), 247–74. See also Phyllis Lewsen, ed., *Selections from the Correspondence of J. X. Merriman, 1890–1898* (Cape Town: Van Riebeeck Society Publications 41, 1963), for insights into parliamentary Cape liberalism of the 1890s.

the British South Africa Company was characterized as a parasite on the populations of Britain and South Africa. On 9 May 1891, *The Economist* opined: 'Sovereign companies are probably the worst possible agencies for developing a new country. Their object is not to open up territory for settlement; it is to close it. They want to make good dividends for themselves, not to see the ordinary emigrant flourishing'.[15] Schreiner's narrative rereads this Hobsonian ideology in ways that partly criticize and partly uphold it. Through the mouthpiece of the 'ordinary emigrant', Peter, Schreiner highlights the unjust way the Company's economic and political monopoly disables potential colonists even before they have arrived. All that is left to them is Company exploitation. Peter complains 'There's not too much cakes and ale up here for those that do belong to it [the Company], if they're not big-wigs, and none at all for those who don't . . . it's not the men who work up here who make the money; it's the big-wigs who get the concessions!' (42).

Schreiner underscores the ways in which his exclusion from colonial capital accumulation fosters Peter's subjective investment in its ideology. The more he experiences Rhodesian exploitation, the stronger his unrealizable fantasy of empowerment. Peter's daydream of wealth and power mimics the model of Rhodes himself, from business success through to parliamentary office:

Peter Halket was not very clear as to how it ought to be started; but he felt certain that he and some other men would have to take shares. They would not have to pay for them. And then they would get some big man in London to take shares. He need not pay for them; they would give them to him; and then the company would be floated. No one would have to pay anything; it was just the name—'The Peter Halket Gold Mining Company, Limited.' (32–3)

For Schreiner, the issue is not only wealth accumulation but also the role of verbal signification within this process. Peter's fantasy consists almost entirely of a stream of proper names; the company is to be magicked up through the invention of names,

---

[15] Porter, *Critics of Empire*, 42. For Schreiner's own non-fictional promotion of the interests of settler colonialism, see The *Political Situation*. For analyses of political economy of imperialism, see Anthony Brewer, *Marxist Theories of Imperialism: A Critical Survey* (London: Routledge 1990).

it is to be empowered through the incorporation of men with 'big names', his trajectory of upward mobility is plotted in terms of names. The information he has absorbed about the process of flotation is italicized as a series of dictums (for example, '*It's the shares that you sell, not the shares that you keep, that make money*')—further pronouncing what for Schreiner seems a strong but indeterminate connection between language itself and the production of surplus value. The power Rhodes attributes to the process of naming (evident in his country's name) is argued to be illusory by Christ who argues for the ephemerality of the proper name (91). Christ is, significantly, never named. His first encounter with Peter involves exposing the political contingency of words like 'rebel', 'Christian'. Schreiner's ambivalence towards signifiers resembles her ambivalence in Peter's fantasy towards 'paper money'. On the one hand, she seems to want to suggest that signifiers do *not* have the power their users claim. They are subordinate to the extra-verbal systems and totalities to which they refer; Schreiner's concern is with those economic and political totalities themselves, attacking the political power that manipulates terms like 'rebel' to carry its own ideological agenda. At the same time however, Schreiner wants to suggest that words have too much autonomous power. Schreiner reveals a suspicion towards verbal signification itself, as materially productive, and able to falsify and fabricate its socio-economic and political referents.

Peter's fantasy continues with an account of 'making money' through selling off his shares at the right moment. His calculations stumble when he considers the question of the fate of other shareholders, those that have actually purchased shares with cash:

Then Peter Halket's mind got a little hazy. The matter was getting too difficult for him, like a rule of three sum at school when he could not see the relation between the two first terms and the third. Well, if they didn't like to sell out at the right time, it was their own fault. Why didn't they? . . . But if they *couldn't* sell them? (33–4)

He reasons:

'The British Government can't let British shareholders suffer.' He'd heard that often enough. The British taxpayer would have to pay for the Chartered Company, for the soldiers, and all the other things, if *it* couldn't, and take over the shares if it went smash, because there were lords and dukes and princes connected with it. And why shouldn't they pay for his company? He would have a lord in it too! (34)

Peter's fantasy does not here recognize labour as the basis of accumulation. It does recognize the structural reliance of companies upon something exterior—the populace at large—to support them. In this emphasis on the category of the nation rather than the labourer as bearer of the burden, Schreiner echoes Hobson's liberal critique.[16] Likewise in her ironic representation of Peter's naive discourse, which underscores the impossibility of his dream ever being realized. This colonial 'rags to riches' fantasy is criticized for being both essentially illusory—the province of the juvenile—and the actuality of a minority who exclude and manipulate others with it.

Schreiner thus protests the gap between free enterprise individualism and the monopoly conditions of the British South Africa Company. She criticizes Peter's exclusion from the benefits of Rhodesian imperial capitalism, and also the English cultural and economic undervaluation of the labouring classes, its rigid class structure. This critique itself combines an economic theory of value with an ethical creed of the dignity of labour and 'service'. The liberalism of Schreiner's protest stance is complicated and undermined by ethical humanist and materialist perspectives that question the legitimacy of an ideology based on the pursuit of self-interest. Schreiner's particular target is the operation of 'instrumental' or 'calculating' 'rationality' that reduces everything and everyone to a 'means'.[17] This instrumentality underlies Peter's attempts to calculate his company's formation, and it flounders when he is unable to satisfactorily 'calculate' the place, and fate, of shareholders that fail to 'sell out' at the right time. Peter's conscience rises to rebut his fantasy of autochthonous production of wealth

---

[16] For discussions of Hobson see Porter, *Critics of Empire*, ch. 7; Daniel Bivona, 'Postscript: Disposing of the Surplus: Capitalism and Empire', *Desire and Contradiction: Imperial Visions and Domestic Debates in Victorian Literature* (Manchester: Manchester University Press 1990), 113–27; and Patrick Brantlinger, *Rule of Darkness: British Literature and Imperialism, 1830–1914*, 236–8.

[17] See Max Horkheimer and Theodor Adorno, *Dialectic of Enlightenment* (1944), trans. John Cumming (New York: Continuum 1972); Max Horkheimer, *Eclipse of Reason* (1947; New York: Continuum 1974), for discussions of the rise in the West of 'instrumental' (in contrast to 'transcendental') reason.

by stressing the human costs of syndication. 'Making everything from nothing', as he elsewhere describes the colonial narrative, is based on bad arithmetic: other people pay. This leads Schreiner away from and back towards a materialist concern with reason as the basis for anti-capitalist critique: from reason towards ethics, and towards a transcendental reason, reformulated as the analysis of the totality and a systematic grasp of its operations. From this angle, what unsettles Peter's daydream is the very attempt to grasp the operations of the capitalist system as a whole, a structure of political economy that straddles metropole and colony.

COLOSSAL CONFUSION: REPRESENTING RHODES

Rhodes's activities spanned the development of monopoly capitalism and the creation of the Chartered British South Africa Company; the acquisition of formal political power as prime minister of the Cape; the orchestration of the Jameson Raid and the violent conquest of 'Rhodesia'. Schreiner's letters throughout the 1890s are full of references to Rhodes, and chart a course from initial enthusiasm to disillusioned critique.[18] Crucial for this discussion is the way in which Schreiner's perceptions pointedly lead her to question Rhodes's responsibility for the system he dominates. For example (from a letter to Betty Molteno, 1 March 1898): 'the common enemy . . . is not a person, but a system. If Rhodes were to die tomorrow, we should be free of the most energetic of the capitalists, but capitalism would be with us still!'[19] Or, from a letter to John Merriman, 3 April 1897: 'We fight Rhodes because he means so much of oppression, injustice, and moral degradation in South

---

[18] For an account of Schreiner's relations with Rhodes, see John van Zyl, 'Rhodes and Olive Schreiner', *Contrast*, volume 6, number 1 (Aug. 1969), 86–90. See also Simon Lewis, 'Graves with a View: Atavism and the European History of Africa', *ARIEL: A Review of International Literature*, volume 27, number 1 (Jan. 1996), 41–60. A contemporary fictional rebuttal of *Trooper Peter*, which presents a spirited defence of Rhodes's ethics, was published by the Princess Catherine Radziwill: *The Resurrection of Peter: A Reply to Olive Schreiner* (London: Hurst and Blackett 1900). Other contemporary fictional representations of Rhodes include Morley Roberts, *The Colossus: A Story of Today* (London: E. Arnold 1899); Sir Gilbert Parker, *The Judgment House* (London: Methuen and Co. 1913); Sarah Gertrude Millin, *The Jordans* (London: W. Collins Sons and Co. 1923).

[19] Rive, *Letters*, i. 326.

Africa;—but if he passed away tomorrow there still remains the terrible fact that something in our society has formed the matrix which has fed, nourished, and built up such a man!'[20]

Her explanations of the genealogy and maintenance of Rhodesian power veer from structural ('the capitalist system') to social-collective ('our society') to the individualist (Rhodes as fallen angel or genius). This plurality of versions finds its way into *Trooper Peter*. Schreiner utilizes an allegorical mode of representation for Rhodes which like her feminist allegories simultaneously articulate and seek to resolve material contradictions.[21] Her choice of allegory contrasts sharply with the realist approach chosen by F. R. Statham in his 1896 fictional portrait of Rhodes, the *roman à clef Mr Magnus*.[22] Statham was a social activist and author of numerous books of analyses of Southern Africa. Schreiner knew his novel. A letter of Schreiner's husband to T. Fisher Unwin of 19 July 1896 states that 'We have both read "Mr Magnus" with pleasure, not from the standpoint of its merit as a novel or for its literary worth, but as a singularly accurate portrayal of Kimberley life'.[23]

A publisher's reader of her own *Trooper Peter* also knew *Mr Magnus*. The reader compares Schreiner's text unfavourably with Statham's, commenting: 'The pity is that, as a tract, the thing is not likely to do a ha'p'orth of good. It is the Statham style that tells best. Mrs Schreiner aims at the heart; Statham aims at the head. And the head is the place to aim at decidedly, if you want to transfer political views'.[24] Statham's novel, as the

---

[20] Rive, *Letters*, i. 308.

[21] Schreiner's feminist shorter fiction and allegories include *Stories, Dreams and Allegories* (London: T. Fisher Unwin 1923); *Dreams* (London: T. Fisher Unwin 1890); *Dream Life and Real Life* (London: T. Fisher Unwin 1893); 'The Buddhist Priest's Wife' (1892), *An Olive Schreiner Reader*, 109–29. For a discussion of Schreiner's use of allegory see Laura Chrisman, 'Allegory, Feminist Thought and the *Dreams* of Olive Schreiner', in *Edward Carpenter and Late Victorian Radicalism*, ed. Tony Brown (London: Frank Cass 1990), 126–50. On allegory as a literary form see Gay Clifford, *The Transformations of Allegory* (London: Routledge and Kegan Paul 1974), and Walter Benjamin, *The Origin of German Tragic Drama*, trans. John Osborne (1963; London: Verso 1977). The latter is illuminating for a reading of Schreiner's allegories in its distinction between allegory and symbol, and its argument for allegory as a fragmented form that dramatizes its rift with the site it gestures towards.

[22] F. R. Statham, *Mr Magnus* (London: T. Fisher Unwin 1896).

[23] Unpublished manuscript, Harry Ransom Humanities Research Center, University of Texas at Austin.

[24] Ibid.

manuscript reader suggests equates political critique with the operations of reason. His style combines novelistic realism with satirical caricature and journalistic empiricism. It is a book-length exposé of the corrupt, exploitative operations of the magnates of South African mineral industries, and of the rise to office through election rigging and bribery of the super-magnate. In Statham's *roman à clef* Rhodes, the colossus, becomes 'Mr Magnus'; 'diamonds' become 'rubies'; Kimberley becomes 'Camberton'. Statham's belief in the easy translatability of referents (intrinsic to *roman à clef* structure) is part of his support for an essentially rationalist politics and hermeneutics.

That Schreiner and her husband (Cronwright-Schreiner) dissent from this mode of fictional rationalism is evident in Cronwright-Schreiner's comments to the publisher. Statham's realism, as Cronwright-Schreiner suggests, is appropriate only for a limited goal such as the depiction of the exploitative practices of a specific mineral company in a specific locality. This is indeed Statham's goal, to protest:

The merciless hours of work, twelve hour shifts practically lengthened out to fourteen hours; the suppression of all freedom of opinion among those employed; the animal herding together of natives; the universal espionage over every man by his fellows; the atmosphere of theft and suspicion; the disregard, in the presence of the interests of the company. (22)

Such a remit excludes consideration of the general origins and process of imperial capitalism itself. Imperialism, then, for Statham, is not a conceptual concern nor representational dilemma and therefore does not impel fictional innovation. Whereas Statham is content to present his material, Schreiner speculates about what she presents. Statham is concerned with one aspect alone of Rhodes's power—his mining industry. Schreiner in contrast is concerned with several elements, political, economic, and epistemological. Where Statham primarily aims to expose corruption, Schreiner seeks to explore the implications of oppositional Christian and humanitarian value systems.

These general contrasts surface in the divergent approaches used by the writers to represent the sexual politics of Rhodes's power. Statham interestingly condemns the political economy of mineral wealth production by linking it to the sexual economy of patriarchy which is, he suggests, its cause and end:

> Had it not been openly said, almost openly boasted, that at least three-fourths, perhaps four-fifths, of the products of that mine went into consumption as the price, or part of the price, paid to women for the surrender of their honour: Was it possible that an industry with such a curse at its end should not be under a curse from its very beginning and through all its stages? . . . The tears of the women betrayed, the slinking brutality of the men who deserted them, seemed part and parcel of the ceaseless workings of the shaft gear and the unending procession of trucks round the floors. (22–3)

Schreiner too explores the links between women's oppression and the process of imperialism; but her focus is on African women and more peripherally on the working-class mother of Peter. These categories of women are a far remove from Statham's: they are underpaid labouring and colonized women placed outside the exclusively sexual commodification to which Statham's womanhood is victim. Schreiner's women are potential agents of opposition to Rhodesian capitalism, as well as its victims; Statham's are only victims. Whereas Statham is content merely to allude to the process of sexual victimization, Schreiner explores it.

It is the figure of Cecil Rhodes that reveals the sharpest differences of the writers. Statham terms Rhodes 'The Napoleon of Finance' (168), and offers a throwaway speculation on the overreacher's constitution, couched in psychological and philosophical terms:

> If anyone said that our friend Magnus was the incarnation of unconditioned acquisitiveness—well, there might be something in it, of course from a purely philosophical point of view. Beddings [i.e., W. T. Stead], by the way, who is one of his worshippers, says something rather like that. He says that Magnus is a man whose moral development has been arrested. I believe that if you consult authorities such as Lombroso you will find the same definition applied to — well, to quite a different set of people. (133)

For Statham, the question of what it is that Rhodes represents is peripheral; it can be answered easily enough by the use of psychological classification codes established by criminal/

medical authorities such as Lombroso.[25] The 'different set of people' coyly alluded to here is not ambiguous: 'criminal' supplies the term. As with the classification system of the *roman à clef* genre itself, it is a matter of exchanging the phony fictional term for the real. Schreiner's allegorical approach to Rhodes involves a more imaginative attempt to explore the question of what it is that Rhodes represents or 'incarnates'. If the proper name is the key to Statham's representation scheme, Schreiner's is more ambivalent: her narrative withholds the names of Christ and Rhodes, not (as with Statham's *roman à clef* logic) to reinforce the centrality of their names but to problematize this very assumption.

Schreiner's allegorical perception of Rhodes was already a feature of her earliest fictional depiction of him. This was a skit, 'The Salvation of a Ministry', which was a protest at Rhodes's support for the Masters and Servants Amendment Bill ('Strop Bill').[26] Rhodes here as in *Trooper Peter* is cast as a figure who poses problems of classification; does he fit into heaven or hell? In *Trooper Peter*, Schreiner extends the number of locations into which Rhodes cannot be fixed: social, economic, and ethical as well as noumenal/phenomenal. Her inability to decide on the cause and the location of Rhodes's material power is played out in the contrast between the allegories about him. The first allegory constructs Rhodes as a lighthouse set up by men to guide them (87). The beam of light turns treacherously inconstant, and leads men to their death on the rocks, a source of destruction instead of instruction and salvation. The second more extended allegory sets Rhodes as a stream that has the choice of routes to the sea; one is down a chasm, the other is along mountain ridges, 'where no path had been' (88–90). The latter route would not only have produced a new path but also ushered in new fertility to the land; the stream chooses the former and turns into a stagnant marsh, unable to meet the sea, productive only of decay.

[25] Cesare Lombroso was a criminologist widely known throughout Europe. In addition to works such as *L'Homme Criminel* (Paris: Alcan 1881) he also published analyses of genius for instance *The Man of Genius* (London: W. Scott 1891). Statham here is playing on this double association here: Stead's Rhodes as genius becomes Statham's Rhodes as criminal.

[26] See S. Cronwright-Schreiner's *Life of Olive Schreiner* (London: T. Fisher Unwin 1924), 202–5.

Rhodes is inscribed by the first allegory in a dialectic of power: he is empowered by the men who set him up, in order that he may assist them, in keeping with the emphasis on his being chosen, elected, and entrusted by the men of South Africa. The stress of the second allegory is different: Rhodes has the power not merely to guide life but to create it. Others (as in the lighthouse image) do not produce him; he is in contrast a potential producer of others. The lighthouse allegory highlights a structural explanation for Rhodes; he is a malfunctioning (if romanticized) manufactured item of equipment, in need of repair. The stream allegory aligns Rhodes with the natural rather than social environment; not a man-made object but an elemental force. Both images put limits to Rhodes's centrality. He is but a stream, after all, that has become a marsh, just as he is one lighthouse, replaceable.

If these allegories attest to Schreiner's inability to fix Rhodes's identity in relation to society and capitalism, her description of Rhodes's ontological status likewise suggests his indeterminacy. Christ instructs Peter that there are certain men born as Genius, who are burdened with a choice between bearing their gifts for themselves or for others. If they choose the former 'let men weep rather than curse' (92). What is important about this Genius figure here is less its romantic Christian morality than the way it formulates mutability as a basic property of Rhodes's subjectivity. Presenting Rhodes as himself transformable, Schreiner opposes Rhodes's essentialism ('how can I be myself and another man?' 90) by asserting the possibility of a transformable subject. Furthermore, by including Rhodes as worthy of spiritual and ideological redemption Schreiner contests the very notions of social fixity and exclusivity themselves. Such notions, Schreiner suggests, are a function of the politico-economic system Rhodes has been so active in. Schreiner's largesse then in considering Rhodes as *worthy* of redemption performs an ethics of democratic inclusivity.

COLONIAL WAR AND RESISTING SUBJECTS

Most critics have focused on the section depicting Peter's fantasies and nightmares, his wartime and peacetime experiences, treating it as a dissection of the phenomenon of 'the colonial man'. This overlooks the important fact that Schreiner is not presenting a generalized image of 'the' colonial psyche. A crucial element of her portrait is its class specificity: Peter is a rural working-class English youth, and Schreiner takes pains to suggest that his fantasies, desires, and resistance result from this particular origin. Peter is among the British poor that British imperialists were anxious to export as a way of preventing potential socialist militancy and class conflict at home.[27] It is especially significant that Schreiner gives Peter a rural not urban background. She is thereby able to link his domestic British practices of land cultivation directly with his Rhodesian experience of the opposite, crop destruction, and through this attack the ideology of colonial pastoralism. Ultimately Schreiner moves to suggest that the only form of settlement possible in Rhodesian conditions is both parasitic and genocidal; there can be no legitimate colonization.[28] What exists turns Africans into metaphorical 'food' even as it literally destroys their own infrastructure of food production.[29]

If his company daydream is Schreiner's vehicle for attacking Rhodes's monopoly capitalism, Peter's subsequent semiconscious nightmare is her medium for attacking Rhodes's brutal colonial war. Peter's mind wanders from images of African destruction to images of his own rural home:

Now, as he looked into the crackling blaze, it seemed to be one of the fires they had made to burn the natives' grain by, and they were throwing in all they could not carry away: then, he seemed to see his

[27] See V. I. Lenin, *Imperialism, the Highest Stage of Capitalism* (Peking: Foreign Languages Press 1975), quoting Rhodes: 'I was in the East End of London . . . yesterday and attended a meeting of the unemployed. I listened to the wild speeches, which were just a cry for "bread", "bread!" and on my way home I pondered over the scene and I became more than ever convinced of the importance of imperialism . . . My cherished idea is a solution for the social problem, i.e., in order to save the 40,000,000 inhabitants of the United Kingdom from a bloody civil war, we colonial statesmen must acquire new lands to settle the surplus population, to provide new markets for the goods produced in the factories and mines'.

[28] Schreiner in *Thoughts on South Africa* deploys various organic images to articulate social vision. See the descriptions of positive and negative empire as, respectively, a tree which shelters and nurtures the land around it, and an upas tree which destroys its environment, 333.

[29] See Schreiner's allegory 'The Sunlight Lay Across My Bed', *Dreams*, 133–82, for a representation of cannibalism as a metaphor for capitalism. The metaphor of physical consumption is a central one in Schreiner's writing; the notion of 'sex-parasitism', in *Woman and Labour*, is a prime example.

mother's fat ducks waddling down the little path with the green grass on each side. Then, he seemed to see his huts where he lived with the prospectors, and the native women who used to live with him; and he wondered where the women were. Then he saw the skull of an old Mashona blown off at the top, the hands still moving. He heard the loud cry of the native women and children as they turned the maxims on to the kraal; and then he heard the dynamite explode that blew up a cave. Then again he was working a maxim gun, but it seemed to him it was more like the reaping machine he used to work in England, and that what was going down before it was not yellow corn, but black men's heads; and he thought when he looked back they lay behind him in rows, like the corn in sheaves. (36)

Peter goes on to recall his recent rape of a young African mother and rationalizes

Well, they didn't shoot her!—and a black woman wasn't white! His mother didn't understand these things; it was all so different in England from South Africa. You couldn't be expected to do the same sort of things here as there. He had an unpleasant feeling that he was justifying himself to his mother, and that he didn't know how to. (36–7)

The very leap of the referent from African woman to his mother contradicts Peter's defensive claim that England and African are distinct and incomparable spheres. Schreiner similarly destabilizes the boundary separating the metropolis from the colony by showing Peter's unconscious nightmare conflation of domestic cultivation and African destruction. Colonialism in Rhodesia thus cannot replicate domestic pastoralism. The colonial setting necessarily reverses the dynamics: from producing food for others to producing others as food.

Stephen Gray argues that Peter is revealed by Schreiner here to be an ethical failure because he fails to achieve rational recognition of his perversions, prejudices, inhibitions, and emotional needs.[30] But this overlooks that Schreiner is, throughout *Trooper Peter*, ambivalent about the nature and function of 'reason', not unequivocally supportive of these. Schreiner intervenes against reductive psychologies of social Darwinism and liberal rationality alike. She takes issue with the notion that imperialism is biologically determined by universal bloodlust

---

[30] Gray, 'The Trooper at the Hanging Tree', 198–208.

lurking within the unconscious of every male.[31] Instead she suggests that the unconscious can oppose the dominatory practices of the rational ego, and be the source of multiple, contradictory impulses including altruism.[32] This is not to suggest that Schreiner is postulating ambivalence as a structural feature of the colonial psyche in relationship to its colonized 'others'. On the contrary, Schreiner presents the splits in Peter's nightmare discomfort with colonial violence and his organic, humanitarian impulses as being particular to his rural mother's humane upbringing. Schreiner consistently highlights the humanitarian legacy of Peter's mother as a dominant influence upon him. As a result Peter's conversion by Christ endorses both a static and an evolutionary notion of subjectivity: it signals a growth of consciousness and a return to his 'original' nature formed and bequeathed by his mother.[33] His conversion, then, is as much a reversion to type as it is a progressive development of consciousness.

Schreiner evidently regarded this *Chimurenga* as a legitimate war of national self-defence. She wrote to Betty Molteno in July 1896 that 'The way they are hounding the Mashonas for what they call *murder*—i.e. for killing people in time of war—is to me far more terrible than anything that is happening in the Colony'.[34] This understanding informs her representation of Shona people in *Trooper Peter*. Although Schreiner's emphasis

[31] See Karl Pearson, *National Life from the Standpoint of Science* (London: A. and C. Black 1901) and *The Ethic of Freethought* (London: T. Fisher Unwin 1888) for examples of his 'socialist' eugenic and social Darwinist thought. Schreiner was a close friend of Pearson. Her thought was in complex and variable intellectual relationship with his ideas, as is evident through her correspondence as well as fiction. For useful discussions of social Darwinist 'scientific' ideology of this period, see Greta Jones, *Social Darwinism and English Thought: The Interaction between Biological and Social Theory* (Brighton: Harvester Press 1982). See Berkman's *Healing Imagination* for a discussion of Schreiner's oppositions to social Darwinism and its versions of evolution. See also Margaret Lenta, 'Racism, Sexism and Olive Schreiner's Fiction', *Theoria*, 70 (Oct. 1987), 15–30; Paula M. Krebs, 'Olive Schreiner's Racialization of South Africa', *Victorian Studies*, volume 40, number 1 (spring 1997), 427–44; also Julia Cleves Mosse, 'Feminism and Fiction: A Study of Nineteenth Century Writing and Contemporary Feminist Literary Theory', unpub. M.Litt. thesis, University of Oxford 1986.

[32] Schreiner's *Woman and Labour* contains many examples of a positive valuation of the unconscious, instinctive aspects of the psyche. Often this occurs when Schreiner is arguing for the simultaneously religious and instinctual motivation of women's struggles for emancipation. See 123–8 for example.

[33] See *Trooper Peter*, 30–1.

[34] Rive, *Letters*, i. 287.

falls on the destructive activities of Rhodes's colonials this does not exclude her recognition of African resistance. What Schreiner does is mediate this resistance through the voice of Peter himself in his campfire story to Christ. This story is Peter's party piece, serving usually to facilitate male–male bonding and to aggrandize his ego. It tells of his betrayal by two African women whom he had bought whilst working for a prospector before becoming a trooper. The women function for him as food producers and sexual partners. One day he catches them in conversation with an African man. When he goes away for a period to his surprise the women desert the house, leaving behind the Western clothes he has given them but taking with them his gun and ammunition:

I hadn't been gone six hours when those two women skooted! It was all the big one. She took every ounce of ball and cartridge she could find in that hut, and my old Martini-Henry, and even the lid off the tea-box to melt into bullets for the old muzzle-loaders they have; and off she went, and took the young one too. The fellow wrote me they didn't touch another thing: they left the shawls and dresses I gave them kicking about the huts, and went off naked with only their blankets and the ammunition on their heads. (46)

He had previously given the older woman some cartridges at her request:

I asked her what the devil a woman wanted with cartridges, and she said the old nigger woman who helped carry in the water to the garden said she couldn't stay and help her any more unless she got some cartridges to give her son who was going up north hunting elephants. The woman got over me to give her the cartridges because she was going to have a kid, and she said she couldn't do the watering without help. (62–3)

Peter concludes that the women have gone back to their community. More specifically, the older woman married and with two children when he took her, has returned to her husband, whom he deduces to be the man he caught in conversation:

I tell you what . . . if I'd had any idea that day who that bloody nigger was, the day I saw him standing at my door, I'd have given him one cartridge in the back of his head more than ever he reckoned for! . . . I shouldn't have minded so much . . . though no man likes to have his woman taken away from him; but she was going to have a kid in a month or two—and so was the little one for anything I know; she looked like it! I expect they did away with it before it came; they've no hearts, these niggers; they'd think nothing of doing that with a white man's child. They've no hearts; they'd rather go back to a black man, however well you've treated them . . . If ever I'm shot, it's as likely as not it'll be by my own gun, with my own cartridges. And she'd stand by and watch it, and cheer them on; though I never gave her a blow all the time she was with me. (47–8)

Peter's story forces on readers the awareness that racial, sexual, and labour domination of women is a central feature of colonial expansionism. It also pronounces the political agency of African women in resisting colonization. Schreiner's representations of African women elsewhere, for example in *The Story of an African Farm*, *From Man to Man*, and *Woman and Labour* inscribe them in a passive and auxiliary relation to white colonial culture.[35] *Trooper Peter* is distinguished from these by the way it acknowledges their autonomy. This perhaps can be explained by the highly visible leadership roles taken by women in the *Chimurengas*.[36] Peter's colonial narrative emerges from conditions that guarantee its eventual defeat; Peter is indeed shot by his own gun, the gun of his story. He acknowledges his misreading of one scene, the episode in which he supplies bullets to the women and thereby facilitates his 'betrayal'. This misreading he can use to his own advantage, to affirm his sentimental capacity ('she got over me'). But his sexual cognitive blindness dooms him to repeated and unrecognized misreading.

Incapable of crediting African women with political capacity or motivation he has inadvertently enabled them to resist. Forced then to acknowledge their agency, Peter nonetheless can only account for it by his recourse to a masculine agenda. The women leave in order, he believes, to serve their men; the man

[35] See Laura Chrisman, 'Colonialism and Feminism in Olive Schreiner's 1890s Fiction', *English in Africa*, volume 20, number 1 (May 1993), 25–38, and 'Empire, 'Race' and Feminism at the *fin de siècle*: The Work of George Egerton and Olive Schreiner', in *Cultural Politics at the Fin de Siècle*, ed. Sally Ledger and Scott McCracken (Cambridge: Cambridge University Press 1995), 45–65. See also Cheryll Walker, ed., *Women and Gender in Southern Africa to 1945* (Cape Town: David Philip 1990)

[36] For a fictional representation of Nehanda, one of the women spirit mediums involved in leading the resistance, see Yvonne Vera, *Nehanda* (Harare: Baobab Books 1993).

is the agent and cause of his downfall, and it is the man who will be the object of his retaliation. The narrative of the women's theft and departure itself gives no such support to this interpretation; it is all conjecture on Peter's part. What the narrative does impel is a different mode of evaluation of what counts as resistance action: the women are resistant to the same degree as their male counterparts. In this context, it is important to recognize the radical tactic of using a white colonial to mediate this African resistance. In adopting this tactic, Schreiner pursues a form of immanent critique. Rather than speaking as or on behalf of the 'other', she allows the 'other' to speak through the cognitive deformations of the colonial 'self'. In this Rhodesian context, Schreiner is suggesting, there cannot be conditions of equal 'self/other' exchange be they narrative, sexual, or political.

The material conditions that preclude colonial comprehension of colonized African subjectivity also preclude for Schreiner her own direct representation of African anti-colonial political activity. These conditions necessarily preclude also the general possibility of interracial love. This is borne out elsewhere by Schreiner's pronouncements on interracial sex, which compound eugenic and liberal racism with sensitivity to power imbalance. An example is her argument in a letter to J. C. Smuts, 1 July 1896 that:

[It] is exactly because of the terrible chasm which in the minds of many men divides them from the dark races that the mixture of bloods in its least desirable form goes on. It was not when the native races were free and richly endowed with social and political rights, that the great fusion took place, and I believe that exactly in proportion as we raise and educate the native races and endow them with social and political rights such fusion will become rare. Where it does occur, it will be as the result of a vast affection and sympathy, and will so lose its worst features.[37]

Peter testifies against himself: his outrage at the women's theft from him enforces the extent of his theft of them; his self-pity emphasizes the degree to which he is guilty of reifying the women. His defence that he never hurt them underscores the actual violence of the colonial situation itself and the (epistemological) violence represented by his very ignorance. Peter's

[37] Rive, *Letters*, i. 286.

relationship is predicated on the exploitation of his women as labourers and on the denial of their subjectivity. The unequal conditions of Rhodesian colonialism, Schreiner suggests, doom any interracial relationship to racist sexual exploitation, self-destruction and non-reciprocity. At the same time, Schreiner is trying to validate Peter's desire and capacity for human intimacy, to present these as proleptic of the humanitarianism that will later prompt Peter to liberate a prisoner and oppose colonialism. But it is only when purged of sexual, possessive qualities that these desires for bonding can 'succeed'. Even within the very expression of Peter's brutalization, then, Schreiner finds qualities of resistance.

CONCLUSION

Schreiner's fictional critique of colonialism stands as an important alternative to the models of representation supplied by Haggard and by Conrad. Her critique refuses the conceptual boundaries that allow metropolitan readers and liberal ideology to remain at a safe remove from the violent expansionist operations of Rhodesian monopoly capitalism. Thus Schreiner denies a distinction between the categories of war and colonial economic settlement. The non-militarized operations of individual settlers, like those of Rhodes's Chartered Company, are necessarily a form of war; Schreiner suggests there is no difference between Peter's pre-trooper status as a private prospector (with his forced sexual, domestic, and agricultural labour of the women he has bought) and Peter's behaviour as a soldier (his rape and murder of African women). No reader can take refuge in the notion then that there is a legitimate narrative of settler colonialism and liberal free trade capitalism against which Rhodes's company and murderous expansionism can be judged as mere parasitic aberrations. Similarly the figure of Rhodes himself cannot be accommodated within a single literary mode of representation that places him at a safe and knowable remove; the spectacular pathology of a Kurtz by contrast allows readers a more comfortable self-location.

Schreiner, like Haggard in *King Solomon's Mines*, is openly concerned with the economic dynamics of imperial accumulation. Unlike Haggard, she is also deliberately engaged in tracing their impact on subject-formation. I have argued of Haggard that the 'dialectic of enlightenment' produces a textual practice in which romantic and rational modalities prove inextricable, synthesized to a project of authoritarian mystique. This serves a capitalist logic of commodity relations through which black bodies are made to mediate value for Haggard's English heroes. In Schreiner, the operations of an instrumental reason are dissociated from an unconscious seen to be capable of radical opposition and resistance to reason's calculations and self-interest. In the simultaneously idealist and materialist directions of Schreiner's presentation, the dissonances themselves open new ways to conceptualize the project of metropolitan anti-colonial subjectivities.

If for Conrad in *Heart of Darkness* there is no representable alternative to imperialism—its totalizing aspirations are successful and can only self-deconstruct—for Schreiner there are viable alternatives. And at the same time, Schreiner features deconstruction as a condition of Peter's colonial narrative, evident in its mis-cognition of the African resistance. Haggard can present such resistance only as a form of *ressentiment*, while Conrad it seems cannot present it at all. Schreiner both recognizes resistance and does not attempt to assimilate it directly into her narrative but lets it speak through Peter's hermeneutic failure. According to Conrad, exposure to the land, people, and customs of Africa can itself contribute to the brutalization of the metropolitan subject. According to Schreiner, the brutalizing agent is Rhodes's Company alone.

6

Alternative Empires? Englishness and Christianity in *Trooper Peter Halket of Mashonaland*

SCHREINER'S novella is distinguished by not only its radical representation of colonialism but also by its equally radical reformulation of the two institutions to which she makes her appeal against Rhodes: Britain and Christianity. In focusing on the British people, her primary concern is not to save the moral soul of British empire; Schreiner is not motivated by the desire to uphold the British as the vanguard race in charge of conferring subject status on Africans. What Schreiner is concerned with is social mobilization, derived from a pragmatic apprehension of the material power of Britain *vis-à-vis* white South African political structures. Likewise, Schreiner's deployment of the figure of Christ and the values of Christianity is as tactical as it is ideological. Christianity is turned into the name for a transcendental humanism capable of commanding recognition and affiliation from across the globe; it is to be harnessed as a viable source of ideological, subjective and material opposition to imperialism. This is not to suggest that Schreiner's representations of oppositional institutions escape contradiction. On the contrary, as this chapter will explore, these contradictions and the unanswered questions they invite are among the most important elements of Schreiner's novella.

REVISIONS OF ENGLISHNESS

In *Trooper Peter* Schreiner takes up notions of Englishness she had developed elsewhere, most fully in 'The Englishman' in *Thoughts on South Africa*.[1] There she presents a defence of

---

[1] 'The Englishman', *Thoughts on South Africa* (London: T. Fisher Unwin 1923), 328–66. For articulations of British imperial ideology see Lord Rosebery, *Questions*

the British empire founded on several standard contradictory tenets. For Schreiner insight into the fundamental 'unity of all human creatures' is, paradoxically, the exclusive birthright and monopoly of the English: 'To us it has been given first among all peoples' (351). Schreiner presents humanity as a single unity, but equally argues man to be a free autonomous individual, 'that profound consciousness of the necessity and importance of the preservation of individual freedom and the liberty of uncoerced personal action' (343), inherited from wild Teutonic ancestors. This English monopoly on the knowledge of man produces the (Kantian) realization that man is an end-in-himself. And this realization is accompanied by the English mandate to make this a reality everywhere:

The deep conviction [is] buried somewhere in our nature, not to be eradicated, that man as man is a great and important thing, that the right to himself and his existence is the incontestable property of all men; and above all the conviction that not only we have a right and are bound to preserve it for ourselves, but that where we come into contact with others we are bound to implant it or preserve it in them. (351)

Contradictions abound. There is the conviction of onto-logical freedom as genetically predetermined and experienced by the English as an involuntary submission to a racial and divine law. Freedom has to be categorically imposed upon subjects who are presumably unfree and therefore nonhuman until it is imparted to them. The violence underlying the imperative to make free/make self is given some interesting amplification when Schreiner considers the place of the Natives of the land:

If it be asked whether we think them our equals, we would reply:

of Empire (London: Arthur L. Humphreys 1900); Lord Milner, *The Nation and the Empire* (London: Constable 1913). For an alternative progressive critique of contemporary England, see Edward Carpenter, *England's Ideal and other Papers on Social Subjects* (London: Swan Sönnenschëin, Lourey and Co. 1887). For discussions of popular and hegemonic constructions of England and Englishness of this period, see R. Colls and P. Dodd, eds., *Englishness: Politics and Culture 1880–1930* (London: Croom Helm 1985). See also H. John Field, *Toward a Program of Imperial Life: The British Empire at the Turn of the Century* (Westport: Greenwood Press 1982); Bernard Semmel, *Imperialism and Social Reform: English Social-Imperial Thought 1895–1914* (London: Allen and Unwin 1960) and Richard Faber, *The Vision and the Need: Late Victorian Imperialist Aims* (London: Faber and Faber 1966).

Certainly in love of happiness and their own lives—perhaps not in some other directions; but we are here to endeavour to raise them as far as it is possible; we are determined to make them a seed-ground in which to sow *all that is greatest and best in ourselves*. (361; emphases added)

The Natives are to be implanted with is a selfhood that clearly comes from the colonizers, who make a gift of themselves (presumably the seed-ground has no seedlings of its own).

These conceptions of imperial Englishness are seriously modi-fied in *Trooper Peter*. Schreiner recognizes her own idealization of the English for what it is, a political fiction, and uses this tactically to simultaneously appeal to and attack an existing English population. Schreiner's insistence on the importance of the English public sphere to *Trooper Peter*'s cultural-political project is clear from her letters. Her combination of rebuke and affirmation is also clear. Her postulation of the ideal English proceeds by differentiating this English from the majority. She wrote to her brother William Schreiner in December 1896:

Now it is to this public, which really is the great British public apart from the speculators and military men on the one hand and apart from the ignorant mass of the street on the other, that my little book is addressed. If that public lifts its thumb there is war, if it turns it down there is peace; if, as in the present case they are indifferent and just letting things drift, there is no knowing what they may be surprised into at the last moment. It is for them and not at all for the South African public (who would not understand it) that the book is written. They must know where the unjustices and oppression really lie, and turn down their thumbs at the right moment.[2]

If Schreiner's snobbish allusions to 'the ignorant mass of the street' are not to be overlooked here, then neither is the con-ditionality of the 'legitimate' 'public', nor Schreiner's impatient and pragmatic perception of their potential agency *vis-à-vis* South African current affairs. The critical tone is evident else-where. As she wrote to W. T. Stead, February 1896:

The future of South Africa lies largely in the hands of England now: if the English public and the English government do not make it perfectly clear that they unrestrictedly and entirely condemn the action of Rhodes, and do not take away the Charter and remove Rhodes from

[2] Rive, *Letters*, i. 299.

all positions of trust, there will never be rest and trust of England in this country.[3]

By July 1897 Schreiner had it seems given up hope of the metropolitan government and turned entirely to the public instead, arguing to her publisher that 'It is . . . for the English public (the people, not the government) to insist upon an official inquiry which shall make clear the conduct of the Chartered Company during the last five years'.[4] This metropolitan subject is put on trial by Schreiner in a process that also turns them into the jury of the trial against Rhodes. She engages with an England construed here as the power ultimately responsible for future administration of Southern Africa and already responsible for granting Rhodes's company the charter that made it the 'British South Africa Company'. It is through the hypothetical speech to the English that Christ implants in Peter, that Schreiner appeals to, and judges, the English. Their brief is to save the world from Rhodes's materialism.

Christ figures England through metonyms of the imperial sword and banner but does not turn England itself into the object of an allegorical tale. This fundamentally distinguishes the political status of England from that of the white South African public and Rhodes. The distinction is between rhetoric and allegory: white South Africa is allegorized as two white beasts fighting in the field, while as already discussed Rhodes is featured as a lighthouse and a stream. Schreiner does not even attempt to appeal to the compassion of white South Africans. Christ's white beast allegory appeals only to the self-interest of the groups involved. Schreiner shows them to be victims of Rhodes's manipulation and divisive misrepresentation. He has caused them to mistake each other as the enemy, instead of recognizing him as the vulture intent on creating them as carcasses on which he can feed.

As with Schreiner's non-fictional representations, England is situated as the maker of subjects, conferring subject status upon other peoples. England is the matrix for allegory just as it is the 'mother' land. This rhetoric presents the British as bearers of a God-given imperial trust that, like the English themselves, stands

---

[3] Rive, *Letters*, i. 266.
[4] Unpublished manuscripts, property of Harry Ransom Humanities Research Center, University of Texas at Austin.

outside the conditions of allegory. Accordingly, it could be argued that Schreiner does not fundamentally challenge this imperial privilege. But this is to overlook the complicated effects of inserting this rhetorical appeal into fiction. Christ's discourse is accordingly fictionalized and its rhetorical status modified. Schreiner's indirect imaginary appeal to an imaginary British public is interesting not only for its contents—whom and what she constructs as the representatives of the nation—but also for the ways in which a structural and ideological conflict emerges between this version of Englishness and the Englishness described and enacted by Peter.

Schreiner postulates the 'great English public' as the national subject, only to break this category down into its constituent parts. The speech formally demarcates and addresses in turn specific interest groups within the nation. This produces fragmentation; national identity is no sooner posited than it is dispersed by the heterogeneity of its members. Who then are the vanguard groups of the vanguard nation, in Schreiner's revision of English imperial supremacy? After the public is addressed, come the queen, intellectuals, women, and the working-classes. Conspicuous by their absence are the elected representatives of the public, namely, members of parliament. Schreiner appears to adhere to a biological rather than political model of the nation: these groups represent the head, womb, and hands, respectively, of the 'race'.

The intellectuals are, as Christ's hypothetical speech demands, to be upbraided for their irresponsibility. They have neglected the analysis of overseas affairs: 'Where the brain of a nation has no time to go, there should its hands never be sent to labour: where the power of a people goes, there must its intellect and knowledge go, to guide it' (82). Schreiner's English womanhood is to be criticized for neglecting its maternal duty towards the 'child-peoples' of the colonies whose cries they ignore (82–3).[5]

[5] On Schreiner's representations of imperial womanhood see Carol Barash, 'Virile Womanhood: Olive Schreiner's Narratives of a Master Race', in *Speaking of Gender*, ed. Elaine Showalter (London: Routledge 1989), 269–81. On English imperial womanhood, see Julia Bush, 'Lady Imperialists and the Cause of British South Africa', paper delivered at 'South Africa 1895–1921: Test of Empire' conference, St Edmund Hall, Oxford, March 1996; Anna Davin, 'Imperialism and Motherhood', *History Workshop Journal*, 5 (1978), 9–65; Nupur Chaudhuri and Margaret Strobel, eds., *Western Women and Imperialism: Complicity and Resistance* (Bloomington: Indiana University Press 1992); Vron Ware, *Beyond the Pale:*

The working people of England—men and women—are alleged to have political sovereignty ('you, who have taken the king's rule from him and sit enthroned within his seat; is his sin not yours to-day?' 83).[6] At the same time, their lack of *economic* self-determination is acknowledged: 'If men should add but one hour to your day's labour . . . would you not rise up as one man?' (83). Christ's hypothetical appeal to the working classes thus proceeds through a double gesture to their authority and simultaneous oppression. Christ suggests that they do not have the monopoly on suffering ('Think you, no other curses rise to heaven but yours?' 83).

Schreiner's portrayal of colonized 'subject peoples' is tactically adjusted to fit the imagined preferences of these different imaginary audience communities. In the context of the workers' appeal, colonized voices can 'curse', an action she expects to elicit empathy from British workers; Schreiner is appealing to a potential transnational affinity between one militant group of workers and another. Christ supplies English mothers with a version of the colonized in which they do not curse but cry. The emphasis on pitiful victimization and infantilization aims to arouse maternal sympathy.

White Women, Racism and Imperialism (London: Verso 1992); Sally Ledger, ch. 5 'Unlikely Bedfellows? Feminism and Imperialism at the *Fin de Siècle*', *The New Woman: Fiction and Feminism at the Fin de Siècle* (Manchester: Manchester University Press 1997), 62–93; Jane MacKay and Pat Thane, 'The Englishwoman', in *Englishness* ed. Colls and Dodd, 191–229.

[6] Schreiner had a complicated relationship to socialism. She tended to advocate a liberal model of individual liberty and self-determination in preference to what she saw as the anti-individualism of socialism. At a 1918 women's meeting to commemorate Mill, Schreiner stated that Mill's lesson was 'that the freedom of all human creatures is essential to the full development of human life on earth', S. Cronwright-Schreiner's edition of The *Letters of Olive Schreiner 1876–1920* (London: T. Fisher Unwin 1924), 402. This echoes an early letter of Schreiner to Havelock Ellis, 29 March 1885: 'Ah, freedom . . . that is the first great want of humanity. That is why I sympathise so much more with the Herbert Spencer school than with the Socialists, so called. If I thought Socialism would bring the subjection of the individual to the whole I would fight to the death', Rive, *Letters*, i. 63. Herbert Spencer's *First Principles* (1862) was a seminal text for Schreiner, and features, as does John Stuart Mill's *Principles of Political Economy* (1848) in *African Farm*. See her letter to Havelock Ellis of 28 March 1884 (Rive, *Letters*, i. 36–7) and her letter to Edward Carpenter of 21 Jan. 1889, Rive, *Letters*, i. 147. On Spencer, see J. D. Y. Peel, *Herbert Spencer: The Evolution of a Sociologist* (London: Heinemann 1971). On J. S. Mill, see William Thomas, *Mill* (Oxford: Oxford University Press 1985) and Eileen P. Sullivan, 'Liberalism and Imperialism: J. S. Mill's Defense of the British Empire', *Journal of the History of Ideas*, volume 44, number 4 (Oct.–Dec. 1983), 599–617.

Even as Schreiner radically redefines the symbolic and moral centres of the British empire, she fails to address the politico-economic centre of the nation. Likewise she neglects the relationship between metropolitan and colonial economic power. A critic of imperial capitalism such as John Hobson would and did attack it for being against the self-interest of the British nation as a whole, and only in the interests of a small international class of speculators. But Schreiner cannot do that, because her idealist definition here of the British empire is predicated on its refusal to consider its own material interests. This is reinforced by her selection as primary custodians of Englishness groups not professionally associated with economic systems or government. Not only are they not parliamentary representatives, they lack substantial political influence upon those representatives. Schreiner's then is an appeal to constituencies whose dereliction of moral duty is not structurally responsible for the rise of monopoly capitalism.

In Schreiner's address to the national public, the material self-interest linking this negligent public and Rhodes's company becomes a possibility in ways that her account of intellectuals, women, and workers preclude. Schreiner/Christ challenges the intellectuals to solve contrary analytical questions: 'to whom has England given her power? How do the men wield it who have filched it from her?' (82). The first question presents an England that has voluntarily handed power over to the reprehensible Rhodes and company. According to the second question this power has been stolen, not given. The questions Christ asks the public are similarly contradictory: 'where is the sword that was given into your hand, that with it you might enforce justice and deal out mercy? How came you to give it up into the hands of men whose search is gold' (81) If they have 'given' away their 'sword', how and why did they volunteer to abdicate power? If their sword has been stolen, how could they have come to be so weak? Schreiner suggests the answer these questions rhetorically disavow; namely, the great English public itself is definable as 'men whose search is gold'.[7]

[7] Deirdre David observes that 'by directing so much of its attack to one undeniably rapacious individual . . . [metropolitan critique of empire] fails to indict the innumerable British businessmen and companies for whom Southern Africa was a personal treasure trove of extraordinary wealth . . . the ruling-class British, through their business affiliations with these enormous imperialistic conglomerates, secured

A final twist comes in the way Christ's imaginary speech to various chosen representatives of England is instantly refused by Peter because, as he explains, he knows that the metropolitan English will not accept such a speech from him. This derives from their social class hierarchy; because of his lowly status, he has no credibility. Schreiner in this way dramatizes the practical constraints, and prejudices, that inhibit proper communication of a text to a projected audience. She also ironizes the idealism of the discourse itself, even while she suggests its political utility. In other words, the Englishness to which she appeals is presented as a fiction, used both to facilitate mobilization against Rhodes and to criticize the existing social relations of real England, the snobbish exclusion and impoverishment of their own subjects. The complexity is sustained by the ways these speeches are mediated: Christ addresses the speeches to Peter, rendering Peter the fictive object of the discourse, in the guise of preparing Peter to be the enunciator of the speeches to the English. The speeches become thereby provisional, hypothetical and relative. At the same time, by mediating the speeches through Christ Schreiner removes herself from direct responsibility and endows them with the absolute authority of the divine figure.

CHRISTIAN EMPIRES?

Schreiner's novella shares its use of Christ as medium of social critique with W. T. Stead's *If Christ Came to Chicago* (1894).[8] Schreiner was in correspondence with Stead throughout her 1890s residence in South Africa. She wrote to him in late 1895, several months before the conception of *Trooper Peter*, 'Our

for themselves their own sizeable pieces of African land', *Rule Britannia: Women, Empire, and Victorian Writing* (Ithaca: Cornell University Press 1995), 187.

[8] W. T. Stead, *If Christ Came to Chicago! A Plea for the Union of All Who Love in the Service of All Who Suffer* (Chicago: Laird and Lee 1894). Stead, a vigorous moral journalist and campaigner, responsible for the exposé of child prostitution in 1880s London, was also an ardent social imperialist and advocate of Cecil Rhodes. According to Richard Rive, Stead promoted Rhodes and Rhodesian imperialism through the *Review of Reviews* from January 1891, and 'succeeded in rescuing Rhodes from the obscurity of colonial politics', Rive, *Letters*, i. 190. See Patrick Brantlinger's discussion of Stead, *Rule of Darkness: British Literature and Imperialism, 1830–1914* (Ithaca: Cornell University Press 1988), 247–50.

history during the last five years has been the saddest that I think has ever been set down on the record of any Anglo-Saxon people. And we had such hopes of Rhodes years ago! We want an "If Christ Came to South Africa" from your pen'.[9] She went on to supply that text herself. *If Christ Came* is a bizarre polemic of a text, an indictment of the city of Chicago's social corruption, depravity, and deprivation, mounted through the medium of the imaginary visitant. He provides the ethical humanitarian standard against which Chicago's reality can be measured. *Trooper Peter* directly takes up the structure and theme of Christ's visitation. But whereas Schreiner personifies Christ, Stead does not. Instead of giving him a fictional character role, Stead makes him a rhetorical device.

The most significant elements of Stead's book for our purposes are his conceptions of social imperialism, humanitarianism, and civic religion. His social imperial ideology, like Schreiner's, takes as its premise the notion that 'Among all the agencies for the shaping of the future of the human race, none seem so potent now . . . as the English-speaking man' (341). For Stead Anglo-Saxon imperial supremacy links to missionary responsibility for the salvation of the universe. From this, he produces an argument for the ethical necessity of social reform to render the Anglo-Saxon race fit to occupy its world position. Here he differs from Schreiner in his prioritization of a state-centralized programme of domestic structural adjustment:

The amelioration of the conditions of life, the levelling-up of social inequalities, the securing for each individual the possibility of a human life, and the development to the uttermost by religious, moral and intellectual agencies of the better side of our countrymen,—these objects follow as necessary corollaries from the recognition of the providential sphere occupied by English-speaking men in the history of the world. (342)

The most striking part of Stead's work is his destruction of the distinctions between the spheres of religion and politics through the invention of what he terms a civic religion. He wishes to invest the institutions of the municipality (City Hall) and the concept of citizenry with spiritual value; to render City Hall the expression of the sacred brotherhood of man,

<hr>

[9] 26 Aug. 1895. Rive, *Letters*, i. 256.

and to render manifest the divinity of the electoral system of representation itself. The state is both medium and end of social/religious action. The exercise of citizenry, through the machinery of elections, is what will establish humane civic values. The concept of the citizen itself provides the equality and fraternity of the civic religion: 'there is neither Greek nor Jew . . . all are one before the ballot-box' (276).

There is a practical as well as an ideological basis for Stead's elevation of City Hall. The sources of 'Assyrian tyranny', corruption and exploitation—for Stead, these consist mainly of capitalist monopolies, corporations such as the Gas Trust and private millionaires. Only civic institutions can check these powers, by legislation and by establishing alternative industries to break their monopolies. Stead recommends for example that the city owns and operates its own gas plant. Whereas Stead embraces the institutions of the state in his civic religion, Schreiner entertains a far more ambivalent position; she is in fact far less destructive of their opposition than Stead, presenting her transcendental humanitarianism as an extra-statal ideal. When she appeals to the English nation-state, as we have seen, she very conspicuously focuses not on its formal governmental institutions but on its population. Some of the groups to which she appeals do not even have the vote.

When it comes to the enemies of humanity Stead's discourse presents a certain double bind. To cast them as Old Testament figures, and to represent the 'evils' in terms of sins of idleness, despotism, greed, luxury, is simultaneously to challenge the hierarchies of capitalism and to endorse them. Stead contests the surface of monopoly capitalism by suggesting that modern capitalism itself is only surface; the Old Testament fills the depths. The assimilation of contemporary oppressors into ancient narratives is also, of course, an empowerment of the opposition, who now find themselves inscribed as biblical heroes. But Stead effectively wrests the ideological, discursive monopoly away from capitalism only to transfer that monopoly to God. Critique, and opposition, are possible only through 'faith in God'; readers are exhorted to surrender to this authority. In Schreiner's *Trooper Peter,* there is much less direct equation of archaic biblical paradigms and contemporary social, cultural practices; Schreiner's technique is to mix and juxtapose these rather than to conflate into a single traditional biblical narrative.

Implicit in Stead is a notion of fidelity to holy writ; beyond that, the supremacy of scripture, of words as more than ideological weapons. They are constitutive of 'value' itself. Crucial to his project is Stead's belief that the precise 'mind' of Christ himself must be named and articulated through his own writing:

> Whatever value it [the book] possesses, whatever help there is in it for the citizens of Chicago, or of any other city, will depend solely upon the fidelity with which I have succeeded in expressing the mind of Christ on the subjects which it treats, and of bringing those who read its pages within the shadow of the presence of the Son of Man. (14)

Only the identity of Christ as word and as spiritual presence can legitimate Stead's project. The selection of the Christ as the central figure is of course overdetermined by such literalism; Christ himself represents the marriage of matter and word, humanity and divinity. Unsurprisingly Schreiner is also far more sceptical about the efficacy and the value of the word, the 'proper name', and about the unifiability of signifier and signified. Christ is never named as such in her text; the practice of Christianity seems reliant upon a notion precisely opposite to Stead's, that 'the spirit' can only operate when disjoined from 'the letter'.

Although Schreiner uses an impersonal figure of 'God' senior in many of her other allegories and fictional texts, at times representing him as a trope for oppressive patriarchy, at times for the benign cosmos itself, *Trooper Peter* is the only text in which she invokes the figure of Christ.[10] The appropriation of the figure of Christ to serve in the campaign against Rhodes's power caused considerable literary and political offence to contemporary critics including the reviewer of *Blackwood's*. The

---

[10] See *The Story of an African Farm* for a negative presentation of God as patriarch. See Schreiner's allegories 'The Sunlight Lay Across My Bed' and 'In a Ruined Chapel', both in *Dreams* (London: T. Fisher Unwin 1890), 133–82 and 98–111 for examples of God as a benign presence. Schreiner's letter to Revd. J. T. Lloyd, 29 Oct. 1892 in Rive, *Letters*, i. 212–3, contains an extensive discussion of her conception of God, while her letter to Karl Pearson of 23 Oct. 1886 outlines her notion of Christ: 'We do need a Christ; but the Christ of one age is not like to that of another . . . Yes, we need to be more Christlike, but in this; After our forty days of solitary contemplation we need to carry the dreams and ideals we have formed out into the world, and incarnate them quietly and simply day by day in action' (Rive, *Letters*, i. 109–10).

readers' reports on the manuscript are also outraged: 'Egoism can go no further in an author than for him to introduce Christ as a personage . . . All Christ's language is bad, ineffective, bombastic, borrowed . . . flat' (reader number one) and 'One is sorry to see so many inflated nothings put in the mouth of his Saviour' (reader number two).[11]

Schreiner's Christ also elicited praise from others for whom her representation was a feat of decorum rather than hubris. For these readers Schreiner's novella was commendable not only for the sentiments expressed by Christ but also for the skilful way Schreiner balanced the supernatural and mundane levels of the text. Thus G. W. Cross in the *Eastern Province Magazine*, Grahamstown, 6 March 1897 enthuses that 'The triumph of the book is the imaginative realization of the Christ. . . [Christ] is not exactly the Christ of our Conventions. Be that as it may, only the simplest and firmest faith could have created him'.[12] A similar affirmation is evident in the unpublished letter of J. Clifford to T. Fisher Unwin, 17 March 1897:

It is intrinsically Christian and brings him who was and is the Saviour of low and despised men into the actual life of the world, as He himself wishes it, and indeed as He himself in His strong love bore it in the days of His flesh, to the places where women were wronged, and men were contemned.[13]

Rhodes, as was well known, identified himself with icons of Roman imperial power. The figure of Christ appeals to Schreiner for his historical relationship with the Roman empire. Both Shelley's 'Essay on Christianity' and Gibbon's *Decline and Fall of the Roman Empire* influenced Schreiner's construction of Christianity as an anti-imperial force.[14] Schreiner twins the two

[11] *Blackwood's Edinburgh Magazine*, quoted in R. First and A. Scott, *Olive Schreiner: A Biography* (London: The Women's Press 1989), 230. Readers' comments from unpublished manuscripts, property of Harry Ransom Humanities Research Center, University of Texas at Austin.

[12] Cherry Clayton, ed., *Olive Schreiner* (Johannesburg: McGraw-Hill 1983), 87.

[13] Unpublished manuscripts, property of Harry Ransom Humanities Research Center, University of Texas at Austin.

[14] Gibbon, The *History of the Decline and Fall of the Roman Empire* (Dublin: Luke White 1789). See John Burrow's *Gibbon* (Oxford: Oxford University Press 1985) for an account of Gibbon's thought. See Schreiner's letter to Edward Carpenter of 21 Jan. 1889, where she emphasizes Gibbon's importance to her thought, (Rive, *Letters*, i. 147). Shelley, 'Essay on Christianity', *Shelley Memorials* (Boston: Tickner and Fields 1859). The edition used here is that of *Shelley's Prose*, ed. David Lee Clark (London: Fourth Estate 1988), 196–214. Shelley's combina-

figures of Rhodes and Christ as geniuses whose gift and privilege it is to mediate between the noumenal and phenomenal spheres. Only Christ can march Rhodes's colossal abilities. Only Christ can pose as altruistic ideal counterpart to Rhodes's choice of a selfish materialism. The contrast and similarity between the two figures is made explicit by Rhodes himself, when he delivers his imaginary response to Peter's hypothetical speech: 'You want me to be Jesus Christ, I suppose? How can I be myself and another man?' (90).

A transnational subject replaces Stead's 'citizen Christ' who is a missionary emblem of Western civilization. Schreiner's Christ is no such emblem, notwithstanding Nadine Gordimer's allegation that Schreiner is a sanctimonious peddler of Victorian missionary values.[15] Schreiner is not guilty of a conventional Victorian religiosity. This much her contemporaries such as G. W. Cross could recognize.

In fact Schreiner's reinvention of biblical discourse belongs to an experimental culture of the 1890s. Christ and his 'company' become a radically polymorphous entity in Schreiner's protest against Rhodes's politico-economic monopoly and her contradictory counter-argument that this colonial capitalism does not command total sovereignty over human subjectivity.[16] These conflicting moves create alternative, oppositional value system that uses the same language as its materialist counterpart. As Christ alleges to Peter, 'my company is the strongest in the world'. Schreiner seeks to attack Rhodes's monopoly on epistemological as well as political and economic grounds.

The shocking frontispiece photograph demonstrates this contest. The photograph was indeed offensive enough to be

tions of political reformism with philosophical idealism, scientific materialism with noumenalism resonate with Schreiner's thought. See her letter to Havelock Ellis, 19 April 1884, on her affinity with Shelley (Rive, *Letters*, i. 38).

[15] Nadine Gordimer, 'Afterword: the Prison-House of Colonialism', in *An Olive Schreiner Reader: Writings on Women and South Africa*, ed. Carol Barash (London: Pandora Press 1987), 221–7.

[16] For Schreiner's contemporary construction of Christ and biblical discourses, see the letter to Pearson of 23 Oct. 1886. That she was well aware of the anachronism of traditional models of religious (and other) ideology and media is clear:

One man might set all Europe in a blaze still, but he must do it in a new way . . . Science has taken the place of Theology, the press has taken the place of the ruler . . . and fiction has taken the place which painting and the drama occupied in other ages (Rive, *Letters*, i. 109).

removed by South African publishers after the first edition. The
picture features three black African men, war prisoners, hanging from a tree; around them stand white Rhodesian men idly
smoking and looking on. The blatant inhumanity of colonial
power is pronounced. As a literary rather than visual device,
however, the photograph introduces a more questionable note.
Juxtaposed against the novella's title it also problematizes the
referent: who is 'Trooper Peter'? Is he one of the men featured
in the photograph?

The single referent of the title and the plural referents of the
photo establish a series of tensions between visual and verbal
elements of meaning; documentary and fictional truth claims;
between ideological valorizations of collectivity and individualism. The photograph's contents remain in a non-specific relationship to the contents of the text until Peter alludes to the
photo in a flash of textual self-reflexivity. Peter mentions a
recent hanging of three black prisoners in Bulawayo:

'I was there,' said the stranger.
'Oh, you were?' said Peter. 'I saw a photograph of the niggers hang-
ing, and our fellows standing round smoking; but I didn't see you in it.
I suppose you'd just gone away?'
'I was beside the men when they were hung,' said the stranger. (51)

The photograph's 'objectivity' and extra-textual veracity are
thus underscored but Christ disrupts the equation of empirical
reality with truth. Christ's invisible and unrecorded 'presence'
has not prevented the men from being unfairly hanged. Christ
has however described how he helped an injured African by
taking him down to the riverside. According to the photograph
episode Christ has only a metaphysical presence. According to
the injured man episode Christ has physical agency also. In
both cases, Christ cannot be contained within colonial power
systems, be they epistemological or military.

The point, in a way, is precisely the clash between the two
representations of Christ's being. Schreiner makes him irre-
ducible to a single ideological code, even the Kantian categorical
imperative. Schreiner could easily have specified the categorical
imperative as 'the' essential maxim of her value system; she
does in other writings, as we have seen. The decision against
privileging any sole maxim in this text corresponds with this

text's insistence upon heterogeneity of modes—itself an ethical stance.

Although the actions of Christ's company are variable, they all involve self-sacrifice. The ethic of 'loving your enemy' rubs shoulders with the principle that all men are brothers. The older African woman sacrificing herself in order to save the younger African woman with her baby deliberately contrasts with the story of the white prospector and his black male servant whose fidelity to his benign master costs him his life when he is shot as a traitor to his people by some African soldiers. African women are portrayed in solidarity with each other, while it is the men who cross ethnic and political divides in their interracial male–male bonding. One story points to racial survival— through the older woman's sacrifice the young African mother can join her people. The other story points to transcendence of political divisions through death.

This latter story is undoubtedly disturbing to modern readers. Not only does it promote a model of loyal *service* by African people to their masters; it presents such service as superior and oppositional to African political solidarity. Both these stories of 'company' action are explicitly shaped to fit the interests of their audience Peter, calculated for maximum appeal to his own sensibility. The women's story impresses him because the young African woman is the very woman he had recently met and raped. The second story strikes a chord, because he can as a white male become sympathetic to the notion of a loyal black servant sacrificing himself for another white male. (It is of course a neat reversal of his own eventual fate, which is to sacrifice himself for a black prisoner.) It wins him over; as he acknowledges to Christ, he has heard of 'niggers' doing that sometimes. Christ's rhetorical practice here conforms to Shelley's description of his discursive practice: 'He accommodated his doctrines to the prepossessions of those whom he addressed'.[17]

To assume that Schreiner endorses the ideology encoded in any one of the inserted narratives is to overlook the particular contexts which Schreiner has worked hard to make us aware of. This bespeaks a commitment to effective communicability, itself a theme of *Trooper Peter* just as is the suspicion of verbal

[17] *Essay on Christianity*, 198.

discourse itself. This is all dramatically borne out in the contradictory sentiments pronounced by Christ. When he tackles Peter
on his use of the concepts of 'rebel', 'Christian', 'nation', his
practice does more than expose the double standards and
political interests which influence the dominant definitions of
these terms: he comes close to demolishing the notion of
linguistic transparency altogether. In liberating the concepts
from dominant usage, he frees them for a more progressive
appropriation. In the process Christ contests the 'right' of
England to own the land and the people of South Africa, turning it into an unresolved question:

'Who gave the land to the men and women of England?' asked the
stranger softly.
'Why, the devil! They said it was theirs, and of course it was,' said
Peter.
'And the people of the land: did England give you the people also?'
Peter looked a little doubtfully at the stranger. 'Yes, of course, she gave
us the people; what use would the land have been to us other-wise?'
(56)

When Christ goes on to contest Peter's claim that the Shona and
Ndebele are 'rebels', arguing through the parallel with contemporary Armenian nationalism that they are fighting to
reclaim their land from those who conquered them, he asks: 'If
these men . . . would rather be free, or be under the British
Government, than under the Chartered Company, why, when
they resist the Chartered Company, are they more rebels than
the Armenians when they resist the Turk?' (58). Yet as we have
seen in Christ's invention of a speech for Peter to deliver to the
English people, the 'sword' of empire is alleged to be 'God-
given', and the subject peoples are alleged to have been given by
God for imperial protection. Not unreasonably, the discursive
appeal to the English expediently enlists the concepts that
resonate with the projected audience.

In discussing African nationalism with Peter, however, Christ
interrogates those same imperial concepts. If this testifies to a
pragmatic view of discourse—that is, that it is necessary to
tailor discourse to fit the interests of the particular occasion—it
is part of a more general pragmatism towards textual artefacts.
For Schreiner there are no limits to 'usability': anything and

everything, from photographs to parliamentary Blue Books, counts as useable media and is convertible to her aesthetic.

Trooper Peter's political radicalism contrasts sharply with *The Political Situation*, a paper that Schreiner wrote during the same period. It was delivered by her husband to the Cape parliament.[18] In it she proposes the establishment of a party in opposition to Rhodes and capitalist monopolies. This party is to consist of a small minority of enlightened progressives under the leadership of a great individual. Its minority size and elite status guarantee its integrity, as does the political impotence Schreiner promotes for it. Schreiner stresses her fear of its potential corruption through bearing government office and by mass membership to the point where one almost suspects that the purpose of the party is simply to supply spiritual capital for its members. Espousal of ethical virtues proves not only an end in itself here but incompatible with any concrete social action.

Trooper Peter in contrast presents an unbounded membership that dissolves denominational definitions altogether:

'We are the most vast of all companies on the earth' said the stranger; 'and we are always growing. We have among us men of every race and from every land; the Esquimo, the Chinaman, the Turk, and the Englishman, we have of them all. We have men of every religion, Buddhists, Mahomedans, Confucians, Freethinkers, Atheists, Christians, Jews. It matters to us nothing by what name the man is named, so he be one of us.' (60–1).

The novella culminates in Peter's liberation of an African prisoner and consequent murder by his troop's captain. Its interpretation has sharply divided South African critics. For Isabel Hofmeyr, Schreiner's fiction is its dissonance with her non-fictional prose.[19] While the latter is optimistic and idealist, the fiction displays Hardyesque pessimism, revealed through the death of the enlightened characters. Peter's death accords with Schreiner's pessimism. According to Stephen Gray, Schreiner exposes Peter's liberation of the prisoner and his death as futile acts.[20] This stems not from pessimism on Schreiner's part about

[18] *The Political Situation* (London: T. Fisher Unwin 1896).

[19] Isabel Hofmeyr, 'South African Liberalism and the Novel', in *Olive Schreiner*, ed. Cherry Clayton (Johannesburg: A. D. Donker 1983), 154–7.

[20] Stephen Gray 'The Trooper at the Hanging Tree', in *Olive Schreiner*, ed. Cherry Clayton (Johannesburg: A. D. Donker 1983), 198–208.

the efficacy of liberal idealism itself, but from the inadequacy of Peter's conversion. Peter's inability to bring both his positive (life-affirming) drives and his residual prejudices into the realm of self-awareness doom him to the performance of pointless acts; his 'failure' of consciousness is necessarily a social and political 'failure'.

For Nadine Gordimer, the failure of consciousness is not Peter's but Schreiner's. Caught within the 'prisonhouse of colonialism', her attempts to overcome the oppressions of colonialism are doomed to repeat the very terms and concepts of that colonialist ideology, while the vague utopianism of her liberal humanism is an evasion, not a resolution, of the social and political complexities of colonial reality. To extend Gordimer: it could be argued that Peter's martyrdom is an imaginary resolution, which forecloses exploration of political resistance. Or, one could argue that Peter's death vindicates English imperialism. His self-sacrifice illustrates perfectly the 'white man's burden'; Peter, England's true representative, redeems her name and imperial credentials.

Gray's misreading of Schreiner's idealism has already been dealt with: rationality is not, contra Gray, the uncontested basis of this idealism. Gray's argument that Peter's actions must of necessity 'fail' because they are the result of insufficiently developed reason not only falsifies the nature, and diminishes the extent, of Peter's progressive anti-colonialism—it also overlooks the fact that Peter does succeed in setting free a prisoner. The fact that his companions fail to fully comprehend Peter's humanitarianism and are also unaware of the fact that their own captain has sneakily shot Peter need not detract from the *material* freedom that Peter has given an African captive. This also challenges Hofmeyr's pessimism. Against Gordimer's view of Schreiner as an imperial apologist, two things need to be pointed out. Schreiner clearly represents the Shona people as *agents* of resistance to Rhodes, not passive beneficiaries of English paternalism. And she gives no support for British claims to African government. If Peter *is* the representative of English imperial largesse, he is a highly atypical one: as already discussed, he is a poor and dispossessed Englishman, who cannot get a hearing within the official arena nor even Schreiner's reconstituted symbolic centre of imperial England.

Schreiner's conclusion is in fact more complex and troubled than any of the above. She presents a critique of the conditions that isolate Peter, rather than a valorization of his martyrdom. Her novella's conclusion portrays a successful but limited resistance that refuses premature resolution of social contradictions and belies a liberal faith that individual action can overturn the socio-economic totality. She affirms the possibility of a social alternative in Southern Africa to Rhodes's monopoly capitalism, but she does not suggest this to be fully realizable now by white agents who inhabit these systems they ideologically resist. White metropolitan and colonial opposition to empire is as necessary as it is inescapably inadequate and partial.[21]

CONCLUSION

'In spite of its immense circulation, I do not believe it has saved the life of one nigger, it had not the slightest effect in forcing on the parliamentary examination into the conduct of affairs in Rhodesia and it cost me everything'.[22] Thus Schreiner laments *Trooper Peter*'s failure to achieve direct political results. But the novella refuses to limit its definitions of political agency in this way. As we have seen, Schreiner articulates a critique of capitalist rationality that simultaneously reinforces and questions a belief in rationality as the source of social transformation—she articulates a humanitarian ethics that at times contests and at times complements this rational faculty. Similarly Schreiner's utilitarian approach to this fictional production, which measures anti-imperial value by social mobilization, is at odds with an anti-imperialism that here works deconstructively by questioning the very utility of the discourses it deploys, introducing a self-consciousness about its own

---

[21] In the letter to Pearson cited above, Schreiner goes on to argue that 'in that action that seems a great failure may lie a great success. I suppose one of the greatest successes the world has ever seen was when the Jew carpenter's son hung alone, and cried "My God, I am forsaken". One can only form one's ideal and strive to live it; success and failure must come as they will' (Rive, *Letters*, i. 110). See also Schreiner's letter to John X. Merriman of 17 Dec. 1897: 'And yet by each man doing his tiny best in his tiny place, humanity does grow slowly and slowly onwards' (Rive, *Letters*, i. 324).

[22] Letter to Will Schreiner, 29 June 1898, quoted in First and Scott, *Biography*, 231.

fictionality. Schreiner criticizes and problematizes the very agents—the English—she appeals to, presenting this appeal in ways that pronounce its contingency and the imaginary basis of her idealized community. The Christian humanism she enlists as an another potential agent of anti-imperial social transformation is unstable in its materiality. At times, its effects are tangible, like Peter's freeing of the prisoner, but at times, like Christ's invisible presence in the photograph, this radical oppositionality derives (for Schreiner) precisely from its refusal of empirical locatibility.

7

Transforming Imperial Romance:
Anti-Colonial Pastoralism and
Sexual Politics in *Mhudi*

ANC founder member Sol Plaatje described his novel *Mhudi* as 'a love story after the manner of romances; but based on historical facts . . . with plenty of love, superstition, and imaginations worked in [between the wars]. Just like the style of Rider Haggard when he writes about the Zulus'.[1] Plaatje evidently has *Nada the Lily* in mind, and there is more than a loose resemblance between the two novels.[2] Indeed Plaatje closely modelled *Mhudi* on *Nada the Lily*, something that has escaped critical attention to date. *Mhudi* dramatically revises, and critiques, the imperialist textual politics of *Nada*. Both books are set in the turbulent *Mfecane* of the 1820s and 1830s, and feature a quasi-imperial monarch, respectively Shaka and Mzilikazi who broke away from Shaka to construct the militaristic Ndebele kingdom.[3] Haggard writes as a British imperialist concerned exclusively with the Zulu people. Plaatje writes from a position which was neither imperialist British nor Zulu; he was Rolong, part of the Tswana people, and one of the

[1] Letter to Silas Molema, Aug. 1920. Quoted in Brian Willan, *Sol Plaatje: South African Nationalist 1876–1932* (London: Heinemann 1984), 254.

[2] Solomon T. Plaatje, *Mhudi* (London: Heinemann 1982), with an introduction by Tim Couzens. The novel has a complicated textual history: it was not until ten years after completion, in 1930, that Plaatje succeeded in finding a publisher, the Lovedale Press, and the published text was bowdlerized. The text used here derives from the original typescript, discovered by Tim Couzens and Stephen Gray in 1976. For details of *Mhudi*'s textual variants, see Tim Couzens and Stephen Gray, 'Printers' and Other Devils: The Texts of Sol T. Plaatje's *Mhudi*', *Research in African Literatures*, volume 9, number 2 (1978), 198–215.

[3] See John Omer-Cooper, 'Aspects of Political Change on the Nineteenth-Century *Mfecane*', in *African Societies in Southern Africa*, ed. Leonard Thompson (London: Heinemann 1969), 207–29, and the editors' introduction to Shula Marks and Antony Atmore, eds., *Economy and Society in Pre-Industrial South Africa* (London: Longman 1980), 1–43. For the history of the Ndebele kingdom see R. Kent Rasmussen, *Migrant Kingdom: Mzilikazi's Ndebele in South Africa* (London: Rex Collings 1978).

early activists of the ANC. The Tswana were early converts to Christianity, and as a result feature in colonial discourses as pacific, industrious, and civilizable in contrast to the 'savage', warrior and autonomous Zulu and Ndebele.[4] This contrast is dramatized—and challenged—in Plaatje's novel. Although one of his protagonists is a military 'emperor', the novel concentrates on the Rolong community. It represents their historical massacre and dispersion by Mzilikazi, and subsequent successful resistance in alliance with the newly arrived Boers.[5] Plaatje thus presents Ndebele imperial domination from the perspective of its victims, and suggests a political correspondence between Ndebele imperialism and the twentieth-century white power that was to replace it. The book reads, as Tim Couzens observes, as an allegorical warning to this white government of its inevitable overthrow by those it oppresses.[6] But Plaatje simultaneously presents this as a narrative of a potential pan-African nation, thwarted by a mistaken collaboration with white colonialism in the form of the Boers. Critics have been slow to notice this proto-nationalism, far more radical than the

---

[4] For Plaatje's discussion of the alleged peacefulness of the Tswana, see the introduction to his *Sechuana Proverbs with Literal Translations and Their European Equivalents* (London: Kegan Paul, Trench, Trübner and Co. 1916). Throughout this chapter, I will use the modern terminology of South Africa: 'Tswana' (formerly 'Bechuana'), 'Ndebele' (formerly 'Matabele'). For typical late 19th-cent. articulation of these ethnic stereotypes see George Stowe, *The Native Races of South Africa* (London: Swan Sönnenschëin and Co. 1905), esp. 417–20 and 552. See also George McCall Theal's classic pro-settler 19th-cent. history, *History of South Africa from 1795 to 1872* (4th edn.; London: George Allen and Unwin Ltd. 1915), esp. i. 444–54 and 471–80. For a corrective to the above, see S. M. Molema, *The Bantu Past and Present: An Ethnographical and Historical Study of the Native Races of South Africa* (Edinburgh: W. Green and Son Ltd. 1920), esp. chs. 5 'Bantu: Bechuana, Basuto (First Ethnical Group)', 35–69, and 6 'Bantu: Xosas, Zulus (Second Ethnical Group)', 70–95, in which Molema accepts the basic opposition between the 'peaceful' nations of the interior and the 'warlike coast' nations, but defends the former against its customary denigration.

[5] See Theal, *History*, for one account of these historical events, but see also S. M. Molema's *Chief Moroka: His Life, His Times, His Country and His People* (Cape Town: Methodist Publishing House 1951), 50, for a refutation of Theal's account of the Rolong/Boer alliance.

[6] See e.g. his introd. to the 1982 edn. of *Mhudi*, 1–20. See also: Tim Couzens, 'Sol Plaatje's *Mhudi*', *Journal of Commonwealth Literature*, volume 8, number 1 (June 1973), 1–19; 'The Dark Side of the World: Sol Plaatje's *Mhudi*', *English Studies in Africa*, volume 15, number 2 (1977), 187–203; 'Sol T. Plaatje and the First South African Epic', *English in Africa*, volume 14, number 1 (May 1987), 41–65.

book's surfaces—or the official discourse of the early ANC—suggest.[7]

If Plaatje decentres Haggard's thematic emphasis on an African 'imperial' people he also challenges Haggard's notion of the feminine, producing an eponymous female protagonist who neatly reverses all that Haggard's eponymous Nada represents. Whereas Haggard's Nada is an empty, passive cipher, Plaatje's Mhudi is the most active subject of the book. Nada is a catalyst of destruction and genocide; Mhudi works to preserve life. Haggard's Nada is a political alibi; fatal sexual attraction and family ties instead of British imperialism cause the downfall of the Zulu. Mhudi's political significance is not one of alibi: her friendship with the Ndebele queen Umnandi is the medium for Plaatje's pan-African critique. Their symbolic relationship undercuts Plaatje's representational ideology of an African masculinity in which African men war against themselves and form personal friendships with white men. Plaatje's sexual politics here present an intervention not only against Haggardian ideology but also, as I shall discuss, against the white-centred feminism of Olive Schreiner, a friend of Plaatje's.

Plaatje's contestation of Haggard's paradigm is evident also in his construction of his narrator. Both Haggard and Plaatje feature elderly male narrators directly connected to the events they narrate: *Nada*'s Mopo had planned and executed the downfall of Shaka, while *Mhudi*'s Half-a-Crown is the son of Mhudi and Ra-Thaga. Mopo's narration occurs in the 1870s when as he states white men are preparing to consume the dying Zulu kingdom. When Mopo finishes his narration, he dies. Half-a-Crown's narration is placed in the 1910s, a period as destructive of black South African society as the 1870s were of the Zulu. But Half-a-Crown does not die with the termination of the narrative. To Haggard the Zulu kingdom is a thing of the past; this generates a final link to be instrumentalized and then killed off. Plaatje emphasizes regeneration instead of death; his

[7] Kolawole Ogungbesan, in 'The Long Eye of History in *Mhudi*', *Caribbean Journal of African Studies*, 11 (1978), 27–42, observes the expansion of Plaatje's sympathy from Rolong to Ndebele, and identified this as a form of nationalism, but does not explore how the imperialism of the Ndebele nation fits in to this scheme. Anthony Chennells, however, in his excellent 'Plotting South African History: Narrative in Sol Plaatje's *Mhudi*', *English in Africa*, volume 24, number 1 (May 1997), 37–58, argues for Plaatje's pan-Africanism and links it to his influence by African-Americans W. E. B. Du Bois and Booker T. Washington.

living narrator is himself a testament to the physical survival and productivity of the Rolong people.

As we saw in chapters 3 and 4, Haggard initially analysed the events in Zululand in a serious work of non-fiction, *Cetywayo*, undertaken while the kingdom was being destroyed.[8] His fictional production occurs only after the destruction was complete. The resort to an historical fiction attempts to escape responsibility for the existing desolate reality, while simultaneously supplying its rationale. Through fiction, Haggard reconstitutes the Zulu as a consumable source of fantasy, creating an imaginary subplot as outlet for the most murderous aspects of that fantasy. Plaatje shares nothing with Haggard here except the timing of his turn to fiction. For he too turns to a fictional form only after completing his non-fictional analysis, *Native Life in South Africa*, which exposes and condemns the white South African government for its destruction of black African life.[9] Rather than retreat from and justify the current political situation, Plaatje's historical fiction confronts its genesis. Haggard, as I have argued, is incapable of establishing causality of action; Plaatje explores the diverse consequences of historical actions. At the same time, he supplies a utopian wish-fulfilment that radically contrasts with Haggard's nihilism. Where there is isolation, moribundity, and absolutism in Haggard, there is dialogue, community, vitality, and relativity in Plaatje. Where there is contradiction and aporia in Haggard there is multiplicity and ambiguity in Plaatje. Finally, where there is parody or simulation of (African) culture in Haggard, there is a cultural syncretism in Plaatje.

LOCATING PLAATJE'S PROJECT

To understand more fully the complexities of Plaatje's literary relations to British imperialism, we must look briefly at the man

---

[8] H. Rider Haggard, *Cetywayo and His White Neighbours. Or, Remarks on Recent Events in Zululand, Natal, and the Transvaal* (London: Trübner and Co. 1882).

[9] The central text here is Plaatje's *Native Life in South Africa before and since the European War and the Boer Rebellion*, introd. Brian Willan, foreword by Bessie Head (1916; Athens: Ohio University Press 1991).

and the period.[10] Plaatje belonged to a small class of mission-educated African intelligentsia that in 1912 founded the South African Native National Congress, the political organization later renamed the African National Congress.[11] Plaatje was the first secretary of the SANNC. He was an accomplished politician; he was also a superb polemicist. Before becoming general secretary he worked as a court interpreter and then in the media as founder, editor, and journalist of some of the earliest African newspapers.[12] He participated in the (Anglo-Boer War) siege of Mafeking; his diary of the events is a valuable historical document, unique in its presentation of an African perspective.[13] He was a committed Christian, responsible for organizing the interdenominational Christian Brotherhood movement devoted to the ideals of fraternity and equality. He was also an accomplished linguist fluent in at least seven languages. With Daniel Jones, the English linguist, he compiled the first Setswana phonetic reader, a bilingual collection of Tswana folklore

[10] For the following information, I am indebted to Brian Willan's definitive biography of Plaatje.

[11] For a documentary history of the African National Congress, see Thomas Karis and Gwendolen Carter, eds., *From Protest to Challenge: A Documentary History of African Politics in South Africa 1882–1964* (Stanford: Hoover Institution Press 1972), esp. i. 111, introd. by Sheridan Johns, *Protest and Hope, 1882–1934*. See also Francis Meli, *South Africa Belongs to Us. A History of the ANC* (Harare: Zimbabwe Publishing House 1988); André Odendaal, *Black Protest Politics in South Africa to 1912* (Totowa: Barnes and Noble 1984); Peter Walshe, *The Rise of African Nationalism in South Africa: The African National Congress 1912–1952* (Berkeley: University of California Press 1971). Gail M. Gerhart, *Black Power in South Africa: The Evolution of an Ideology* (Berkeley: University of California Press 1978), considers Plaatje to be an exceptional member of the black bourgeoisie of this period, which she characterizes as remaining faithful to liberal ideology even when the basis for such faith had been destroyed. Plaatje, however, revealed 'an unusual absence of illusion'; attributable to the fact that he was entirely self-educated, unlike his colleagues who had European or US university education (35). This view of the ANC is contentious; for an alternative view see Shula Marks's *The Ambiguities of Dependence in South Africa: Class, Nationalism, and the State in Twentieth-century Natal* (Baltimore: Johns Hopkins Press 1986), esp. ch. 2 on the ANC's first president, 'John Dube and the Ambiguities of Nationalism', 42–73.

[12] Plaatje's newspapers included *Koranta ea Becoana* (The Bechuana Gazette), founded 1902, and *Tsala ea Becoana* (The Friend of the Native), from 1910. See the special issue on Plaatje's journalism of *English in Africa*, volume 3, number 2 (1976). And see Brian Willan, ed., *Sol Plaatje: Selected Writings* (Athens, Ohio University Press 1996). See Benedict Anderson for the role of newspapers within nationalism, *Imagined Communities: Reflections on the Origin and Spread of Nationalism* (London: Verso 1983).

[13] John Comaroff, ed., *The Boer War Diary of Sol T. Plaatje* (London: Macmillan 1973).

(1915). He also collected Tswana proverbs, producing a book in 1916.[14] Another of his achievements was the translation of Shakespeare's *Comedy of Errors, Much Ado about Nothing, Merchant of Venice, Julius Caesar*, and *Othello* into Setswana.[15]

Born in 1876, Plaatje belonged to an era and a class that perceived the British empire as supplying cultural elevation and a system of liberal equality, epitomized in the Cape franchise and contrasted with the oppressive society of the Boers in the Transvaal and Orange Free State.[16] But the 1910 Union of South Africa challenged such perceptions by its alliance of British and Afrikaner interest groups only formally accountable to the metropolitan government. This set the stage for the onslaught on African rights throughout the Union, beginning with the Natives' Land Act of 1913. This devastating legislation aimed to dispossess Africans of the land they owned and rented; to segregate them into disproportionately small 'Native Areas', and to transform them into wage labourers.[17] The

[14] *Sechuana Proverbs*. Plaatje with Daniel Jones, *A Sechuana Reader in International Phonetic Orthography (with English translations)* (London: University of London Press 1916).

[15] On Plaatje and Shakespeare, see Stephen Gray, 'Plaatje's Shakespeare', *English in Africa*, volume 4, number 1 (March 1977), 1–6; the excellent paper by David Schalkwyk and Lerothodi Lapula, 'Solomon Plaatje, William Shakespeare, and the Translations of Culture', delivered at the 'Shakespeare Postcoloniality' conference, University of the Witwatersrand, July 1996. See also David Johnson, *Shakespeare and South Africa* (Oxford: Clarendon Press 1996). See Ali Mazrui, 'The Patriot as Artist', in *African Writers on African Writing*, ed. G. D. Killam (London: Heinemann 1973), esp. 'literature and transnationalism', 86–90, which discusses President Julius Nyerere of Tanzania's translation of *Julius Caesar* into Swahili. This translation, Mazrui argues, vindicates African languages as a literary medium, and 'enrich[es] the creative versatility of the . . . languages themselves'. Such transnationalism thereby belongs to a movement of nationalism. For a recent theatrical exploration of Shakespeare in South Africa, see Michael Picardie's play *The Cape Orchard* (Cardiff: Pant-teg Press 1987), 41–4, in which characters engage with *The Tempest*.

[16] For the history of Cape liberalism, see Stanley Trapido, ' "The Friends of the Natives": Merchants, Peasants and the Political and Ideological Structure of Liberalism in the Cape, 1854–1910', in *Economy and Society in Pre-Industrial South Africa*, ed. Shula Marks and Antony Atmore (London: Longman 1980), 247–74. See Willan's biography for Plaatje's Cape liberal formation, and his essay 'An African in Kimberley: Sol T. Plaatje, 1894–1898', in *Industrialisation and Social Change in South Africa: African Class Formation, Culture and Consciousness 1870–1930*, ed. Shula Marks and Richard Rathbone (London: Longman 1982), 238–58.

[17] On the Natives' Land Act, see Plaatje's *Native Life*. See also Tim Keegan, 'The Sharecropping Economy, African Class Formation and the Natives' Land Act of 1913 in the Highveld Maize Belt', in *Industrialization and Social Change in South Africa*, ed. S. Marks and R. Rathbone (London: Longman 1982), 195–211.

SANNC organized a major campaign against the Act; it sent a delegation including Plaatje over to England to petition parliament in an attempt to nullify the Act. The appeal to the British government failed. Plaatje stayed on alone to campaign in England until 1917. When he returned to South Africa, the SANNC was now divided. The heavily industrialized Transvaal branch had become militant. Plaatje was among the older guard that opposed this spread of 'black bolshevism'.[18] It was during this fraught period of 1917–20—in which Plaatje's relations with both the British and the African nationalist movement were, effectively, in a state of crisis—that he completed the novel *Mhudi*.

Plaatje's aesthetic intervention needs to be understood as a product of his dominant preoccupations with law, aesthetic culture, media, and Christianity. As an institution predicated on abstract principles of justice and equality, law was important to Plaatje, who was an in all respects an extremely litigious man. Throughout his discursive and political activities he positions himself as a lawyer: for the defence, representing African people; and for the prosecution, attacking white racism, its injustice, poor reasoning, and double standards. If Plaatje is both defence and prosecution, he is also judge. Throughout his oeuvre and activities he is concerned always to contest 'one-sidedness' by balancing, deliberating, and finally dispensing judgement.[19] At times this seems to stem less from a commitment to an 'objective' even-handedness and more from an ironic strategy to contain opposition by presenting its voice(s) before it can present them itself. For Plaatje, law is then both an arena and a container of battles; Plaatje's preference was always for constitutional and peaceful over militant ('bolshevik') action. But what happened when the domain of law proved

---

[18] Quoted in Willan, *South African Nationalist*, 224. For the militancy of the Transvaal branch, see Willan. See also Philip Bonner, 'The Transvaal Native Congress, 1917–1920: The Radicalisation of the Black Petty Bourgeoisie on the Rand', in *Industrialization and Social Change in South Africa*, ed. S. Marks and R. Rathbone (London: Longman 1982), 270–313.

[19] These strategies are ubiquitous in Plaatje's writings, and frequently play on the judgement tradition associated with his biblical namesake Solomon. See e.g. 'The Mote and the Beam. An Epic on Sex-Relationship 'Twixt White and Black in British South Africa', originally published in New York, 1921, reprinted in a special issue on Plaatje's journalism of *English in Africa*, volume 3, number 2 (1976), 85–92. Also reprinted in Willan, ed., *Sol Plaatje: Selected Writings*, 274–82.

itself to be just as violent? Much of Plaatje's life from 1913 to 1920 was spent in battling against the 'revolutionary single stroke of the pen', the Natives' Land Act, a piece of legislation whose passage by government was an outrage.[20] If previously Plaatje's litigiousness had been limited to testing and using the constitutional channels open to him, it now extended to querying the very constitutionalism of that legislation.

Media and culture constitute other major concerns for Plaatje, whose involvement ranged from his newspapers to his cultural translations, dictionaries, and anthologies. These indicate his commitment to the modernity, universality, and impersonality of print. This accompanies Plaatje's construction of a new nationalism—the bi- and tri-lingual newspapers must be seen as contributions to 'imagining a nation' across ethnic and linguistic divisions. In translating Tswana proverbs into their literal and idiomatic European equivalents, Plaatje situates himself as medium through which the law of the universal equivalence of languages is revealed. Simultaneously his work bears witness to a counter drive towards the individual and the particular, 'difference' instead of 'identity'.[21] This aspect of Plaatje's cultural production is focused instead on a smaller, orally-derived collectivity: he wishes to protect Rolong and Tswana cultures against the European cultures that threaten them. His allegiance to African cultural traditions and their preservation thus runs in interesting counterpoint to his commitment to modernity and the invention of a national collective. A distinctive individualism cuts across his political, cultural and legal activities, accompanied by Plaatje's concern for self-authorization. Plaatje's work as a translator openly affirms not only the cultural difference of the Setswana language, but also the brilliance of his own talents. Operating as a writer enables Plaatje to flaunt his talents for irony and rhetoric. His argumentative virtuosity finds a showcase in his work as political representative and litigant.

[20] *Native Life*, 6.

[21] See Willan's ch. 14 'Language and Literature: Preserving a Culture' for a detailed explication of these tensions, 324–48. See also Jane Starfield's superb 'The Lore and the Proverbs: Sol Plaatje as Historian', University of the Witwatersrand African Studies Institute Seminar paper, Aug. 1991, on Plaatje's complex literary/cultural negotiations of an ethnic, Rolong/Tswana nationalism and a broad pan-ethnic South African nationalism.

The sphere of Christianity is clearly crucial to Plaatje in supplying a set of 'universal' ethical standards with which to judge and fight others.[22] It also supplies, by extension, a paradigm of fraternity that corresponds to that presented by the SANNC. And it fits the description of the British empire given by Plaatje's Christian Brotherhood Movement, a federation of peoples 'founded upon unity, toleration, justice, and liberty', infinitely expandable.[23] Most crucial to us here is the importance, for Plaatje, of Christianity as a literary tool. A system based upon resourceful reversal of ethical values and semantic definitions, paradox, and parable supplies Plaatje in writing *Mhudi* with a literary style through which traditional African prophetic and parabolic structures can operate. If imperialism impels, Christianity licenses Plaatje to code his text as a multiple allegory, as a story of collective defeat and regeneration combined.[24]

NARRATORIAL HERMENEUTICS

Mhudi supplies a sophisticated lesson in anti-colonial critical judgement, embedded in the narrator's and characters' hermeneutic activities. Plaatje simultaneously exposes the limited interpretative skills of contemporary white power and their historical proxies here, the Ndebele. The myopic, monological practices associated with an imperial hermeneutic are

[22] For analysis of the emergence of Christianity as a tool of the oppressed, see Nietzsche's *The Genealogy of Morals: An Attack*, trans. F. Golfing (1887; New York: Doubleday Anchor Books 1956). Recent South African criticism has begun to re-evaluate the meanings of Christian missionary discourse for black South Africans of the 19th- and early 20th-cents. See the work of Leon de Kock, *Civilising Barbarians: Missionary Narrative and African Textual Response in Nineteenth-Century South Africa* (Johannesburg: Witwatersrand University Press 1996); David Attwell, 'Intimate Enmity in the Journal of Tiyo Soga', *Critical Inquiry*, volume 23, number 3 (spring 1997), 557–77, and 'Reprisals of Modernity in Black South African "Mission" Writing', *Journal of Southern African Studies*, volume 25, number 2 (June 1999), 267–85; Piniel Viriri Shava in ch. 1 'Commitment or Reaction? The Writings of the Mission-Educated Elite and other Early Black Writers', *A People's Voice: Black South African Writing in the Twentieth Century* (London: Zed Books 1989), 5–28. 　　　[23] *Native Life*, 267.

[24] I do not mean to imply here the valorization of Christian over African literary forms. Only a Tswana language and literature specialist would be able to establish the full extent of Plaatje's utilization of these literary forms; I can only be receptive to those areas (fables, proverbs, folklore, prophecies) which are expressly designated African by Plaatje.

evident in the narrative formulations of Haggard's *Nada*: its style remains stuck in a monotonous, essentializing simulation of Zulu orality, and assumes semantic transparency. Haggard's storytelling mode cannot endorse linguistic ambiguity or diversity. In contrast, Plaatje's storytelling exploits semantic complexity, through the protean modalities of a narrator who marries the collective authority of oral history and the individual authority of modern fiction. Interior monologue, third person, and dramatic transcription all feature as narrative approaches, the last replete with stage directions. *Mhudi* is a compendium of rhetorical practices.[25] It contains formal ceremonial situations in which epideictic rhetoric is deployed; legal occasions in which forensic rhetoric occurs; pastoral scenes, presented in the idioms of traditional pastoral prose and verse; and comic scenes, exploiting a 'low' style appropriate to the occasion. The diction appropriates Renaissance models including Shakespeare and the King James Bible. These feature throughout,as also do contemporary social Darwinist language, and a variety of African oral discourses including fables, similes, and proverbs.[26]

It is in his direct practice of translating African idioms that we are made most aware of the narrator's mediatory role, and the ethical and social judgements he exercises in the process. He mediates not only between past and present, as oral historian and son of Mhudi, but also between black and white English speakers. If he affirms his personal relation to his characters—'my father being a trained hunter' (60)—he also establishes ironic distance from them—'they [the Ndebele] . . . introduced manners that were extremely offensive even for these primitive people' (29). At certain key moments, the narrator quietly withdraws his translation function. Careless readers may not be fully aware of the judgements that are being exercised against them, and the linguistic strategies through which they occur.

[25] For an attack on Plaatje's style as purely imitative of Western culture, see the (anonymous) essay on Sol Plaatje's *Mhudi* in S. Christie, G. Hustings, D. MacLennan, eds., *Perspectives on South African Fiction* (Johannesburg: A. D. Donker 1980), 76–82, and Gerald Moore's review of *Mhudi*, *Research in African Literatures*, volume 11, number 2 (summer 1980), 248–50.

[26] See Ruth Finnegan, ch. 14 on proverbs, *Oral Literature in Africa* (Oxford: Clarendon Press 1970), 389–425. See also Jane Starfield's detailed discussion of Plaatje's proverb book projects.

This is the more reprehensible because semantics and judgement feature as themes throughout the book; they furnish the
novel with many of its seemingly incidental episodes. During the
Rolong festive sports, a fight erupts when one relay runner
omits to take the emblem over from another. Is the winner he
who runs fastest or he who is the first carrying the sign?
(Chapter 12, 'A Sportive Dawn and a Gloomy Dusk', 104–6).
Similarly, the marital dispute that chief Moroka is called
upon to judge is semantic at base. It is a question of whether
marriage is to be defined by the contractual sign or the affection
(Chapter 13, 'With the Boers at Moroka's Hoek', 121–4).
Moroka's ruling, like the Koranna's chief's ruling concerning
the murderous Ton-Qon, signals a break from precedent to
establish a new judgement appropriate to the modernity of the
period. Good judgement requires reflexivity, strategic flexibility,
and receptiveness to the specific context; blind adherence to old
protocol is inadequate.

An imperial hermeneutics is what the Ndebele practice.
Blindness is their flaw; they are poor readers of new situations.
They are oblivious to the possibility that their enemies may be
spying on them. We are in danger of aligning ourselves with
the blind, imperial Ndebele—and becoming victims of our
hermeneutic incapacities—if we do not cultivate the linguistic
skills of the Rolong. This involves becoming receptive to the
surveillance operating upon us by the narrator, by Plaatje, and
the black South African nation of which he positions himself as
representative.

ROMANTIC MODULATIONS

Like Haggard, Plaatje bases his novel on events of the early
nineteenth century.[27] These events are juxtaposed against the
realm of fictionality—comprised mainly of the central protagonists, Mhudi and Ra-Thaga. By placing them both within and
outside the historical action he provides a critical perspective to

---

[27] See Georg Lukács, *The Historical Novel*, trans. H. and S. Mitchell (Harmondsworth: Penguin 1976). Plaatje's text is not a 'novel' in the sense that Lukács uses the
term. The historical fiction *Chaka*, by another African literary pioneer, Thomas
Mofolo, trans. Daniel Kunene (1910; London: Heinemann 1986), is an equally
hybrid mixture of genres.

analyse those factual events. At the same time through his treatment of their imaginary pastoral narrative, Plaatje establishes
the limits of the individualist ideology associated with British
imperialism in both its conservative (Haggardian) and liberal
Cape variants. He introduces Mhudi and Ra-Thaga as dispossessed, isolated individuals; the novel sees their eventual
integration into collectivity. Even before this social inter-
pellation occurs, Ra-Thaga and Mhudi as bearers of romantic
individualism are displaced by the *dramatic* form of the novel,
which alternates between scenes at the Ndebele camp and
scenes with the Rolong pair. In other words, Plaatje turns the
individualism of Haggard's heroes Umslopogaas and Galazi, in
their splendid pastoral isolation, into an object of provisional
utility and critique.

For all its generic diversity, the predominant form of *Mhudi*
is a romance.[28] Indeed, it is more faithful than Haggard's *Nada
the Lily* to the orthodox structure in beginning with an idyllic
world and closing with a semi-cyclical resolution that sharply
contrasts with Haggard's absolute, genocidal closure. Whereas
Haggard's characters are cast into the wilderness through an
individual or familial crisis, Plaatje's crisis is social in origin: the
massacre of a whole community. Haggard's twosome consists
of young men, who form an adolescent homosocial brother-
bond and become wolf-monarchs. Plaatje's twosome is a
heterosexual couple, Mhudi and Ra-Thaga. The pastoral adventures of the aristocratic wolf-brothers in *Nada* are conducted
for the pleasure of conquest. Plaatje's romance adventure is a
matter of survival rather than aggrandizement. There are the
customary romance adventures in the pastoral exile, the quests
and trials of suffering, the family reunions, the 'resurrections' of

[28] On romance, see Gillian Beer, *The Romance* (London: Methuen 1970), and
Northrop Frye, *The Secular Scripture: A Study of the Structure of Romance*
(Cambridge: Harvard University Press 1976). On romance in Mhudi, see Brian
Walter's excellent 'The Romance of Protest: Sol Plaatje's *Mhudi*', in *Literature,
Nature and the Land: Ethics and Aesthetics of the Environment. Papers given at the
Annual Conference of the Association of University English Teachers of Southern
Africa*, University of Zululand, 7–10 July 1992, ed. Nigel Bell and Meg Cowper-
Lewis (1993), 193–99. Walter argues Plaatje as 'strongly influenced by the romance
vision in Shakespeare', 193. See also Chennells, 'Plotting South African History',
40–3, for a discussion of the romantic pastoral episodes of Mhudi and Ra-Thaga.
And see Graham Pechey, ' "Cultural Struggle" and the Narratives of South African
Freedom', in *Altered State? Writing and South Africa*, ed. Elleke Boehmer, Laura
Chrisman, and Kenneth Parker (Hebden Bridge: Dangaroo Press 1994), 25–36.

those believed dead. But the traditional romance emphasis on masculine action is reversed when female protagonists, especially Mhudi, take the centre stage.

Plaatje's pastoral scenes contain Shakespearean elements: in the natural environment, characters comment on the politics of the public sphere from which they are temporarily removed. Mhudi and Ra-Thaga's sojourn evokes also the originary narratives of Eden and Robinson Crusoe. Together they construct their comfortable life from scratch. Ra-Thaga soon begins to enjoy a proprietorial relationship to his environment: he 'was already beginning to regard himself as a king reigning in his own kingdom, and the animals of the valley as his wealth' (60). Naturally this king identifies his 'queen' as both a fellow proprietor *and* as property: 'He felt that she—his queen—should be free as the birds of the air were free, nay, even more so; she should be a queen ruling over her own dominion, and he her protector guarding her safety and happiness' (61). Mhudi meanwhile enjoys her 'monopoly' on her husband's time and affections, thinking 'Did they not say that man is by nature polygamous and could never be trusted to be true to only one wife? But here is one as manly as you could wish, and I have never, never seen a husband of any number of wives as happy as mine is with me alone!' (60–1).

Even as Plaatje sets up this paradigm, he gives it a suspiciously comical twist. Mhudi ends her private eulogy on Ra-Thaga and their absolute self-sufficiency by asking herself 'How can I help him to be more manly!' (61). Masculinity is a project in which Mhudi has an active involvement, rather than a natural condition to which she bears witness. Having begun to deflate the paradigm, Plaatje continues; this is where the full force of his critique of Haggardian romanticism can be seen. Ra-Thaga mistakenly identifies six lions as wood-bearing men, but Mhudi's superior reasoning rejects that possibility. On realizing that they are lions, Ra-Thaga registers his dismay: 'he could not claim the sole proprietorship of Re-Nosi. It would be a case of the survival of the fittest'. Mhudi is unperturbed, explaining 'Why should I feel fear . . . while fear is afraid of you?' This challenge to their royal monopoly by the king of the beasts is enough to ruin their whole isolated existence. They cease to venture out to hunt, and Mhudi falls ill from malnutrition. Ra-Thaga steals away while she is asleep to get her a herb; when he returns, a lion is about to enter the hut.

Rather than demonstrating a Haggardian warrior instinct of attack, Ra-Thaga recalls the story of a man who seized a lion by the tail and held on to it until some 'trekkers who chanced to come that way speared the lion for him'. Accordingly Ra-Thaga creeps up, grabs the lion's tail, and shouts to Mhudi, who has just woken up, to come out with his assegai.

Most Bechuana women in such circumstances would have uttered loud screams for help. Mhudi yielded to the humour of the picture of her husband having a tug of war with the lion; highly amused, she gripped the situation, stepped forward in obedience to Ra-Thaga, and summoning all her strength, she aimed a stab at the lion's heart. The infuriated beast fell over with a growl that almost caused the earth to vibrate. (64)

After this success, Mhudi's 'adoration' of Ra-Thaga increases; 'she forgot that she herself was the only female native of Kunana who had thrice faced the king of the beasts, and had finally killed one with her own hand' (66). The intrusion of the lion is the stuff of pastoral allegory; one critic sees this lion as emblem of British imperialism.[29] But Plaatje's presentation emphasizes the scene's material modality and the resolutely practical, unromanticized responses of the protagonists.[30] Plaatje's evocation and denial of a conventional romantic register subjects the 'dream' world of romance to a rationalist scrutiny, while simultaneously putting the category of the empirical into question. Plaatje sustains this dual modality throughout the novel, by presenting numerous characters who question their own perceptions, uncertain whether they belong to dream or reality.[31]

[29] Stephen Gray, *Sources of the First Black South African Novel in English: Solomon Plaatje's Use of Shakespeare and Bunyan in Mhudi* (Pasadena: Munger Africana Library, California Institute of Technology 1976), 23: 'In the nicest possible way, cheeky Mr Plaatje is laughing at the Georgian lions that have set up their flag over Southern Africa, and the message is that they have to be tiptoed past, and killed when they trespass'.

[30] The allegorical register accrues from their discussion of the Rolong legacy: the great leader of their past was Tau, whose name is literally 'lion' while his status as 'the Lion of the North' has a symbolic ring; therefore when the pair do battle with a lion this previous king and his terrain is evoked.

[31] This occurs on a number of levels. Environment: in Mhudi's quest for Ra-Thaga after the war, the landscape is invested with both natural and supernatural

In mocking the pair's royal proprietoriness, Plaatje also mocks the language and ideology of possessive individualism. The corresponding pastoral ideal of self-sufficiency is exposed as an impossibility. The pair cannot permanently survive as a society unto themselves. Although the lion-death is a triumph of teamwork even here the social collective is given affirmative priority over the duo: it is by recalling a narrative from his cultural bank that Ra-Thaga obtains an idea for action. The lion is gripped by two tails—the second being the Tswana 'tale' (Plaatje would have certainly been alert to such a pun). In this feat, Mhudi plays as great a part as Ra-Thaga.[32] Plaatje presents female weakness to be a fiction and mocks Mhudi's own fiction of Ra-Thaga's supreme masculinity.

SEXUAL POLITICS: THE GENDERING OF SUBJECTIVITY

That *Mhudi* presents a woman-centredness rather threatening to later ANC models of nationalism is suggested by the response of Mazisi Kunene in 1980.[33] This ANC activist, poet, and

status. Events: people's fake deaths—Mhudi's, Ra-Thaga's, Umnandi's, are given both naturalist and providential explanation. Perceptions: Mhudi's 'cool judgement', we are told, was 'the secret of the charmed life she bore' (74), which neatly balances romance and realism, as does the episode when Mhudi hears the jabber of monkeys which to her 'native superstition' is a bad omen; while the narrator sneers at this, the omen is vindicated as Mhudi finds Ra-Thaga badly injured.

[32] Myrtle Hooper remarks on 'Plaatje's deliberate substitution of a woman for a man as "hero" in the folktale', 'Rewriting History: The "Feminism" of *Mhudi*, *English Studies in Africa*, volume 35, number 1 (1992), 78.

[33] Mazisi Kunene, review article on Plaatje, *Research in African Literatures*, volume 11, number 2 (summer 1980), 244–7. On gender in Plaatje, see Laura Chrisman, 'Fathering the Black Nation of South Africa: Gender and Generation in Sol Plaatje's *Native Life in South Africa* and *Mhudi*', *Social Dynamics*, volume 23, number 2 (summer 1997), 57–73. On gender and nationalism in the ANC, see Deborah Gaitskell and Elaine Unterhalter, 'Mothers of the Nation: A Comparative Analysis of Nation, Race and Motherhood in Afrikaner Nationalism and the African National Congress', in *Woman–Nation–State*, ed. Nira Yuval-Davis and Floya Anthias (London: Macmillan 1989), 58–78; Frene Ginwala, 'Women and the African National Congress, 1912–1943', *The Societies of Southern African in the 19th and 20th Centuries* vol. 16, University of London Institute of Commonwealth Studies Collected Seminar Papers 1990, 57–69; Anne McClintock, ch. 10 'No Longer in a Future Heaven', *Imperial Leather: Race, Gender and Sexuality in the Colonial Contest* (London: Routledge 1995), 352–89; Julia C. Wells, *We Now Demand! The History of Women's Resistance to Pass Laws in South Africa* (Johannesburg: Witwatersrand University Press 1993).

mythographer of nineteenth-century Zulu history is outraged by the novel's equal attention to the operations of romance, femininity, and the domestic along with the historical representations of military conflict. Kunene claims that

Basically he (Plaatje) wanted to tell a story about a notorious and skilful general (Mzilikazi) whose raids on the Tswana had made him both hated and admired. Because Plaatje was writing the story down and not narrating it verbally *à la africaine*, he thought it necessary to include a little romantic episode (or did someone suggest it?). The episode itself is totally infantile and hangs loosely in between the violent actions of the warring parties. In fact, it is totally incongruous.[34]

For this ideologue, Plaatje's female-centred scenes and themes are an inevitable, regrettable consequence of his capitulation to European aesthetic and political values. They seriously detract from the proper stuff of novels and nationalism, that is, the narration of military history.

This judgement complements that passed by the editor of the 1930 Lovedale Press first edition of *Mhudi*. The very last sentence of the novel is Ra-Thaga's announcement to his wife that 'from henceforth, I shall have no ears for the call of war or the chase; my ears shall be open to one call only—the call of your voice'. In the Lovedale edition this is altered to 'my ears shall be open to one call only *besides the call of the chief*, namely the call of your voice—Mhudi' (emphasis added).[35] For this editor, Plaatje's privileging of feminine/domestic bonds over those of traditional chiefly authority is an unacceptable transgression of a properly 'native' ideology. These anxious responses suggest just how provocative Plaatje's text is. Against an ideology that equates national history and culture with masculinity and warfare, the novel argues for the value of the spheres of the domestic, and the feminine, in building a national narrative. Plaatje presents these as the basis for an alternative pan-African history.

Plaatje not only valorizes the domestic sphere, he also offers a critique of African women's restriction to that sphere and

[34] Kunene, 'Plaatje', 246. Criticism of the 'clash of romance and realism' is also found in S. Christie *et al.* eds., *Perspectives on South African Fiction* (Johannesburg: A. D. Donker 1980).
[35] Sol Plaatje, *Mhudi* (1930; Broadway: Quagga Press 1982), 165.

their exclusion from decision-making office.[36] Plaatje's novel does not romanticize an 'essential' life-affirmative femininity. What it does do is situate African women as having access to more diverse forms of subjectivity than men have, ironically at times as the result of their very exclusion from public power.

We have already seen how Mhudi's actions in the pastoral wilderness challenge the stereotypes of female weakness and submissiveness that she herself articulates. We have also seen the superiority of Mhudi's judgement. From the opening prologue, Plaatje establishes women as the active and creative forces of their society.[37] Plaatje represents men as mainly reactive, their hunting and pastoral duties described as 'perfunctory' capitalization upon the material amply supplied by 'mother earth'. In contrast, Plaatje asserts, women are constantly industrious, their workload combines agricultural, domestic, and reproductive labour. So far, so traditional; European anthropologists were fond of characterizing African men as lazy patriarchs and their women as exploited drudges.[38] However, Plaatje goes on to challenge this evaluation:

[36] Willan and Ogungbesan both comment upon Plaatje's friendship with Olive Schreiner, after whom he named his daughter. Plaatje's Schreiner connection extended to her husband and one of her brothers, politicians who belonged to the group of South African liberal 'Friends of the Natives' with whom the ANC liaised. Willan also outlines a circle of women, including Georgina Solomon, the Colensos, Betty Molteno, Alice Werner, and Jane Cobden Unwin, who were some of Plaatje's closest friends and supporters while he was in England (*South African Nationalist*, 360). These women were active suffragettes as well as campaigners for African rights in South Africa. For examples of Plaatje's correspondence with these women, see *Sol Plaatje: Selected Writings*, ed. Brian Willan (Johannesburg: Witwatersrand University Press 1996).

[37] Olive Schreiner venerates African women for their productive maternity and its respected role, in her accounts of 'traditional' African society. She does not emerge with much credit if compared with Plaatje here, who presents the 'venerated' role of African maternity in *Mhudi* but goes on to supply a critique of the political disempowerment that attends such veneration. Schreiner requires a notion of static African maternity on which to ground her exclusively white female evolutionism. See her *Woman and Labour*, preface by Jane Graves (1911; London: Virago 1978), ch. 1 'Parasitism', esp. 56–65.

[38] See Rosalind Coward's account of 19th-cent. European anthropology, *Patriarchal Precedents: Sexuality and Social Relations* (London: Routledge and Kegan Paul 1983). By the time Plaatje was writing, anthropologists had rejected the idea that 'primitive' society was matriarchal and argued for primitive patriarchal supremacy. In Britain, a definition of power as political rights and property ownership had become dominant; as women in 'primitive' societies appeared to lack these, they were interpreted as lacking power altogether. This was accompanied by the belief that the status of women had improved under Western civilization. Lubbock,

Fulfilling these multifarious duties of the household was not regarded as a drudgery by any means; on the contrary, the women looked upon marriage as an art . . . the simple women of the tribes accepted wifehood and transacted their onerous duties with the same satisfaction and pride as an English artist would the job of conducting an orchestra. (25–7)

As usual in Plaatje, the ironies are multiple and some of them rebound upon the 'simple' society he describes. However, the equation of women with creativity—more precisely, with resourcefully turning the quotidian necessities of life into expressions of individual artistic freedom—is one that Plaatje unconditionally sustains. This novel presents men as reflexive rather than reflective. In Ra-Thaga's argument with Mhudi over Mzilikazi's ownership rights, Ra-Thaga operates on the principle that 'might is right'; that is, he accepts the status quo. This does not prevent him and his fellow Rolong from mobilizing to avenge themselves against Mzilikazi. But their reaction is just that, structured as revenge for the loss of their reproducing 'stock'—women—as well as the loss of their cattle. Mhudi instead proposes a resistance derived from moral and political principles.

Men's re-activeness as Plaatje presents it stems from their investment in the existing patriarchal order. Ra-Thaga's poor judgement originates in masculine myopia. It fails him in his dealing with the Koranna headman; his refusal to heed Mhudi's warning is based upon a misguided machismo. He allows a sexist proverb—'never be led by a female lest thou fall over a precipice' (73)—to determine his decision to go hunting against her advice. Mhudi's doubts are vindicated when the headman tries to have Ra-Thaga killed; it is Mhudi's bravery that saves him. Frequently Plaatje contests Rolong people's masculinist assumptions. Mhudi's arrival at the war camp after her second solo quest is another instance: Ra-Thaga is embarrassed and annoyed by her incursion into this masculine space, fearing humiliation by his fellow fighters. But the novel itself celebrates

for example, asserts that 'Nothing, perhaps, gives a more instructive insight into the true condition of savages than their ideas on the subject of relationship and marriage; nor can the great advantages of civilisation be more conclusively proved than by the improvement which it has effected in the relation between the two sexes', *The Origin of Civilisation and the Primitive Condition of Man: The Mental and Social Condition of Savages* (London: Longmans, Green, and Co. 1870), 58.

Mhudi's arrival, the heroic culmination of a difficult trek. Plaatje presents Mhudi's quests as voluntary acts that transgress customary feminine limits. Her second quest takes Mhudi into Lear territory:

In spite of the fury and rage of the storm the brave woman struggled along her chosen route. There being neither trees nor shelter of any description, she had to endure in full the heavy onslaughts of these angry elements. It was as though the legions of nature were in conflict, and she—poor little human wreck—a mere plaything at their mercy. (153)

It is women who are the most curious about new phenomena (including Boers) and the most communicative. In a text which is itself persistently and pervasively interrogative, it is significant that women should ask more questions. Mhudi's range from the sublime (about cosmology) to the mundane (about the clothes of the Boer women). However Plaatje considers women also be myopic, as emphasized in the behaviour of Ndebele women during their victory celebrations:

No one, much less a woman, cared to know the cause of the raid, for the end had amply justified the means . . . Today, especially, the booty more than counter-balanced the loss of the good Matabele blood spilled in the enterprise. With this magnificent addition to the national wealth and the national food supply, it should be impossible in future for the sister, wife or mother of a spearman to run short of beef; so the women of the city were in high glee. (51)

Instead of lamenting the loss of their offspring, their long-term racial investment, the women are celebrating the immediate material benefits of the massacre. Plaatje suggests that the 'imperial' Ndebele women's structural dependency upon the already parasitic activities of cattle-raiding men devalues their reproductive labour and debases their subjectivity. There is, it seems, no necessary connection for Plaatje between maternal function and maternal sentiment. This is also suggested by the converse case of Ndebele queen Umnandi, who is childless but the most socially nurturant queen of Mzilikazi's house.

Plaatje thus echoes Olive Schreiner's argument that an imperial, parasitic society produces parasitic female subjects.[39] At the same time, he argues that imperial expansion reinforces patriarchal domination. Thus he represents Mzilikazi's 'harem'

[39] *Woman and Labour*, ch. 2 'Parasitism Continued', 69–110.

as a dysfunctional space producing insecurity, rivalry, scheming and homicidal ambitions among the wives who depend upon the whimsical tyranny of their husband. The destabilizing violence of Mzilikazi's foreign imperial policy recurs in his household regime. The destructive social relations of this 'harem' force Umnandi, the favourite wife, into exile to preserve her life from the jealous scheming of the other wives. Plaatje criticizes both Mzilikazi's favouritism and the system of polygamy as unjust.[40] That Plaatje terms Mzilikazi's domestic arrangement a harem is significant: it associates polygamy with an 'Oriental' political despotism and sexual excess. An attempt to articulate a critique from a proto-African nationalist perspective, then, involves Plaatje's problematic reinforcement of an Asian stereotype.

AFRICAN WOMEN AND PAN-AFRICANIST VISION

Plaatje uses African women as the vehicle of a pan-African political vision.[41] While Mhudi and Umnandi pursue their respective quests they meet and become friends. Through this friendship across political enmity Plaatje questions the basis of that enmity itself in African self-destructiveness. Through it he extends the critique to include the exclusion of women from political representation. In their formal farewell Umnandi anticipates for herself an uncertain future, the 'blank gloom' of a shattered and dispossessed nation, but anticipates a positive future for Mhudi. Mhudi replies 'How wretched . . . that men

[40] Elsewhere in his writing Plaatje defends polygamy, like Molema, to the extent that the official status and protection accorded to women within it contrasts favourably to the exploitative practices of prostitution and sexual degradation ushered in through 'civilized' monogamy. See e.g. *Native Life*, ch. 7 'Persecution of Coloured Women in the Orange "Free" State', 110–20.

[41] Walter remarks on the symbolic implications of this transethnic women's friendship: 'In each of their cultures the women symbolize similar values. They recognize each other's virtue across the barriers of race and enmity. Their friendship is the symbol of a possible new social order' ('The Romance of Protest', 195). Hooper ('Rewriting History', 77) argues this female bonding to 'speak for all women, regardless of race'. Phaswane Mpe, ' "Naturally These Stories Lost Nothing By Repetition": Plaatje's Mediation of Oral History in *Mhudi*', *Current Writing. Text and Reception in Southern Africa*, volume 8, number 1 (April 1996), 75–89 discusses Mhudi and Umnandi's exchange as 'an allegory of the possibility of ethnic and racial unity, and of gender equality' (82). Mpe argues that Mhudi's anti-war convictions here combine critique of patriarchy with critique of imperialism.

in whose counsels we have no share should constantly wage war, drain women's eyes of tears and saturate the earth with God's best creation—the blood of the sons of women. What will convince them of the worthlessness of this game, I wonder?' (165).

Umnandi is pessimistic: 'Nothing, my sister . . . so long as there are two men left on earth there will be war' (165). But Mhudi has the last word; wishing Umnandi success in her search for Mzilikazi she instructs her to 'urge him, even as I would urge all men of my acquaintance, to gather more sense and *cease warring against their kind*' (emphases added) (167). The reference to 'their own kind' is, I would argue, a specific reference to black Africans; the political corollary is the plea for black Africans, like these two women, to recognize their commonality and unite against a shared white oppressor rather than fight their own people. Mhudi's proto-pan Africanism, like her implicit plea for African women's access to political representation, prevails over Umnandi's universalizing fatalism. Plaatje suggests that African women's suffrage serves the interests both of self-determination and racial survival.

In this he echoes the arguments of Olive Schreiner against war, and for women's suffrage; like Schreiner, Plaatje seems here to advocate a social project centred on feminised nurture as opposed to masculinised war.[42] Schreiner derives an argument for women's political equality from a conviction of their psychological and physiological 'difference', arguing that all women, by nature of their reproductive function, have an 'instinctive antagonism' to war. Men's bodies are their 'works of art' which women would never care to squander.[43] It is on this vital point alone that women are essentially different from men and thereby are enabled to contribute to the public weal through enfranchisement. (The contradictions in Schreiner's arguments need not detain us here.) But Plaatje's pro-feminism differs from Schreiner's in its premises if not its pro-suffrage conclusions. There is nothing in Plaatje's novel to sustain

---

[42] Plaatje's attitude to other, European, wars was quite different. He expresses support for African participation in the Anglo-Boer War and World War I, in *Native Life*, ch. 19 'Armed Natives and the South African War', 284–94; ch. 20 'The South African Races and the European War', 295–315; ch. 21 'The Offer of Assistance by the South African Coloured Races Rejected', 316–32.

[43] *Woman and Labour*, ch. 4 'Woman and War', 153–78.

Schreiner's biological essentialism; his account of gendered subjectivity is social constructionist. And if he deviates from her biologism he also dissents from its corresponding universalism. His arguments against war here do not concern war as an abstraction (his support for participation in the First World War earned sharp criticism from Schreiner) but only intra-racial war which damages the cause of pan-African unity.

This scene's racial unity sentiments gain clarity when juxtaposed to another farewell scene, that features the Boer couple, Mhudi, and Ra-Thaga. Ra-Thaga's friendship with the white de Villiers superficially corresponds with the early ANC's liberal humanistic view that social and cultural difference between black and white can be transcended within interpersonal relationships. It also appears to signify the prospect of a non-racial South African society. But Plaatje criticises this perception, questioning its realizability within a society of economic inequality. The two men have learned each other's languages; their farewell is affectionate. Mhudi has become friendly with de Villiers' fiancee Hannetjie, but the limits to this inter-racial unity quickly become apparent:

De Villiers vainly tried to persuade Ra-Thaga to break with his people and remain with him. Hannetjie too had fallen in love with Mhudi. She said if she lived to have little ones of her own, surely they would be proud to have for an ayah such a noble mosadi as Mhudi. But, unlike the two of them, they knew not each other's language, consequently she made a less favourable impression on Mhudi than de Villiers did on her husband. (183–4)

Plaatje's narrator usually translates African words in brackets. Here he withdraws his translative function. At the very moment of female 'intimacy', the Boer woman inscribes Mhudi as a domestic servant.[44] Plaatje's mixing of languages

[44] Walter ('The Romance of Protest', 197) comments that 'like the Hannetjie in Native Life in South Africa, she automatically assumes a mistress-servant relationship'. Starfield ('The Lore and the Proverbs', 14) observes that: 'Plaatje . . . concludes, with bitter hindsight, that the Boers did not look upon their former military allies as partners on the land, but as a ready labour supply. Plaatje depicts the Boers as incapable of understanding Mhudi's heroism. They see her only as potential *ayah* material for their own passive wives'. Hooper ('Rewriting History', 77) remarks that 'Mhudi is subordinate to no-one, man or woman, and she is able to resist, with grace and determination, Hannetjie's attempts to apply to her the categories of master-servant relationship'. See *Native Life*, chs. 6 'Our Indebtedness to White Women', 100–9, and 7 'Persecution of Coloured Women in the Orange "Free"

juxtaposes 'ayah' and 'mosadi' (Setswana for 'woman') in such a way as to emphasize the words' non-equivalence. The discourse mimics the incomprehension between the two women.

A further effect of this sentence is to indict the English reader, as well as Hannetjie, of racism. The reader who does not know the meaning of 'mosadi' is put in the position of 'othering' Mhudi. At the same time, Plaatje's refusal to translate preserves Mhudi's subjectivity from contamination by the racist discourse into which she is being written. The scene could not contrast more strongly with the affectionate, equal,—and translated—exchange between Mhudi and Umnandi (167).

This scene further underscores Plaatje's interdependent pan-Africanism and pro-feminism. It suggests that the inter-racial bonding achieved by Ra-Thaga and de Villiers is a privilege of their masculinity, facilitated by military conditions that have only temporarily equalized their status. No such equalization is available to the women; they cannot escape structures of socio-economic inequality and their racist ideological correlatives. Plaatje's materialism exposes inter-racial liberalism as a politically limited and sexually exclusive ideal.

CONCLUSION

Like many subsequent African writers Plaatje is involved in establishing an African mythology, creating in the activities and characters of his novel a repository of strong, affirmative heroes and heroines who function to elevate African consciousness, and self-regard, and provide thereby a model and motor for nationalist struggles. But Plaatje at the very same time is involved in interrogating 'myth' and 'legend'. His characters are emphatically not the two-dimensional constructed by Haggard. Such stereotyping and idealization is not completely resisted—it is, rather, shown up for what it is, a human construction. If Plaatje goes beyond unqualified legendizing, with his ironic and rationalist orientation, he also goes beyond the liberalism associated with black South African nationalism of this period. His presentation of the friendship between Ra-Thaga and the

State', 110–20, which highlight the particular tensions between white and black women.

Boer de Villiers both affirms and problematizes this liberalism, by revealing the limits of the ideal of interracial harmony within an emergent colonial society. As with a moral liberalism, so too with a corollary individualism: Plaatje's critique of romantic pastoralism situates individuals as members of collectives who cannot sustain capitalist and colonial narratives of private, competitive, or solipsistic subjectivity.

In revising these—Haggardian—models of an imperial romance, Plaatje offers a radical reformulation of sexual politics. He situates African women as self-determining subjects of a potential oppositional political culture, one that critiques African patriarchy and its attendant notions of sexual difference along with white colonialism. At the same time, African women function as a vehicle for a pan-African utopian vision of nationalism.

8

Complex Relations:
African Nationalism, Imperialism,
and Form in *Mhudi*

THE previous chapter explored Plaatje's revision, in *Mhudi*, of the Haggardian imperial romance. This chapter focuses on Plaatje's critical historiography. His reinterpretation of the events of the *Mfecane* articulates a complex vision of the inter-relations of British imperialism and African nationalism; this complexity is at once historical, theoretical, and literary. In the novel's diachronic and synchronic form Plaatje suggests the multiple, and split, narratives that emerge from the contra-dictions of British imperialism, and the consequently divided meanings of African nationalism itself.

All Plaatje's writings are occasional, determined by the exigencies of the political moment. Writing of proverbs, Plaatje reveals his view of narrative acts in general:

The whole truth about a fact cannot always be summed up in one pithy saying. It may have several different aspects, which, taken separately, seem to be contradictory and have to be considered in connexion with their surrounding circumstances. To explain this connexion is the work of a sermon or essay, not of a proverb. All the latter can do is express each aspect by itself and let them balance each other.[1]

We can see Plaatje's own oeuvre as a series of miniature narra-tives, condensed and isolated like proverbs. *Mhudi* presents an opportunity for Plaatje to supply the full narrative that like the 'sermon or essay' connects and explains the various aspects. But if in *Mhudi* Plaatje frees himself to develop an extended narra-tive, he is also bound to a more general theme, that of European imperialism, whose own master narrative was now fragmented. What happens, then, when the constitutional game is up, when

[1] *Sechuana Proverbs with Literal Translations and their European Equivalents* (London: Kegan Paul, Trench, Trübner and Co. 1916).

two trips and two appeals to the British home government have
failed to secure any protection against the newly introduced
system of segregation and exploitation? The call now to revise
the meanings of the British empire is made loudly by Plaatje's
friend and compatriot S. M. Molema in his book *The Bantu
Past and Present* (1920).[2] In a brilliant penultimate chapter,
Molema proposes two definitions of this British intervention in
South Africa. The first continues the liberal-meliorist view with
which Plaatje started his intellectual life. This sees the original
brutality of colonization—lasting up to the mid-nineteenth
century—as having been replaced by Christian morality and
British altruistic paternalism. It concedes that the present
horrors of 'native life' under South African legislation break the
moral–evolutionary trajectory, but explains this as a temporary
reversion to the old dark days created by South African unifi-
cation and subsequent loss of British civilizing influence. The
situation reinforces dependence on British imperialism as a
bulwark of idealism and as salvation; it is the only hope. The
second view diametrically opposes this first view; it replaces
optimism with an explicitly Nietzschean pessimism. The British
languages of liberalism and altruism have been just that, abstract
professions, contradicted by the operations of imperialism
which follow social Darwinian laws of self-interest, physical
competition and domination through conquest.[3] Under South

---

[2] S. M. Molema, *The Bantu Past and Present: An Ethnographical and Historical
Study of the Native Races of South Africa* (Edinburgh: W. Green and Son Ltd.
1920), ch. 29, 'Social and Economic Prospects', 342–55. See Jane Starfield, 'The
Lore and the Proverbs: Sol Plaatje as Historian', University of the Witwatersrand
African Studies Institute Seminar paper (1991), for analysis of Plaatje's historio-
graphy. Wolfgang R. L. Gebhard makes a comparative analysis of Plaatje's *Native
Life* and Molema's *The Bantu Past and Present*, in 'The Dazzling Light: Impinge-
ments on the Visions of Plaatje and Molema', paper delivered at 'People, Power, and
Culture: the history of Christianity in South Africa, 1792–1992' conference,
University of the Western Cape, Bellville, 8–12 Aug. 1992. For another early 20th-
cent. black South African ethnography, see Magema M. Fuze, *The Black People and
Whence They Came: A Zulu View*, ed. A. T. Cope, trans. H. C. Lugg (1922; Pieter-
maritzburg: University of Natal 1986).

[3] See the address by Meshach Pelem, 26 Feb. 1919, document 29, *From Protest
to Challenge: A Documentary History of African Politics in South Africa
1882–1964*, i: *Protest and Hope, 1882–1934*, by Sheridan Johns, 111, ed. Thomas
Karis and Gwendolen M. Carter (Stanford: Hoover Institution Press 1972), 101–3,
in which he discusses the European scramble for Africa as dancing to the tune of
'survival of the fittest'. This address shares several of Plaatje's and Molema's themes.
The British government in surrendering African rights to Afrikaners has 'imposed a
terrific strain upon our loyalty' (101). The British government, in fact, through its

African home rule the true colours of British power now emerge.

Molema's first Christian model is based upon an ideal that it admits to be very fragile. His Darwinian second view supplies no possibility of positive action, resistance and transformation, by either oppressed or oppressor.[4] The tensions between these two (equally non-economic) perspectives further problematize the genesis and process of European imperial history, its laws and modes. Is it progressive, cyclical, regressive, or static? Is its course determined by absolute necessity, or is there—and has there been—room for chance and choice? Could the present disaster, then, have been prevented by different actions by Africans, Boers, and English in the initial periods of colonial incursion?

REPLOTTING THE HISTORICAL MEANINGS OF BRITISH IMPERIALISM

Plaatje's novel explores the questions that Molema's analysis raises. Plaatje's choice of the early nineteenth century allows him to analyse the arrival of the Voortrekkers into his part of Southern Africa. Plaatje interrogates that process, examines its genesis, and asks whether its present oppressive expression could have been avoided. He challenges the received settler-colonial South African version of history by presenting the Voortrekkers as aliens who are dependent upon black assistance for survival and for their military operations. In established

1903–5 Lagden Report was responsible for developing the notion of segregation that animated the 1913 Natives' Land Act. Plaatje quotes the Colonial Secretary Harcourt in this connection in *Native Life in South Africa Before and Since the European War and the Boer Rebellion*, ed. B. Willan, foreword by B. Head (1916; Athens: Ohio University Press 1991) 229–31, but prefers to take issue with this view of British complicity. See also Pixley Seme, *The Regeneration of Africa* (New York: Columbia University Press 1906).

[4] There is a critical risk, that is, in accepting the very tenets that were being used to justify the oppression. The ideology here is related to the late 19th-cent. social Darwinism that had taken over from liberalism as the legitimating tool of colonialism in South Africa. For the use of social Darwinism in South Africa see Saul Dubow, 'Race, Civilisation and Culture: The Elaboration of Segregationist Discourse in the Inter-War Years', *The Politics of Race, Class and Nationalism in Twentieth Century South Africa*, ed. Shula Marks and Stanley Trapido (London: Longman 1987), 71–94.

white historiography, that assistance consisted of a few herd-boys, not the military alliance Plaatje represents. This is the case in George McCall Theal's work, which summarizes this episode in a lengthy footnote specifying the 'sixty Barolong on foot' who 'engaged their services with a view to sharing the spoil' of the Boer attack upon the Ndebele.[5] Interestingly, Theal is very defensive here; the Rolong had already challenged his version and he has here to answer that charge with a full arsenal of authorities. Theal is in no doubt of the 'redemptive' role of the Voortrekkers, come to 'deliver' the Rolong from the fear of the Ndebele.[6]

Plaatje's fiction is not confined to historical exploration. If under the current early twentieth-century situation the past is in crisis, so also is the future. Plaatje examines the future, fore-seeing in the overthrow of Mzilikazi a predetermined victory over imperial oppression. As historical analyst identifying a causal, linear relation between that past and the present, Plaatje belongs to an Enlightenment trajectory. But in his capacity as allegorist and prophet he sustains a pre-'Enlightenment' mode, in which history becomes both cyclical and apocalyptic.[7]

---

[5] George McCall Theal, *History of South Africa from 1795 to 1872* (4th edn.; London: George Allen and Unwin Ltd. 1915), ii. 300–2. For an intelligent dis-cussion of Theal, see Deryck Schreuder, 'The Imperial Historian as Colonial Nationalist: George McCall Theal and the Making of South African History', in *Studies in British Imperial History: Essays in Honour of AP Thornton*, ed. Gordon Martel (London: Macmillan 1986), 95–159.

[6] See Theal, *History*, 296, for his view of the redemptive role of the Voortrekkers come to 'deliver' the Rolong from the terror of the Ndebele. For a contrast see Plaatje's own accounts of his people and their history. In ch. 8 'At Thaba Ncho: a secretarial Fiasco' of *Native Life*, 121–35, he outlines Moroka's assistance to the Voortrekker Boers, their alliance and the subsequent Boer betrayal. See too his bio-graphy of Chief Moroka in T. D. Mweli Skota, ed., *The African Yearly Register: Being an Illustrated National Biographical Dictionary (Who's Who) of Black Folks in Africa* (Johannesburg: R. L. Esson and Co. 1932), 60–4, for a more strongly worded account of these events. This biography is reprinted in Brian Willan, ed., *Sol Plaatje: Selected Writings* (Athens: Ohio University Press 1996), document 102, 406–13. Two critical discussions of Plaatje's historiography have recently been published: Michael Green, *Novel Histories: Past, Present, and Future in South Africa* (Johannesburg: Witwatersrand University Press 1997) and Phaswane Mpe, ' "Naturally These Stories Lost Nothing by Repetition": Plaatje's Mediation of Oral History in *Mhudi*', *Current Writing. Text and Reception in Southern Africa*, volume 8, number 1 (April 1996), 75–89.

[7] Plaatje had a strong interest in prophecy, in African and Christian spiritual traditions. See for example *Native Life*, ch. 9 'The Fateful 13', 136–51. His interest in prophecy was common to other early 20th-cent. African writers. Tim Couzens's introduction to *Mhudi* quotes R. V. Selope-Thema in 1929: 'a writer is a prophet,

Through the medium of fiction, then, Plaatje's material becomes simultaneously historical and allegorical, negative (a story of the advent of colonialism, aided by the Rolong) and positive (a story of the inevitable overthrow of imperialism).

The very preface of the book shows Plaatje in hermeneutic battle, challenging an image of the Ndebele that might come straight out of Haggard, or Theal:

In all the tales of battle I have ever read, or heard of, the cause of the war is invariably ascribed to the other side. Similarly, we have been taught almost from childhood to fear the Matabele—a fierce nation—so unreasoning in its ferocity that it will attack any individual or tribe, at sight, without the slightest provocation. Their destruction of our people, we were told, had no justification in fact or in reason; they were actuated by sheer lust for human blood. By the merest accident, while collecting stray scraps of tribal history, later in life, the writer incidentally heard of 'the day Mzilikazi's tax collectors were killed'. Tracing this bit of information further back, he elicited from old people that the slaying of Bhoya and his companions, about the year 1830, constituted the *casus belli* which unleashed the war dogs and precipitated the Barolong nation headlong into the horrors described in these pages. (21)

Plaatje is evidently displaying a scrupulous 'even-handed-ness', and disinterested concern for ethical justice. He does not, however, emphasize this historical provocation simply to remedy a popular misconception of Ndebele savagery, nor merely for the dramatic possibilities it supplies. Such an event enables him to keep unresolved the definition of Ndebele power, and by extension, the nature of imperialist and nationalist identities. Such a starting-point for *Mhudi*'s plot—in which the motivation for Bhoya's murder is never explained, but presented as a rash and autocratic decision by the chief Tauana—leaves it open whether this Rolong act was justified, inevitable, or a freak, and whether the Ndebele backlash was typical, mistaken, or an aberration.[8] And the meanings of Ndebele imperial rule become indeterminate in turn.

and his duty is not only to prophesy but also to rebuke, when necessary, the people for wrongdoing', 19. On Plaatje's relations, in *Native Life*, to 18th-cent. English 'Enlightenment' cultures, see A. E. Voss, 'Sol Plaatje, the Eighteenth Century, and South African Cultural Memory', *English in Africa. 21st birthday issue. 'Revisions'*, volume 21, numbers 1 and 2 (July 1994), 59–76.

[8] Mpe on 85–6 discusses the ambiguities attached to the representation of the

Plaatje stages two scenes to dramatize these ambiguities, each one balancing the other. One is set within the Ndebele camp, where Ndebele military leaders analyse and disagree about the recent Rolong resistance to their imperial rule. The other is set in the Rolong camp, where Mhudi and Ra-Thaga display equally conflicting views concerning the Ndebele as an imperial force. The Ndebele jingoistic patriots use a social Darwinian rhetoric of racial supremacy; Sitonga and Dambuza emphasize the Rolong political transgression in murdering Bhoya as a member of the ruling race. The more temperate Gubuza privileges the category of class over race, and uses a language of their imperial responsibility towards their subjects. He suggests that Bhoya may have stepped outside his class function as emissary of the government to provoke the Rolong. Mzilikazi himself affirms that Gubuza commands political centrality as one of the main agents of his expansionist scheme, responsible for training their young men to chase 'human buffaloes' (58). Gubuza's power is such that he can later prevent Mzilikazi from executing the defeated Ndebele soldiers; his careful dedication to the nation's physical preservation contrasts with Mzilikazi's extravagant expenditure of Ndebele life. In making Gubuza a major, not dissident, figure in the Ndebele government, Plaatje suggests that his paternalist discourse is as authentic an expression of Ndebele power as the 'new' racial supremacy discourse of Sitonga and Dambuza.[9]

Social Darwinism looms again in the argument between Mhudi and Ra-Thaga about the nature of Mzilikazi's imperial rule. Ra-Thaga's thesis is that 'might is right' and that Mzilikazi is therefore entitled to his rule. Mhudi counters this with a moral argument against the original Ndebele usurpation of their land, and the injustice of the massacre itself. Ra-Thaga defends Mzilikazi's reign as a fair one, which exacted a primarily

murder and massacre. For an intelligent discussion of Plaatje's representation of African political structures, see J. M. Phelps, 'Sol Plaatje's *Mhudi* and Democratic Government', *English Studies in Africa*, volume 36, number 1 (1993), 47–56. See also David Schalkwyk, 'Plaatje Reviewed', forthcoming in *Scrutiny 2*.

[9] See Phelps ('Sol Plaatje's *Mhudi*', 51) who comments that Plaatje's overall effect in this scene is 'not only to expose the limitations of the narrow nationalism which fuels the autocratic power of Mzilikazi, but, more cogently to reveal how autocracy disrupts the body politic by fostering the autocratic ambitions of others. The scene of the revels exposes how personal and social relations in this society have become conditioned by the abuse, and the fear, of absolute power'.

symbolic tribute: 'all the tribes who quietly paid their dues in kind were left unmolested. Mzilikazi did not even insist that larger tribes should increase the value of their tax in proportion to their numbers. So long as each tribe sent something each spring in acknowledgement of its fealty, he was satisfied' (66). In contrast, Mhudi claims that the parasitic Ndebele were and are motivated by economic need (66). As in the Ndebele scene, Plaatje does not privilege one interpretation as more accurate or politically representative than the other; he gives equal weight to both, suggesting that there is valid evidence for both perspectives.

Thanks to the introduction of firearm technology, the Boer/ Rolong victory over the Ndebele is indeed a social Darwinian narrative of 'might is right'. However, the battle equally confirms Mhudi's contrasting ethical vision of a righteous Rolong revenge, with rather different allies from those she had foreseen. Prophesied by Ndebele soothsayers, who saw in Halley's comet a sign of military disaster, the battle is yet an event Mzilikazi could have escaped had he taken their advice to resettle north. When defeat occurs it carries the double weight of metaphysical fate and unforeseeable technology, or in other words, tradition and modernity. One might expect Plaatje to depict the battle as a triumph for 'the allies'—after all, it is the overthrow of imperialist oppression.[10] Instead, his description privileges the experience and perception of the Ndebele, in particular the heroic efforts and military 'genius' of the general Gubuza. The lengthy passage concludes:

The battle was a one-sided affair; only Matabele could keep on rushing at such certain death, and even they discovered that they were engaged in a struggle hitherto unknown in human warfare. The devastating machines of war had spread a pall of death and desolation

[10] Plaatje also records the positive effects of this anti-imperial victory or liberation but displaces their expression from the 'Allies' themselves to non-participant, neighbouring Tswana who enjoy the Allies' beef. Here Plaatje's diction becomes distinctly redemptive: 'Villages in the vicinity resounded with a thrilling song of joy. The inhabitants told one another that the hour of deliverance from Matabele domination had already struck . . . In other villages where there were converted Natives, they gathered in their grass-thatched chapels and sang other songs to the God of Moses, of Joshua and of Gideon. Their supplications were for new priests to blow the ramhorn and the trumpet, bring down the walls of the modern Jericho on the banks of the Marico, and thus hasten the emancipation of all the Bechuana tribes' (148).

over the plains. The new moon, expected to make all things new, had instead brought an appalling revolution, for blood and terror had taken the place of the peace of yesterday. The stillness of the woods which had enjoyed peace and tranquillity for a thousand years was suddenly broken by a new and hitherto unknown din of war. (145–6)

Plaatje's figure of the new moon carries more than stylistic importance, with its word play on revolution. The event is a revolution in both senses: a completion of the revenge cycle, and a total transformation of African life.

If Plaatje were concerned to depict the successful overthrow of oppression, this moment would be the obvious closure point for the novel. The novel's opening massacre has been avenged and resolved. Instead Plaatje extends the novel to cover the future Ndebele nation; and he begins this shift towards the Ndebele not after, but during, the very overthrow itself.[11] As the transfer of narrative emphasis towards the Ndebele develops, Plaatje simultaneously makes them the bearers of his biblical diction. A first their situation is lamentable: they are 'strangers in a strange land' (149), who 'hope against hope' (168). Then they commence their 'exodus' (title of chapter 20) to find 'the land of plenty' up north (175). In the meantime Umnandi is 'going into the wilderness' in her quest for Mzilikazi (167). She succeeds and the nation is reborn: the narrator departs from the present tense to gives us a full romance resolution, going on to outline the future powerful reign that the son of Umnandi and Mzilikazi (Lobengula) comes to enjoy in this, the new Matabeleland.[12]

---

[11] Plaatje takes the poetic license of condensing two attacks upon the Matabele, by the Boer/Rolong alliance, into one. See Theal, *History*, ii. 302, for an account of the first attack, 17 June 1837, and 318–19 for the second, in October of that year. Plaatje also unifies the Ndebele exodus, which was historically split into two parts. See R. Kent Rasmussen, *Migrant Kingdom: Mzilikazi's Ndebele in South Africa* (London: Rex Collings 1978), for details.

[12] On the romance resolution of Ndebele nation, see Brian Walter, 'The Romance of Protest: Sol Plaatje's *Mhudi*', in *Literature, Nature and the Land: Ethics and Aesthetics of the Environment. Papers given at the annual conference of the Association of University English Teachers of Southern Africa*, University of Zululand, 7–10 July 1992, ed. Nigel Bell and Meg Cowper-Lewis, 1993, 193–9. See also Anthony Chennell's 'Plotting South African History: Narrative in Sol Plaatje's *Mhudi*', *English in Africa*, volume 24, number 1 (May 1997), 37–58, and Mpe, ' "Naturally these Stories Lose Nothing by the Telling" '. Chennells argues this romance closure as an unambiguously comic mode through which Plaatje explores the possibility of pan-Africanism within South Africa. His view of the social order of this reborn African kingdom is that it is 'centred on a domestic rather than a

The complexities of interpreting an African imperialism now become the complexities of interpreting an African nationalism for which the Ndebele here assume primary symbolic status.[13] These complexities are written in to the historical subject, and overdetermined by the participation of the third party, the Boers. Their alliance with the Rolong prevents that battle from functioning exclusively as a symbol for the overthrow of oppression. Plaatje selects Mzilikazi, the vanquished oppressor, to articulate the political role played by the Boers.

RECONSTRUCTING AFRICAN 'IMPERIALISM' AS PAN-AFRICAN NATIONALISM

Plaatje gives Mzilikazi, the 'imperial' historical figure, a mono-logue of a length and substance to be found nowhere else in the book. If the monologue represents a specifically novelistic tech-nique, it is also a piece of drama, moving from the private to the public sphere, beginning with inner reflection and developing into a public address. The shift in form is also a shift in consciousness: we watch Mzilikazi progress from a personal to a national definition of this tragedy. Plaatje manipulates the king's speech—especially his prophecy—to articulate a new definition of African political identity. Unlike the other prophecies of *Mhudi,* this one explores a future beyond the

militaristic king, and with marriage and birth as the principles of its unity, the nation turns from hierarchy, obedience and death to reciprocity, love and regenera-tion as the sources of its new identity' (40). This contrasts sharply with Mpe's view in which the future society established (historically) by Mzilikazi's son Lobengula is a 'large empire', that 'wields more power' than Mzilikazi's; this 'is a testimony to the fact that Umnandi's good nature is not sufficient influence on her own son' (87).

[13] On theories of African nationalism, see Amilcar Cabral, *Return to the Source* (New York: Monthly Review Press 1973); Wilfred Cartey and Martin Kilson, eds., *The Africa Reader: Independent Africa* (New York: Vintage Books 1970); Frantz Fanon, *The Wretched of the Earth*, trans. C. Farringdon (1961; Harmondsworth: Penguin 1971), and *Toward the African Revolution: Political Essays*, trans. Haakon Chevalier (1964; New York: Grove Press 1988). See also Benita Parry, 'Resistance Theory/Theorising Resistance or Two Cheers for Nativism', in *Colonial Discourse/ Postcolonial Theory*, ed. Francis Barker, Peter Hulme, and Margaret Iversen (Manchester: Manchester University Press 1994), 172–96. On African-American nationalism of this period, see Wilson Jeremiah Moses, *The Golden Age of Black Nationalism, 1850–1925* (Oxford: Oxford University Press 1978). See also Robert Chrisman and Nathan Hare, eds., *Contemporary Black Thought* (New York: Bobbs Merrill 1973).

time-scheme of the novel, reaching forward to the extra-textual present of the reader. Its synthesis of subjective and objective, past and future, history and romance itself effects of kind of commentary on our own contemporary understanding of Southern African power. Its contemporaneity of reference was evident to the Lovedale editors: Mzilikazi's references to super-expansionism were considered too topical for inclusion, and were removed.[14]

Plaatje begins by positioning Mzilikazi as a classic tragic hero granted his anagnorisis after the fatal peripeteia.[15] He owns the disappointment of his 'beautiful dream': 'he had hoped to rule over the most terror-inspiring nation of death-defiers that ever faced an enemy . . . but now he saw the Imperial structure of his super-expansionist dream shattered and blown away like so many autumn leaves at the mercy of a violent hurricane' (170–1). Mzilikazi next discovers the death of his son Langa, who had been the triumphant leader of the attack against the Rolong. This prompts a painful reflection upon 'the patriotic speeches of Dambuza and the others, now killed, and the poignancy of the new situation in which Gubuza, who in the heyday of their rejoicings was accused of being a coward, now remained his sole pillar of strength. "Where is that bombastic spirit now," he asked himself' (171).

Through the Kent-like Gubuza Plaatje refutes the irresponsible and reckless social Darwinist rhetoric espoused by the deceased men, and affirms instead Gubuza's alternative brand of 'imperial' language. Asking 'who was responsible for this calamity?' Mzilikazi realizes that he is: 'notwithstanding that my magicians warned me of the looming terrors, I heeded them not. Had I only listened and moved the nation to the north, I could have transplanted my kingdom there with all my impis still intact' (171–2). He further moves to a greater appreciation of the importance of his poor, and suffering, people, in the figures of women and children: 'He saw anxious mothers press-

---

[14] On the censorship of Mzilikazi's speech, see Tim Couzens and Stephen Gray, 'Printers' and Other Devils: The Texts of Sol T. Plaatje's *Mhudi*', *Research in African Literatures*, volume 9, number 2 (1978), which discusses the cutting of this passage. They suggest that 'Mzilikazi's rhetoric . . . bore a marked resemblance to the rhetoric of his successor—the archetypal British imperialist . . . Cecil Rhodes' (214).

[15] On Shakespearean dynamics of Mzilikazi's speech, see Walter, 'The Romance of Protest'.

ing their empty breasts into the mouths of crying babies, but the teats of starving mothers failed to still the gnawing pangs of hunger and the little ones kept up their discordant wail. All this seemed to affect Mzilikazi tremendously' (172).

This Lear-like realization is a further challenge to the social Darwinist instrumental ethic and its calculated loss of life (including that of one's own side). Mzilikazi moves here from an aggressive to a defensive position, in which he realizes the importance of preserving the blood of the nation. His realization gives a new emphasis to women as the bearers of life, condensed in the figure of his exiled wife Umnandi whom Mzilikazi now characterizes as a 'talisman' for the nation. Her loss is thus constructed as collective as well as personal (172).

Mzilikazi's thought here is paralleled by the novel itself. In the last chapter, I discussed Plaatje's political articulation of the bond between Mhudi and Umnandi. In privileging women both as agents and as objects of Mzilikazi's thought here, Plaatje further reinforces their objective importance for the nation. Plaatje also sets up correspondences between Mhudi's subjectivity and Mzilikazi's. This entire speech of his formally balances the long monologue Plaatje gives Mhudi near the opening of the book. Mhudi too, like Mzilikazi, has progressed from a primarily ethnic to an African allegiance. From wishing vengeance against the Ndebele, she has progressed to wishing for the preservation of African life: she asks Umnandi to do as she will do, tell all men 'to cease warring against their kind' with the emphasis on the pronoun 'their'—an inter-African war is a self-destructive war (167).

Mzilikazi responds to the realization of collective loss with anger, further reminiscent of Lear:

Surveying the ruins of all his hopes and remembering the rich, red Matabele blood sacrificed so lavishly, in hopes that the end would justify the means, and contemplating the inevitable gloom with which he stood face to face, Mzilikazi heaved a deep sigh and wished that he held the keys to open the gateways of the elements of thunder and lightning, so as to command these forces to hurry down and annihilate and blot out forever the armies of his tormentors. (174)

The lesson in humanism is not, then, a lesson in the relinquishment of warfare but the opposite, a lesson in the necessity of sensible African self-protection. This involves more than a nation of one's own people; it extends to a multi-ethnic, pan-African nation:

Have I not been kind to these Bechuana traitors? It was my desire to incorporate them with ourselves so that together we could form one great nation; they pretended to be willing, yet they have always played me false. When they failed to bring tribute I slew them not; yet at the first opportunity they did not hesitate to abuse my kindness. (174)

Through the medium of the Ndebele monarch, then, Plaatje introduces this broad African nationalism as a conceptual and political possibility. But he also presents evidence that the king's past practice compromises and calls into question such a possibility: the past was less pan-African than dominatory. His alleged 'kindness' is not an adequate basis for government. It is also self-deluding, blinding Mzilikazi from the political reasons for their discontent. Mzilikazi himself acknowledges the regular resistance of those peoples to his rule: 'He had repeatedly sent out armies, but not a single tribe had been subdued; their most outstanding success had been to make for him fresh enemies every time. Even the weakest of his Bechuana vassals only remained quiescent for a time in order the better to revolt at the first favourable opportunity' (171).

Mzilikazi's speech allows the reader to assign a broader significance to the novel's opening murder of Ndebele men by the Rolong. Plaatje's carefully sustained indeterminacy surrounding that act now gives way; the act takes its place in a system of anti-imperial resistance. At the very moment Plaatje introduces the theoretical possibility of pan-Africanism, that is, he emphasizes its unrealizability when articulated by an unreliable ruler whose empire is regularly contested by the very peoples with whom he claims national unity. When Mzilikazi introduces the topic of the Boers, however, the political definitions undergo a further transformation. Mzilikazi's past empire now demands to be read a historical opportunity for nation-building permanently thwarted by the Rolong/Boer alliance.

This becomes clearer if we examine the final prophetic part of Mzilikazi's speech:

The Bechuana know not the story of Zungu of old. Remember him, my people; he caught a lion's whelp and thought that, if he fed it with the milk of his cows, he would in due course possess a useful mastiff to help him . . . The cub grew up, apparently tame and meek, just like an ordinary domestic puppy; but one day Zungu came home and found, what? It had eaten his children, chewed up two of his wives, and in destroying it, he himself narrowly escaped being mauled . . . The Bechuana are fools to think that these unnatural Kiwas (white men) will return their so-called friendship with honest friendship. Together they are laughing at my misery. Let them rejoice; they need all the laughter they can have today for when their deliverers begin to dose them with the same bitter medicine they prepared for me . . . They will despoil them of the very lands they have rendered unsafe for us; they will entice the Bechuana youths to war and the chase, only to use them as pack-oxen; yea, they will refuse to share with them the spoils of victory. They will turn Bechuana women into beasts of burden to drag their loaded waggons to their granaries, while their own bullocks are fattening on the hillside and pining for exercise. They will use the whiplash on the bare skins of women to accelerate their paces and quicken their activities: they shall take Bechuana women to wife and, with them, breed a race of half man and half goblin, and they will deny them their legitimate lobolo. With their cries unheeded these Bechuana will waste away in helpless fury till the gnome offspring of such mis-cegenation rise up against their cruel sires. (175)

The mode is as important as the content: prophecy as deployed here is a perfect expression for political agency and paralysis. This prophecy is the final one of the book; the future Mzilikazi outlines has indeed come to pass. Mzilikazi's pre-diction makes use of a historical example and cultural tradition; new though the Boer situation is, the fable of Zungu can be applied to its analysis. If oral tradition supplies one form of precedent, Mzilikazi's own personal experience supplies another; the dispossession he foresees for the Tswana is a repe-tition of what he has himself already experienced. Strengthened as it is by double weighting from history, Boer exploitation is yet unprecedented in its horror. It is far worse than anything Mzilikazi has visited upon his conquered peoples: the bestiali-zation, sexual degradation and propagation will radically trans-form African society.

THE DOUBLE POLITICS OF JANUS FORM

Mzilikazi had the choice of listening to his soothsayers'
prophecy and acting to avoid disaster; he chose to forego this
opportunity. Likewise, the future prophesied by Mzilikazi could
have been avoided had the Rolong not chosen to assist the
Boers, their future enslavers. Just as Mzilikazi's speech here
looks both forward and backward, simultaneously, drawing
from the past the source of the future, whilst at the time seeing
in the past the possibility of averting that now certain future, so
too we must apply that double hermeneutic code to the text of
Mhudi up to this point, looking for narrative warnings, and for
ways in which it self-corrects its former condition. This Janus-
faced pattern is clearest in the fate of particular speech-acts,
most markedly the intertextual use of Shakespeare, African
proverbs, and fables. I want to revisit the council session in
which the Rolong debate whether to ally with the Boers and go
to war against the Ndebele. 'Every man bent forward expectant
how the question, War, to be or not to be, was to be decided'
(110). On the first reading, the allusion (*Hamlet*, III. i. 56)
effects a rewriting of Hamlet's individual dilemma as a collective one.

This is what *Mhudi*'s various Shakespeareanisms do: they
extend and redefine the domain of Shakespeare, offering simultaneously a corrective to the original. In this case, Hamlet like
the Rolong councillors debates taking 'arms against a sea of
troubles'. However, unlike the Africans', Hamlet's combat is
self-directed; it is suicide, rather than war against another.
Hamlet's decision 'to be' is a decision *not* to enter into combat;
the men's decision 'to be' is on the contrary one of entering *into*
combat. A retrospective reading redefines the condition yet
again, bringing it back to its origin, without relinquishing the
collectivism: the council's decision to 'be', to ally with the Boers,
will eventually prove to be a form of social suicide after all. And
when we recall the exchange between Mhudi and Umnandi we
can see how from a pan-African perspective the war itself is a
form of suicide, when the Ndebele are recognized as members
of the same black family and nation.

The whole council takes on a rebarbative cast. All of Chief

Moroka's proverbs are structured to rebound upon the council, which believes itself tackling one enemy but in the process fails to perceive the real (white) source. Thus when Moroka advises alertness, the general force of the proverb remains while the application stands corrected: 'Old people say that the foolish dam suckles her young while lying down; but the wise dam suckles hers standing up and looking out for approaching hunters' (112). And again when he concludes by advocating alliance, the truth hold but rebounds upon the speaker for choosing the wrong alliance: 'Old people say the quarry of two dogs is never too strong' (113).

The reader's initial judgements over the Boers now demand retrospective reversal. This is more comically the case with the Rolong man who in his ignorance begins to flee from the Boers, crying to some women he meets to do likewise: ' "I have seen a milk-white house filled with a load of blood-red devils . . . Women, run I say! The monsters are almost here." But the girls, far from running away, stood and scrutinized the horizon in the direction whence the man came and demanded ocular proof of the existence of these monsters' (89–90). When the girls realize that he is in his ignorance referring to the Boers, they laugh him into shame and his name thereafter becomes a synonym for timidity (90). However, future events vindicate this man's judgement; the Boers' inhuman technology and behaviour indeed align them with 'devils'. This historical irony is also a set of literary ironies. It was Othello who demanded 'ocular proof' of his wife's infidelity (III. iii. 361). Like Othello, the girls are sceptical; unlike him, they are not convinced by the 'proof' with which the man supplies them. However, the proof proves to be correct, and the source of Othello's tragedy becomes neatly reversed.

Similarly, the scene in which the neighbouring peoples celebrate the victory of the 'allies' takes on a retrospective irony. The Rolong are thrilled by the quantities of beef, taken from Ndebele cattle, freely offered to all by the Boers:

Prolific beef-eaters like the Bechuana thought that war was a blessing indeed if one's sympathies were on the winning side . . . No people who were allied to these Boers need be poor, they said. In fruitful years folk could revel in plenty; and when supplies ran short they could always raid their neighbours, kill off the people with little opposition,

round up their stock and distribute the raided cattle among the needy.
(147)

After this sensory gratification and congratulation the Rolong
turn to a redemptive language of political emancipation. If we
recall the materialism of the Ndebele women, in a similarly
vicarious celebration of victory and beef, we should read this as
a deliberate, direct echo of that scene. The myopia of the
women there was proved by subsequent results (the very war
here celebrated), their callousness also shown to be rebarbative
(recall the starving women noticed by Mzilikazi).

These ironic duplicities apply to the entire narrative leading
up to the Ndebele exodus. The novel up to the exodus emerges
as neither pure irony nor pure allegory, constructed to read
both literally and symbolically. The rebarbative ironies are
visible only after the interventions of the war and Mzilikazi's
prophecy. Nonetheless, Plaatje's novel refuses the pessimism of
a closed ironic system. Up to the war, the Ndebele are registered
as an oppressive imperialist force. The war itself consequently
reads as a successful revenge resolution (the completion of the
'revolution' or cycle); a terrible, necessary, historical revolution;
and an unfortunate, avoidable, misalliance that thwarts the
course of African nationalism. That is, it marks an allegorical
triumph over imperialism, and is in that sense a wish-fulfilment.
At the same time, the episode marks quite literally the advent of
white colonialism. Neither possibility is privileged over the
other.

CONDITIONAL FUTURES: READING THE END

All of the above form the domain of fiction.[16] It is a historical
irony which impels the rereading, but it is an irony made

[16] On the relationship of narrative fiction and nationalism, see Tim Brennan, 'The
National Longing for Form', in *Nation and Narration*, ed. Homi K. Bhabha
(London: Routledge), 44–70. Other examples of early 20th-cent. Anglophone black
South African literature include: Tim Couzens and Essop Patel, eds., *The Return of
the Amasi Bird: Black South African Poetry 1891–1981* (Braamfontein: Ravan Press
1982); H. I. E. Dhlomo, *Collected Works*, ed. Nick Visser and Tim Couzens
(Johannesburg: Ravan Press 1985). See Tim Couzens, *The New African: A Study of
the Life and Work of H. I. E. Dhlomo* (Johannesburg: Ravan Press 1985). See also
Ursula Barnett, *A Vision of Order: A Study of Black South African Literature in
English 1914–1980* (London: Sinclair Browne 1983).

possible, and effected through, specifically literary structures, both local (rhetorical acts, literary allusions and diction) and general (the shaping of the narrative sequence). What happens next, in the narrative following the war, is a fiction that refutes irony: Mzilikazi's resettlement and reconciliation with Umnandi provide a fully non-ironized, conventional and perfect *romance* closure. His dream of empire shattered, he is given an escape clause, a magical fiction and a utopian image of hope rewarded. This national rebirth is not simply romance fiction but real history; the new Matabeleland went on to become a political entity. What is important is not so much the triumph of romance but its convergence with a historical mode. Nowhere else in *Mhudi* does Plaatje unite the fictive and the real in this way; elsewhere the romance scenes are not synchronous with the historical scenes. The novel's account of the migrant Ndebele goes far out of the present tense of possibility into the future, describing the greatness which Lobengula, the son of Umnandi and Mzilikazi, comes to achieve. We are given a future viewpoint from which it is impossible to effect a retroactive irony.

This closure contrasts sharply with the open-endedness of the situation of Mhudi and Ra-Thaga, who leave the book literally in transit. The book's aesthetic and political conclusion, such as it is, emerges in the contrast between the two situations. The final scene of Mhudi and Ra-Thaga gives the last word on the Boers. We should note the significance of the romance between de Villiers and Hannetjie. Unlike the totally non-ironized romance reconciliation of Mzilikazi and Umnandi, and the ironized-but-affirmed romance of Mhudi and Ra-Thaga, this young Boer couple's romance receives no elevation. Plaatje presents the pair's ecstasy in terms much more hyperbolic than any so far encountered ('their spirits lost in a newfound bliss', 187). De Villiers asks Hannetjie with romantic impatience when the minister shall arrive to 'merge our two souls into one'. She tells him to be patient: 'depressing the immature swell of her bosom in order the better to hide the intensity of her own impatience. The proverb says, "a hasty dog always burns his mouth". Is it not enough to know that while my heart yearned for yours . . . your soul, too, was yearning to mingle itself with mine?' (187).

It is not a matter of 'souls,' evidently, but bodies—their desire is exposed and ironized as bathetic lust, with the aid of the highly incongruous 'hasty dog' proverb. Plaatje consistently mocks Boer romantic and associated religious aspirations in this novel.[17] The Boers themselves are physically reduced to homely and ridiculous domestic imagery even as they physically reduce Africans, while it is their physical cruelty which receives the most attention. Even in the case of this young pair, Plaatje's deflation overrules any superficial impression we might have of a liberal Afrikanerdom.

The concluding scene of Mhudi and Ra-Thaga picks up the two senses of their battle's 'revolution'. De Villiers remarks to Ra-Thaga: 'Yes, I always told you that this world was round and you refused to believe me; but now that you see that is has spun round like a waggon wheel at Mzilikazi's expense, you must believe that it is indeed round' (186). Ra-Thaga acknowledges that whether the world is round or flat, they have had their revenge; Mzilikazi will not strike again. The circle has been completed; the revenges have cancelled each other out. However, there is no return to an original condition. Ra-Thaga remarks 'the proverb says "there's always a return to the ruins, only to the womb there is no return"' (186–7). He and Mhudi literally take up de Villiers's wagon-wheel ideology but their wheels represent movement, not circularity; they go off in the waggon which the Boer has given them, Ra-Thaga musing 'over the hallowed glories of being transported from one end of the country to the other like White people . . . Gone were the days of their primitive tramping over long distances, with loads on their heads. For them the days of the pack-ox had passed, never to return again' (187–8). The novel ends with this pair in open transition. Their future—it seems—is indeterminate, unresolved, the only certainty being the new mode of transportation which itself signals migratory flux.

Against the certainty of the Ndebele's national resurrection is the uncertainty of the Rolong future. Both aspects—the one,

[17] Examples are legion, including the fact that the Boers' romance quest for God has led them to the Ndebele instead, as Moroka wryly comments (112). The Boers interrogate the heavens, like Mhudi and Ra-Thaga, concerning the cosmological justice of their suffering, but this too is deflated—the question is asked 'as though expecting an answer by return pigeon-post' (134). Plaatje pointedly makes De Villiers illiterate 'like many other young Boers' (131).

closed, collective, the other, open, individual—are essential components of Plaatje's ideology. Yet open as the Rolong future seems, it is simultaneously sealed. For Ra-Thaga and Mhudi, 'the days of the pack-ox had passed' but what awaits them is their own debasement: the Boers will 'entice the Bechuana youths to war . . . only to use them as pack-oxen . . . They will turn Bechuana women into beasts of burden to drag their loaded waggons to their granaries' (175). The repetition of 'pack-ox' imagery is no accident.

The extra-textual future of the respective African peoples should not prevent us from acknowledging and analyzing the force of the book's conclusion. *Mhudi* supplies an unambiguously positive vision of a reborn African nation in the form of the Ndebele. However this national narrative is not comprehensive; alongside it runs the counter-narrative of the soon-to-be-subjugated Rolong. This symbolic interpretation of the Ndebele nation is one that Plaatje simultaneously invites and refuses, by decentring its authority and denying it a temporal/spatial totality.

Just as the Ndebele nation cannot be taken as a pure symbol, neither can women function as a pure romantic source or alternative solution, emblem of the nation. Mzilikazi may construct Umnandi as a magic talisman, whose departure from court was responsible for its reversal of fortunes, and whose return permits the rebirth of the nation, but even while Plaatje reveals the power of such a mythic/romantic role, he shows its subjective basis along with its limitations. Umnandi's exile may be symptomatic of a fall in Ndebele fortune, but it is not the source; Plaatje shows that such an interpretation prevents Mzilikazi from confronting the real sources of his fall, namely, political absolutism and the arrival of the Boers. Umnandi and Mhudi can become friends and take on broader significance as representatives of African solidarity, but this bonding is possible only after the fact of the war, the disruption of the material possibility of such a nationalism. Likewise, as subjects they can articulate an alternative feminine model of evolution that replaces destruction with life preservation, competition with co-operation, militarism with pacifism, but only after the intervention and action of those masculine modes.

What Plaatje refuses, then, is not symbolization itself but its monopoly. The terms of the symbol, the romance, and the feminine, are used but rendered non-self-identical, through their deferral and contingency. Plaatje subjects an essentially meta-phoric mode to a metonymic displacement. This means that his narrative is not reducible to any one-to-one allegorical meaning, *nor* is it reducible to a single ironization. The novel up to the 'fall', the battle, can be read in ironic reverse, but only after the metonymic rupture of the war itself; the irony is not synchronous with the original material, and does not totally subjugate it or diminish its allegorical force as a conquest over imperialism. When read a third time, neither mode monopolizes or prevails.

This applies not only to the condition and movement of the narrative as a whole, but to scenes, and concepts—none can be read in isolation, from its relations to the narrative totality. Plaatje explores the concept of 'tradition' for example, as a material structure and a cultural institution expressed through proverbs, fables, folklore, customary law. But by selecting a period in which these cultures are undergoing transformation through internal and external forces, Plaatje gives them a dia-lectical, not static, reified identity.

CONCLUSION

The socio-economic and political consequences of the Union of South Africa in 1910 and the Natives' Land Act of 1913 forced on Plaatje an awareness of the overdetermined dissonances within the formation he knew as British imperialism. *Mhudi* sees him making creative use of these dissonances—in parti-cular, the semantic confusions stemming from the divisions between ideology and practice—as resources for fiction. The contradictory meanings of British imperialism both impel and enable the complexity of Plaatje's form. Let us go back to the difficulties of imperial definition outlined by S. M. Molema at the start of this chapter. If British imperialism was to be seen essentially as a political oxymoron of ideological idealism and dominatory rule, then Plaatje in the form of the surrogate Ndebele matches and transforms that articulation. If however British imperialism was to be seen as an unambiguous form of white racist oppression, now exposed through the Lands' Act (giving the lie to its previous liberal rhetoric), then Plaatje also supplies that reading, in the form of the Boers, whose racial fixity and, it seems, innate inhumanity signify here less a Boer than a generically white proto-imperial power. And if British imperialism is given a cyclical inflection, its overthrow guaranteed by cyclical laws, its own definition as a circle from barbarity through to liberal humanism and back again—Plaatje presents us with these cyclical dynamics in the overthrow of the Ndebele, and in the shift of imperial semantics from Ndebele to Boer. In other words, for Plaatje both the fluidities of socio-economic, political power and the fixities of race function as possible motors of imperial history.

   It is important to note the precise nature of these historical and conceptual determinants of Plaatje's multilayered and radically decentred narrative, with its reversible, divided and deferred signification codes, its irreducibility to a single hermeneutic dynamic or allegorical interpretation. The models for interpreting anti-colonial literature based on 'writing back to the centre', 'mimicry' or 'hybridity' do not adequately account for the formal, linguistic, and ideological textures of his novel.[18] Likewise, *Mhudi* does not simply subvert European imperialism by reversing the negative valuation placed on Africans, nor does it simply supply an ambassadorial presentation of the equality and parallels of African with English cultures. The triangulated elements of the historical situation on which Plaatje bases his narrative, together with the semantic contradictions of British imperialism of the 1910s, mean that his representations are multiply mediated and more complex than any of the above approaches can suggest.

   Similarly, the objective and subjective complexities of Plaatje's African nationalism preclude the interpretation of this narrative as the demonstration of a nationalist subjectivity that repeats the totalizing subjectivity of British imperialism.[19] The

---

   [18] On 'writing back' as a model, see the book of that name: Bill Ashcroft, Gareth Griffiths, and Helen Tiffin, *The Empire Writes Back: Theory and Practice in Post-colonial Literatures* (London: Methuen 1989). On 'hybridity' and 'mimicry' as models, see Homi K. Bhabha, 'Of Mimicry and Man: The Ambivalence of Colonial Discourse', in *The Location of Culture* (London: Routledge 1994), 85–92.

   [19] On this argument concerning nationalism—as repeating the totalizing moves of imperialism—see Partha Chatterjee, *Nationalist Thought and the Colonial World: A Derivative Discourse* (London: Zed Books 1986), and his *The Nation and*

nationalism Plaatje articulates is constitutively multiple: its designators, like its constituents, shift. The diverse ethnic, gender, and political inflections of Plaatje's nationalism here give rise to diverse temporalities for the African nation (past, utopian/potential, thwarted, achieved in future Ndebele). This is like Plaatje's range of imperialist definitions: historically specific.

Its Fragments: Colonial and Postcolonial Histories (Princeton: Princeton University Press 1993). See also *Selected Subaltern Studies*, ed. Ranajit Guha and Gayatri Spivak, foreword by Edward Said (Oxford: Oxford University Press 1988), and Neil Lazarus, 'National Consciousness and the Specificity of (post)Colonial intellectualism', in *Colonial Discourse/Postcolonial Theory*, ed. Francis Barker, Peter Hulme, and Margaret Iversen (Manchester: Manchester University Press 1994), 197–220, and ch. 2 'Disavowing Decolonization: Nationalism, Intellectuals, and the Question of Representation in Postcolonial Theory', in his *Nationalism and Cultural Practice in the Postcolonial World* (Cambridge: Cambridge University Press 1999), 68–143.

Bibliography

AHMAD, A., *In Theory: Classes, Nations, Literatures* (London: Verso 1992).

—— 'The Politics of Literary Postcoloniality', in *Contemporary Post-colonial Theory: A Reader*, ed. P. Mongia (London: Arnold 1996), 275–93.

ALDERSON, SIR E. A. H., *With Mounted Infantry and the Mashona-land Field Force, 1896* (London: Methuen 1898).

ANDERSON, B., *Imagined Communities: Reflections on the Origin and Spread of Nationalism* (London: Verso 1983).

ARENDT, H., *The Origins of Totalitarianism* (1951; London: André Deutsch 1986).

ASHCROFT, B., G. GRIFFITHS, and H. TIFFIN, *The Empire Writes Back: Theory and Practice in Post-colonial Literatures* (London: Methuen 1989).

ATTWELL, D., 'Intimate Enmity in the Journal of Tiyo Soga', *Critical Inquiry*, volum 23, number 3 (spring 1997), 557–77.

—— 'Reprisals of Modernity in Black South African "Mission" Writing', *Journal of Southern African Studies*, volume 25, number 2 (June 1999), 267–85.

AUSUBEL, H., *The Late Victorians: A Short History* (London: Anvil 1955).

BACON, E., ed., *The Great Archaeologists* (London: Secker and Warburg 1976).

BARASH, C., 'Virile Womanhood: Olive Schreiner's Narratives of a Master Race', in *Speaking of Gender*, ed. E. Showalter (London: Routledge 1989), 269–81.

BARNETT, U., *A Vision of Order: A Study of Black South African Literature in English 1914–1980* (London: Sinclair Browne 1983).

BASS, J. D., 'The Romance as Rhetorical Dissociation: The Purification of Imperialism in *King Solomon's Mines*', *The Quarterly Journal of Speech*, 67 (1981), 259–69.

BECKER, P., *Rule of Fear: The Life and Times of Dingane, King of the Zulu* (London: Longman 1964).

BEER, G., *The Romance* (London: Methuen 1970).

—— *Darwin's Plots* (London: ARK 1983).

BEETON, R., *Olive Schreiner: A Short Guide to her Writings* (Cape Town: Timmins 1974).

BENJAMIN, W., *The Origins of German Tragic Drama*, trans. J. Osborne (1963; London: Verso 1977).

BERKMAN, J. A., *The Healing Imagination of Olive Schreiner: Beyond South African Colonialism* (Amherst: University of Massachusetts Press 1989).

BERNAL, M., *Black Athena: The Afroasiatic Roots of Classical Civilization*, i: *The Fabrication of Ancient Greece 1785–1985* (New Brunswick: Rutgers University Press 1987).

BHABHA, H. K., *The Location of Culture* (London: Routledge 1994), 85–92.

BIDDISS, M. D., ed., *Images of Race* (Leicester: Leicester University Press 1979).

BIRD, J., ed., *The Annals of Natal 1495–1845* (Cape Town: C. Struik 1965).

BIVONA, D., *Desire and Contradiction: Imperial Visions and Domestic Debates in Victorian Literature* (Manchester: Manchester University Press 1990).

BJØRHOVDE, G., *Rebellious Structures: Women Writers and the Crisis of the Novel, 1880–1900* (Oslo: Norwegian University Press 1987).

BLAU DUPLESSIS, R., 'The Rupture of Story and *The Story of an African Farm*', in *Writing Beyond the Ending: Narrative Strategies of Twentieth-Century Women Writers* (Bloomington: Indiana University Press 1985), 20–30.

BLYDEN, E. W., *Christianity, Islam and the Negro Race* (London: W. B. Whittingham 1887).

—— *Africa and the Africans* (London: C. M. Phillips 1903).

—— *West Africa Before Europe* (London: C. M. Phillips 1905).

—— *African Life and Customs* (London: C. M. Phillips 1908).

BOEHMER, E., *Colonial and Postcolonial Literature* (Oxford: Oxford University Press 1995).

—— ed., *Empire Writing: An Anthology of Colonial Literature 1870–1918* (Oxford: Oxford University Press 1998).

BOLT, C., *Victorian Attitudes to Race* (London: Routledge and Kegan Paul 1971).

BONNER, P., 'The Transvaal Native Congress, 1917–1920: The Radicalisation of the Black Petty Bourgeoisie on the Rand', in *Industrialisation and Social Change in South Africa: African Class Formation, Culture, and Consciousness 1870–1930*, ed. S. Marks and R. Rathbone (London: Longman 1982), 270–313.

BOOTH, General W., *In Darkest England and the Way Out* (London: International Headquarters 1890).

BRANTLINGER, P., *Rule of Darkness: British Literature and Imperialism, 1830–1914* (Ithaca: Cornell University Press 1988).

BRENNAN, T., 'The National Longing for Form', in *Nation and Narration*, ed. H. K. Bhabha (London: Routledge 1990), 44–70.

BREWER, A., *Marxist Theories of Imperialism: A Critical Survey* (London: Routledge and Kegan Paul 1990).

BRISTOW, J., *Empire Boys: Adventures in a Man's World* (London: Harper Collins 1991).

BROOKS, C. and P. FAULKNER, eds., *The White Man's Burdens: An Anthology of British Poetry of the Empire* (Exeter: University of Exeter Press 1996).

BRYCE, J., *Impressions of South Africa* (London: Macmillan and Co. 1897).

BUCHAN, J., *Prester John* (1910; Harmondsworth: Penguin 1961).

BUCKLEY, J., *William Ernest Henley: A Study in the 'Counter-Decadence' of the 'Nineties* (Princeton: Princeton University Press 1945).

BUNN, D., 'Embodying Africa: Woman and Romance in Colonial Fiction', *English in Africa*, volume 15, number 1 (May 1988), 1–28.

BURDETT, C., 'Olive Schreiner Revisited', *English in Africa. 21st birthday issue: 'Revisions'*, volume 21, numbers 1 and 2 (July 1994), 221–32.

BURNESS, D., *Shaka: King of the Zulus in African Literature* (Washington, DC: Three Continents Press 1976).

BURROW, J., *A Liberal Descent: Victorian Historians and the English Past* (Cambridge: Cambridge University Press 1981).

—— *Gibbon* (Oxford: Oxford University Press 1985).

BUSH, J., 'Lady Imperialists and the Cause of British South Africa', paper delivered at 'South Africa 1895–1921: Test of Empire' conference, St. Edmund Hall, Oxford, March 1996.

CABRAL, A., *Return to the Source* (New York: Monthly Review Press 1973).

—— 'National Liberation and Culture', in *Colonial Discourse and Post-Colonial Theory: A Reader*, ed. P. Williams and L. Chrisman (Hemel Hempstead: Harvester Wheatsheaf 1993), 53–65.

CALLAWAY, BISHOP H., *The Religious System of the Amazulu* (Springvale: J. A. Blair 1869).

CANTLIE, J. A., *Degeneration Amongst Londoners* (London: Field and Tuer, the Leadenhall Press 1885).

CARPENTER, E., *England's Ideal and Other Papers on Social Subjects* (London: Swan Sonnenschein, Lourey and Co. 1887).

CARTEY, W. and M. KILSON, eds., *The Africa Reader: Independent Africa* (New York: Vintage Books 1970).

CÉSAIRE, A., 'From *Discourse on Colonialism*', in *Colonial Discourse and Post-Colonial Theory: A Reader*, ed. P. Williams and L. Chrisman (Hemel Hempstead: Harvester Wheatsheaf 1993), 172–80.

CHAMBERLAIN, M. E., *The Scramble for Africa* (London: Longman 1974).

CHAPPLE, J. A. V., *Science and Literature in the Nineteenth Century* (London: Macmillan 1986).

CHATTERJEE, P., *Nationalist Thought and the Colonial World: A Derivative Discourse* (London: Zed Books 1986).

—— *The Nation and Its Fragments: Colonial and Postcolonial Histories* (Princeton: Princeton University Press 1993).

CHAUDHURI, N. and M. STROBEL, eds., *Western Women and Imperialism: Complicity and Resistance* (Bloomington: Indiana University Press 1992).

CHENNELLS, A., 'Plotting South African History: Narrative in Sol Plaatje's *Mhudi*', *English in Africa*, volume 24, number 1 (May 1997), 37–58.

CHRISMAN, L., 'The Imperial Unconscious? Representations of imperial discourse', *Critical Quarterly*, volume 32, number 3 (autumn 1990), 38–58.

—— 'Allegory, Feminist Thought and the *Dreams* of Olive Schreiner', in *Edward Carpenter and Late Victorian Radicalism*, ed. T. Brown (London: Frank Cass 1990), 126–50.

—— 'Colonialism and Feminism in Olive Schreiner's 1890s Fiction', *English in Africa*, volume 20, number 1 (May 1993), 25–38.

—— 'Empire, "Race" and Feminism at the *fin de siècle*: The Work of George Egerton and Olive Schreiner', in *Cultural Politics at the Fin de Siècle*, in ed. S. Ledger and S. McCracken (Cambridge: Cambridge University Press 1995), 45–65.

—— 'Inventing Post-Colonial Theory: Polemical Observations', *Pretexts: Studies in Writing and Culture*, volume 5, numbers 1 and 2 (1995), 205–12.

—— 'Journeying to Death: A Critique of Paul Gilroy's *The Black Atlantic*', *Race and Class*, volume 39, number 2 (Oct.–Dec. 1997), 51–64.

—— 'Fathering the Black Nation of South Africa: Gender and Generation in Sol Plaatje's *Native Life in South Africa* and *Mhudi*', *Social Dynamics*, volume 23, number 2 (summer 1997), 57–73.

—— 'Gendering Imperial Culture: Problems in Feminist Post-Colonial Criticism', in *Cultural Readings of Imperialism: Edward Said and the Gravity of History*, ed. K. Ansell-Pearson, B. Parry, and J. Squires (London: Lawrence and Wishart 1997), 290–304.

—— 'Questioning Robert Young's Postcolonial Criticism', *Textual Practice*, volume 11, number 1 (spring 1997), 38–45.

—— 'Local Sentences in the Chapter of the Postcolonial World', *Diaspora: Journal of Transnational Studies*, volume 7, number 1 (spring 1998), 87–112.

—— 'Imperial Space, Imperial Place: Theories of Culture and Empire in Fredric Jameson, Edward Said and Gayatri Spivak', *New Formations*, 34 (summer 1998), 53–69.

CHRISMAN, R., and N. HARE, eds., *Contemporary Black Thought* (New York: Bobbs Merrill 1973).

——eds., *Pan-Africanism* (New York: Bobbs Merrill 1974).

CHRISTIE, S., *et al*, eds., *Perspectives on South African Fiction* (Johannesburg: A. D. Donker 1980).

CLAYTON, C., ed., *Olive Schreiner* (Johannesburg: McGraw-Hill 1983).

CLIFFORD, G., *The Transformations of Allegory* (London: Routledge and Kegan Paul 1974).

COBBING, J., 'Jettisoning the *Mfecane* (with Perestroika)', University of the Witwatersrand African Studies Institute Seminar Paper (1988).

COETZEE, J. M., *White Writing: On the Culture of Letters in South Africa* (London: Yale University Press 1988).

COHEN, M., *Rider Haggard, His Life and Works* (London: Macmillan 1960).

COLBY, V., *A Singular Anomaly* (New York: New York University Press 1970).

COLLS, R. and P. DODD, eds., *Englishness: Politics and Culture, 1880–1930* (London: Croom Helm 1985).

COMAROFF, J., ed., *The Boer War Diary of Sol T. Plaatje* (London: Macmillan 1973).

CONRAD, J., *Heart of Darkness* (1899; New York: Norton 1963).

COOMBES, A. E., 'The Recalcitrant Object: Culture Contact and the Question of Hybridity', in *Colonial Discourse/Postcolonial Theory*, ed. F. Barker, P. Hulme, and M. Iversen (Manchester: Manchester University Press 1994), 89–114.

——*Reinventing Africa: Museums, Material Culture and Popular Imagination in Late Victorian and Edwardian England* (London: Yale University Press 1994).

COUZENS, T., 'Sol Plaatje's *Mhudi*', *Journal of Commonwealth Literature*, volume 8, number 1 (June 1973), 1–19.

——'Literature and Ideology: The Patterson Embassy to Lobengula 1878 and *King Solomon's Mines*', University of London Institute of Commonwealth Studies, Collected Seminar Papers, 5 (1977).

——'The Dark Side of the World: Sol Plaatje's *Mhudi*', *English Studies in Africa*, volume 15, number 2, 1977, 187–203.

——'Introduction', *Mhudi* by Sol Plaatje (London: Heinemann 1982), 1–20.

——*The New African: A Study of the Life and Work of H. I. E. Dhlomo* (Johannesburg: Ravan Press 1985).

COUZENS, T., 'Sol T. Plaatje and the First South African Epic', *English in Africa*, volume 14, number 1 (May 1987), 41–65.

——and S. GRAY, 'Printers and Other Devils: The Texts of Sol T. Plaatje's *Mhudi*', *Research in African Literatures*, volume 9, number 1 (spring 1978), 198–215.

——and E. PATEL, eds., *The Return of the Amasi Bird: Black South African Poetry 1891–1981* (Braamfontein: Ravan Press 1982).

COWARD, R., *Patriarchal Precedents: Sexuality and Social Relations* (London: Routledge and Kegan Paul 1983).

CRAMB, J. A., *Reflections on the Origins and Destiny of Imperial Britain* (London: Macmillan 1900).

CRONWRIGHT-SCHREINER, S., *Letters of Olive Schreiner 1876–1920* (London: T. Fisher Unwin 1924).

——*Life of Olive Schreiner* (London: T. Fisher Unwin 1924).

CROOK, D. P., *Benjamin Kidd: Portrait of a Social Darwinist* (Cambridge: Cambridge University Press 1984).

CROZIER, J. B., *Civilization and Progress* (London: Longmans, Green and Co. 1892).

CRUMMELL, A., *The Future of Africa* (New York: Charles Scribner 1862).

——*Africa and America* (1891; New York: Negro Universities Press 1969).

——'Culture of the Horrible', *Christian Quarterly Review*, 125 (Jan. 1888), 389–411.

CUNNINGHAM, H., 'The Language of Patriotism', in *Patriotism: The Making and Unmaking of British National Identity*, i: *History and Politics*, ed. R. Samuel (London: Routledge 1989), 57–89.

DARWIN, C., *The Origin of Species by Means of Natural Selection, or the Preservation of Favoured Races in the Struggle for Life* (London: John Murray 1859).

DAVENPORT, R., 'Olive Schreiner and South African Politics', in *Olive Schreiner and After: Essays in Honour of Guy Butler*, ed. M. van Wyk Smith and D. MacLennan (Cape Town: David Philip 1983), 93–107.

DAVID, D., *Rule Britannia: Women, Empire, and Victorian Writing* (Ithaca: Cornell University Press 1995).

DAVIDSON, A., *Cecil Rhodes and His Times*, trans. C. English (USSR: Progress Publishers 1988).

DAVIDSON, J., *The Testament of an Empire Builder* (London: Grant Richards 1901).

DAVIN, A., 'Imperialism and Motherhood', *History Workshop Journal*, 5 (1978), 9–65.

DAWSON, G., *Soldier Heroes: British Adventure, Empire and the*

Imagining of Masculinities (London: Routledge 1994).

DE KOCK, L., *Civilising Barbarians: Missionary Narrative and African Textual Response* (Johannesburg: Witwatersrand University Press 1996).

DE THIERRY, C., *Imperialism*, introd. W. E. Henley (London: Duckworth and Co. 1898).

DELANY, M., *Official Report of the Niger Valley Exploring Party* (New York: T. Hamilton 1861).

DHLOMO, H. I. E., *Collected Works*, ed. N. Visser and T. Couzens (Johannesburg: Ravan Press 1985).

DIRLIK, A., 'The Postcolonial Aura: Third World Criticism in the Age of Global Capitalism', in *Contemporary Postcolonial Theory: A Reader*, ed. P. Mongia (London: Arnold 1996), 294–321.

DOUGLAS, LADY F., *A Defence of Zululand and Its King* (London: Chatto and Windus 1882).

DU BOIS, W. E. B., *The Souls of Black Folk* (1903; Harmondsworth: Penguin 1989).

DUBOW, S., 'Race, Civilisation and Culture: The Elaboration of Segregationist Discourse in the Inter-War Years', in *The Politics of Race, Class and Nationalism in Twentieth Century South Africa*, ed. S. Marks and S. Trapido (London: Longman 1987), 71–94.

'Edward Said's *Culture and Imperialism*: A Symposium', *Social Text*, 40 (1994).

ELDRIDGE, C., *Victorian Imperialism* (London: Hodder and Stoughton 1981).

ENGELS, F., *The Origin of the Family, Private Property and the State*, introd. E. B. Leacock, trans. A. West (1884; New York: International Publishers 1975).

ETHERINGTON, N., 'South African Origins of Rider Haggard's Early African Romances', *Notes and Queries*, 222 (Oct. 1977), 436–8.

FABER, R., *The Vision and the Need: Late Victorian Imperialist Aims* (London: Faber and Faber 1966).

FANON, F., *The Wretched of the Earth*, trans. C. Farringdon (1961; Harmondsworth: Penguin 1985).

—— *Toward the African Revolution: Political Essays*, trans. H. Chevalier (1964; New York: Grove Press 1988).

—— *Black Skin, White Masks*, trans. C. L. Markmann (1967; London: Pluto 1986).

FIELD, H. J., *Toward a Program of Imperial Life: The British Empire at the Turn of the Century* (Westport: Greenwood Press 1982).

FINCHAM, G. and M. HOOPER, eds., *Under Postcolonial Eyes: Joseph Conrad after Empire* (Cape Town: University of Cape Town Press 1996).

FINNEGAN, R., *Oral Literature in Africa* (Oxford: Clarendon Press 1970).

FIRST, R., and A. SCOTT, *Olive Schreiner: A Biography* (London: The Women's Press 1989).

FREEDEN, M., ed., *J. A. Hobson. A Reader* (London: Unwin Hyman 1988).

FRYE, N., *The Secular Scripture: A Study of the Structure of Romance* (Cambridge: Harvard University Press 1976).

FRYER, P., *Staying Power: The History of Black People in Britain* (London: Pluto Press 1984).

FUZE, M. F., *The Black People and Whence They Came: A Zulu View*, ed. A. T. Cope, trans. H. C. Lugg (1922; Pietermaritzburg: University of Natal 1986).

FYNNEY, F. B., *Zululand and the Zulus: Being an Enlargement upon Two Lectures* (1880; Pretoria: the State Library 1967).

GAITSKELL, D., and E. UNTERHALTER, 'Mothers of the Nation: A Comparative Analysis of Nation, Race and Motherhood in Afrikaner Nationalism and the African National Congress', in *Woman–Nation–State*, ed. N. Yuval-Davis and F. Anthias (London: Macmillan 1989), 58–78.

GANDHI, L., *Postcolonial Theory: A Critical Introduction* (Edinburgh: Edinburgh University Press 1998).

GEBHARD, W. R. L., 'The Dazzling Light: Impingements on the Visions of Plaatje and Molema', paper delivered at 'People, Power, and Culture: The History of Christianity in South Africa, 1792–1992' conference, University of the Western Cape, Bellville, 8–12 August 1992.

GERHART, G., *Black Power in South Africa: The Evolution of an Ideology* (Berkeley: University of California Press 1978).

GIBBON, E., The *History of the Decline and Fall of the Roman Empire* (Dublin: Luke White 1789).

GIKANDI, S., *Maps of Englishness: Writing Identity in the Culture of Colonialism* (New York: Columbia University Press 1996).

GILBERT, S., and S. GUBAR, *No Man's Land: The Place of the Woman Writer in the Twentieth Century*, ii: *Sexchanges* (London: Yale University Press 1989).

GILROY, P., *There Ain't No Black in the Union Jack* (London: Unwin Hyman 1978).

——*The Black Atlantic: Modernity and Double Consciousness* (London: Verso 1993).

GINWALA, F., 'Women and the African National Congress, 1912–1943', *The Societies of Southern African in the 19th and 20th Centuries*, University of London Institute of Commonwealth Studies, Collected Seminar Papers, 16 (1990), 57–69.

GOLDSTEIN, L., *Ruins and Empire* (Pittsburgh: University of Pittsburgh Press 1977).

GORDIMER, N., 'Afterword: The Prison-House of Colonialism', in *An Olive Schreiner Reader: Writings on Women and South Africa*, ed. C. Barash (London: Pandora Press 1987), 221–7.

GRAY, S., *Sources of the First Black South African Novel in English: Solomon Plaatje's Use of Shakespeare and Bunyan in Mhudi* (Pasadena: Munger Africana Library, California Institute of Technology 1976).

—— 'Plaatje's Shakespeare', *English in Africa*, volume 4, number 1 (March 1977), 1–6.

—— *Southern African Literature: An Introduction* (London: Rex Collings 1979).

—— 'The Trooper at the Hanging Tree', in *Olive Schreiner*, ed. C. Clayton (Johannesburg: A. D. Donker 1983), 198–208.

GREEN, M., *Novel Histories: Past, Present, and Future in South Africa* (Johannesburg: Witwatersrand University Press 1997).

GREEN, R. L., *Andrew Lang: A Critical Biography* (Leicester: Edmund Ward 1946).

GRIMSHAW, A., *The C. L. R. James Reader* (Oxford: Blackwell 1992).

GROGAN, E. S. and A. H. SHARP, *From the Cape to the Cairo* (London: Hurst and Blackett 1900).

GUHA, R. and G. SPIVAK, eds., *Selected Subaltern Studies*, foreword E. Said (Oxford: Oxford University Press 1988).

GUY, J., *The Destruction of the Zulu Kingdom: The Civil War in Zululand. 1879–1884* (London: Longman 1979).

'H. Rider Haggard and the New School of Romance', *Time*, 16 (May 1887), 513–24.

HAGGARD, H. R., 'A Visit to the Chief Secocoeni', *Gentleman's Magazine*, 243 (1877).

—— 'A Zulu War Dance', *Gentleman's Magazine*, 243 (1877).

—— *Cetywayo and His White Neighbours. Or, Remarks on Recent Events in Zululand, Natal, and the Transvaal* (London: Trübner and Co. 1882).

—— *King Solomon's Mines* (1885; Harmondsworth: Penguin 1972).

—— 'About Fiction', *The Contemporary Review*, 51 (Feb. 1887), 172–80.

—— *Allan Quatermain* (London: Longmans, Green and Co. 1887).

—— *Jess* (London: Smith, Elder and Co. 1887).

—— *She* (London: Longmans, Green and Co. 1887).

—— *Cetywayo and His White Neighbours. Or, Remarks on Recent Events in Zululand, Natal, and the Transvaal* (London: Trübner and Co. 1888).

HAGGARD, H. R., *Nada the Lily* (London: Longmans, Green and Co. 1892).

—— 'Preface' to A. Wilmot, *Monomotapa (Rhodesia): Its Monuments, and its History from the most Ancient Times to the Present Century* (London: T. Fisher Unwin 1896), pp. xiii–xxiv.

—— 'The Death of Majajie', *The African Review*, 19 Sept. 1896.

—— *A Farmer's Year* (1899; London: Longmans, Green and Co. 1906).

—— *Rural England* (London: Longmans, Green and Co. 1902).

—— 'Introductory Address' to T. Adams, *Garden City and Agriculture: How to Solve the Problem of Rural Depopulation* (London: Garden City Press Ltd. 1905), 1–11.

—— *The Poor and the Land: Being a Report on the Salvation Army Colonies in the US and at Hadleigh, England with the Scheme of National Land Settlement* (London: Longmans, Green and Co. 1905).

—— *Marie* (London: Cassell 1911).

—— *Child of Storm* (London: Cassell 1912).

—— *Finished* (London: Macdonald and Co. 1917).

—— *Heu-Heu, or The Monster* (London: Hutchinson and Co. 1923).

—— *The Days of My Life*, i–ii (London: Longmans, Green and Co. 1926).

—— and A. LANG, *The World's Desire* (New York: Ballantyne Books 1890).

HALL, S., 'Gramsci's Relevance for the Study of Race and Ethnicity', in *Stuart Hall: Critical Dialogues in Cultural Studies*, ed. D. Morley and K.-S. Chen (London: Routledge 1996), 411–40.

—— and B. SCHWARZ, 'State and Society, 1880–1930', in *Crises in the British State 1880–1930*, ed. M. Langan and B. Schwarz (London: Hutchinson and Co. 1985), 7–32.

HAMILTON, C., 'The Character and Objects of Chaka: A Re-consideration of the Making of Shaka as *Mfecane* "Motor" ', University of the Witwatersrand African Studies Institute Seminar paper (1991).

—— 'Theophilus Shepstone and the Making of Rider Haggard's Shaka', University of Cape Town Centre for African Studies Seminar paper (1995).

HAMMOND, D., and A. JABLOW, *The Africa That Never Was: Four Centuries of British Writing about Africa* (New York: Twayne 1970).

HARRIS, M., *The Rise of Anthropological Theory: A History of Theories of Culture* (London: Routledge and Kegan Paul 1969).

HASTINGS, J., ed., *Dictionary of the Bible* (New York: Charles Scribner's Sons 1909).

HAYFORD, J. E. C., *Gold Coast Native Institutions: With Thoughts upon a Healthy Imperial Policy for the Gold Coast and Ashanti* (London: C. M. Phillips 1903).

—— *Ethiopia Unbound: Studies in Race Emancipation* (London: C. M. Phillips 1911).

HENLEY, W. E., *Poems* (London: David Nutt 1898).

History Workshop Journal 36. Special Issue: Colonial and Post-Colonial History, 1993.

HOBHOUSE, L., *Democracy and Reaction* (London: T. Fisher Unwin 1904).

HOBSBAWM, E., *The Age of Empire. 1875–1914* (London: Weidenfeld and Nicolson 1987).

—— and T. RANGER, eds., *The Invention of Tradition* (Cambridge: Cambridge University Press 1983).

HOBSON, J., *The War in South Africa: Its Causes and Effects* (London: J. Nisbet and Co. 1900).

—— *Imperialism: A Study* (London: J. Nisbet and Co. 1902).

HOFMEYR, I., 'South African Liberalism and the Novel', in *Olive Schreiner*, ed. C. Clayton (Johannesburg: A. D. Donker 1983), 154–7.

—— '*We Spend Our Years as a Tale that is Told*'. *Oral Historical Narrative in a South African Chiefdom* (Johannesburg: Witwatersrand University Press 1993).

HOLDEN, REVD. W. C., *The Past and Future of the Kaffir Races: In Three Parts: I Their History. II Their Manners and Customs. III The Means needful for their Preservation and Improvement* (London: Pub. for the Author 1866).

HOOPER, M., 'Rewriting History: The "Feminism" of *Mhudi*', *English Studies in Africa*, volume 35, number 1 (1992), 68–79.

HORKHEIMER, M., *Critical Theory: Selected Essays*, trans. M. J. O'Connell and others (New York: Continuum 1972).

—— *Eclipse of Reason* (New York: Continuum 1974).

—— and T. ADORNO, *Dialectic of Enlightenment*, trans. J. Cumming (1944; New York: Continuum 1972).

HORTON, J. A., *West African Countries and Peoples, British and Native: with the Requirements Necessary for Establishing that Self-government recommended by the Committee of the House of Commons, 1865; and a Vindication of the African race* (London: W. J. Johnson 1868).

—— *Letters on the Political Condition of the Gold Coast* (London: W. J. Johnson 1870).

HOWE, S., *Anticolonialism in British Politics: The Left and the End of Empire 1918–1965* (Oxford: Oxford University Press 1993).

HOWKINS, A., 'Rider Haggard and Rural England: An Essay in Literature and History', in *The Imagined Past: History and Nostalgia*, ed. C. Shaw and M. Chase (Manchester: Manchester University Press 1988), 81–94.

HULME, P., 'The Locked Heart: The Creole Family Romance of *Wide Sargasso Sea*', in *Colonial Discourse/Postcolonial Theory*, ed. F. Barker, P. Hulme, and M. Iversen (Manchester: Manchester University Press 1994), 72–88.

JACKSON, R., *Fantasy: The Literature of Subversion* (London: Methuen 1981).

JAFFE, H., *A History of Africa* (London: Zed Books 1985).

JAMESON, F., *The Political Unconscious: Narrative as a Socially Symbolic Act* (London: Methuen and Co. 1981).

—— 'Modernism and Imperialism', *Field Day Pamphlet number 14* (Derry: Field Day Theatre Co. Ltd. 1988).

JOHNSON, D., 'Literature for the Rainbow Nation: the case of Sol Plaatje's *Mhudi*', *Journal of Literary Studies*, volume 10, numbers 3 and 4 (1994), 345–58.

—— *Shakespeare and South Africa* (Oxford: Clarendon Press 1996).

JONES, G., *Social Darwinism and English Thought: The Interaction between Biology and Social Theory* (Brighton: Harvester Press 1982).

KARIS, T. and G. CARTER, eds., *From Protest to Challenge: A Documentary History of African Politics in South Africa 1882–1964* (Stanford: Hoover Institution Press 1972).

KATZ, W., *Rider Haggard and the Fiction of Empire: A Critical Survey of British Imperial Fiction* (Cambridge: Cambridge University Press 1987).

KEANE, A. H., *The Gold of Ophir: Whence Brought and by Whom?* (London: Edward Stanford 1901).

KEEGAN, T., 'The Sharecropping Economy, African Class Formation and the Natives' Land Act of 1913 in the Highveld Maize Belt', in *Industrialisation and Social Change in South Africa: African Class Formation, Culture and Consciousness 1870–1930*, ed. S. Marks and R. Rathbone (London: Longman 1982), 195–211.

KIDD, B., *Social Evolution* (1894; London: Macmillan and Co. 1898).

KIERNAN, V. G., *The Lords of Human Kind: European Attitudes to the Outside World in the Imperial Age* (Harmondsworth: Penguin 1972).

KILLAM, G. D., ed., *African Writers and African Writing* (London: Heinemann 1973).

'King Plagiarism and His Court', *Fortnightly Review*, NS 279 (1 March 1890), 421–39 .

KOEBNER, R., and H. D. SCHMIDT, *Imperialism: The Story and Significance of a Political Word 1840–1960* (Cambridge: Cambridge University Press 1964).

KREBS, P. M., 'Olive Schreiner's Racialization of South Africa', *Victorian Studies*, volume 40, number 1 (spring 1997), 427–44.

KUNENE, M, 'Plaatje', *Research in African Literatures*, volume 11, number 1 (summer 1980), 244–7.

—— *Emperor Shaka the Great*, trans. the author (London: Heinemann 1986).

LANE, C., *The Ruling Passion: British Colonial Allegory and the Paradox of Homosexual Desire* (Durham: Duke University Press 1995).

LANG, A., *The Secret of the Totem* (London: Longmans, Green and Co. 1905).

LANGAN, M., and B. SCHWARZ, eds, *Crises in the British State, 1880–1930* (London: Hutchinson 1985).

LAZARUS, N., 'Disavowing Decolonization: Fanon, Nationalism, and the Problematic of Representation in Current Theories of Colonial Discourse', *Research in African Literatures*, volume 24, number 3 (winter 1993), 69–98.

—— 'Doubting the New World Order: Marxism and Postmodernist Social Theory', *differences: a journal of feminist cultural studies*, 3: 3 (1991), 94–138.

—— 'Postcolonialism and the Dilemmas of Nationalism: Aijaz Ahmad's critique of Third-Worldism', *Diaspora: A Journal of Transnational Studies*, volume 2, number 3 (winter 1993), 373–400.

—— 'National Consciousness and the Specificity of (post)Colonial Intellectualism', in *Colonial Discourse/Postcolonial Theory*, ed. F. Barker, P. Hulme, and M. Iversen (Manchester: Manchester University Press 1994), 197–220.

—— *Nationalism and Cultural Practice in the Postcolonial World* (Cambridge: Cambridge University Press 1999).

—— 'Transnationalism and the Alleged Death of the Nation State', in *Cultural Readings of Imperialism: Edward Said and the Gravity of History*, ed. K. Ansell-Pearson, B. Parry, and J. Squires (London: Lawrence and Wishart 1997), 28–48.

LEDGER, S., *The New Woman: Fiction and Feminism at the Fin de Siècle* (Manchester: Manchester University Press 1997).

—— and S. MCCRACKEN eds., *Cultural Politics at the Fin de Siècle* (Cambridge: Cambridge University Press 1995).

LENIN, V. I., *Imperialism, the Highest Stage of Capitalism* (1917; Peking: Foreign Languages Press 1975).

LENTA, M., 'Racism, Sexism and Olive Schreiner's Fiction', *Theoria*,

70 (Oct. 1987), 15–30.

LESLIE, D., *Among the Zulus and the Amatongas* (Glasgow: printed for private circulation 1875).

LEWIS, R., *Gendering Orientalism: Race, Femininity and Representation* (London: Routledge 1995).

LEWIS, S., 'Graves with a View: Atavism and the European History of Africa', *ARIEL: A Review of International English Literature*, volume 27, number 1 (Jan. 1996), 41–60.

—— 'The Violence of the Canons: A Comparison between Conrad's *Heart of Darkness* and Schreiner's *Trooper Peter Halket of Mashonaland*', paper delivered at 'Conrad and Postcoloniality: Heart of Darkness Centenary', conference, Universities of Potchefstroom and Cape Town, March–April 1998.

LEWSEN, P., ed., *Selections from the Correspondence of J. X. Merriman, 1890–1898* (Cape Town: Van Riebeeck Society Publications, 41 1963).

LIVINGSTON, T. W., *Education and Race: A Biography of Edward Wilmot Blyden* (San Francisco: The Glendessary Press 1975).

LOMBROSO, C., *L'Homme Criminel* (Paris: Alcan 1881).

—— *The Man of Genius* (London: W. Scott 1891).

LOOMBA, A., 'Overworlding the Third World', *Oxford Literary Review*, volume 13, numbers 1 and 2 (1991), 164–92.

—— *Colonialism/Postcolonialism* (London: Routledge 1998).

LOW, G., *White Skins, Black Masks: Representation and Colonialism* (London: Routledge 1996).

LUBBOCK, J., *The Origin of Civilisation and the Primitive Condition of Man: Mental and Social Condition of Savages* (London: Longmans, Green and Co. 1870).

LUKÁCS, G., *The Historical Novel*, trans. H. and S. Mitchell (Harmondsworth: Penguin 1976).

LUXEMBURG, R., *The Accumulation of Capital*, trans. A. Schwarzschild (1913; London: Routledge and Kegan Paul 1951).

LYNCH, H. R., *Edward Wilmot Blyden: Pan-Negro Patriot 1832–1912* (New York: Oxford University Press 1967).

—— ed., *Black Spokesman: Selected Writings of Edward Wilmot Blyden* (London: Frank Cass 1971).

McCLINTOCK, A., '*Maidens, Maps and Mines*: King Solomon's Mines and the Reinvention of Patriarchy in Colonial South Africa', in *Women and Gender in Southern Africa to 1945*, ed. C. Walker (London: James Currey 1990), 97–124.

—— 'The Angel of Progress: Pitfalls of the Term "Post-Colonialism"', in *Colonial Discourse and Post-Colonial Theory: A Reader*, ed. P. Williams and L. Chrisman (Hemel Hempstead: Harvester Wheat-

sheaf 1993), 291–304.
——*Imperial Leather: Race, Gender and Sexuality in the Colonial Contest* (London: Routledge 1995).

McClure, J. A., *Late Imperial Romance* (London: Verso 1994).

MacIver, D. R., *Medieval Rhodesia* (London: Macmillan and Co. 1906).

MacKay, J. and P. Thane, 'The Englishwoman', in *Englishness: Politics and Culture 1880–1930*, ed. R. Colls and P. Dodd (London: Croom Helm 1985), 191–229.

MacKenzie, J. M., *Propaganda and Empire: The Manipulation of British Public Opinion, 1880–1960* (Manchester: Manchester University Press 1984).

——ed., *Imperialism and Popular Culture* (Manchester: Manchester University Press 1986).

Marks, S., *The Ambiguities of Dependence in South Africa: Class, Nationalism, and the State in Twentieth-Century Natal* (Baltimore: Johns Hopkins Press 1986).

——and A. Atmore, eds., *Economy and Society in Pre-Industrial South Africa* (London: Longman 1980).

——and R. Rathbone, eds., *Industrialisation and Social Change in South Africa: African Class Formation, Culture, and Consciousness 1870–1930* (London: Longman 1982).

——and S. Trapido, eds., *The Politics of Race, Class and Nationalism in Twentieth Century South Africa* (London: Longman 1987).

Masilela, N., 'The "Black Atlantic" and African Modernity in South Africa', *Research in African Literatures*, volume 27, number 4 (spring 1997), 88–96.

Masterman, C., ed., *The Heart of Empire* (London: T. Fisher Unwin 1901).

Mazrui, A., 'The Patriot as Artist', in *African Writers on African Writing*, ed. G. D. Killam (London: Heinemann 1973), 73–90.

Meli, F., *South Africa Belongs to Us: A History of the ANC* (Harare: Zimbabwe Publishing House 1988).

Michalski, R., 'Divine Hunger: Culture and the Commodity in Rider Haggard's *She*', *Journal of Victorian Culture*, volume 1, number 1 (spring 1996), 76–97.

Mill, J. S., *On Liberty* (London: John W. Parker and Son 1859).

Miller, H., *The Books in My Life* (London: Peter Owen 1952).

Millin, S. G., *The Jordans* (London: W. Collins Sons and Co. 1923).

Mills, S., *Discourses of Difference: An Analysis of Women's Travel Writing and Colonialism* (London: Routledge 1993).

Milner, Lord A., *The Nation and the Empire* (London: Constable 1913).

MITFORD, B., *John Ames, Native Commissioner; a Romance of the Matabele Rising* (London: F. V. White 1900).

MNGADI, S., 'The Politics of Historical Representation in the Context of Global Capitalism', in *Rethinking South African Literary History*, ed. J. A. Smit *et al.* (Durban: Y Press 1996), 196–208.

'Modern Marvels', *The Spectator*, 58 (17 Oct. 1885), 1365–6.

'Modern Men. Mr H. Rider Haggard', *The Scots Observer*, volume 1, number 23 (27 April 1889), 631–2 .

MOFOLO, T., *Chaka*, trans. D. Kunene (1922; London: Heinemann 1981).

MOLEMA, S. M., *The Bantu Past and Present: An Ethnographical and Historical Study of the Native Races of South Africa* (Edinburgh: W. Green and Son Ltd. 1920).

—— *Chief Moroka. His Life, His Times, His Country and His People* (Cape Town: Methodist Publishing House 1951).

MONGIA, P., ed., *Contemporary Postcolonial Theory: A Reader* (London: Arnold 1996).

MONSMAN, G., 'Olive Schreiner: Literature and the Politics of Power', *Texas Studies in Literature and Language*, volume 30, number 4 (winter 1988), 583–610.

MOORE, G., review of *Mhudi, Research in African Literatures*, volume 11, number 2 (summer 1980), 248–50.

MOORE-GILBERT, B., *Postcolonial Theory: Contexts, Practices, Politics* (London: Verso 1997).

MORRIS, W., *News From Nowhere or an epoch of rest being some chapters from a utopian romance*, ed. J. Redmond (1891; London: Routledge and Kegan Paul 1970).

MOSES, W. J., *The Golden Age of Black Nationalism, 1850–1925* (Oxford: Oxford University Press 1978).

MOSSE, J. C., 'Feminism and Fiction: A Study of Nineteenth Century Writing and Contemporary Feminist Literary Theory', M.Litt. thesis (University of Oxford 1986).

MPE, P., ' "Naturally These Stories Lost Nothing by Repetition": Plaatje's Mediation of Oral History in *Mhudi*', *Current Writing*, volume 8, number 1 (1996), 75–89.

'Mr Punch's Prize Novels', *Punch* (17 Jan. 1892), 28.

MUDIMBE, V. Y., *The Invention of Africa: Gnosis, Philosophy, and the Order of Knowledge* (London: James Currey 1988).

MURRAY, S.-A., 'Introduction', *Trooper Peter Halket of Mashonaland* (Johannesburg: A. D. Donker 1992), 9–25.

NEWBURY, C., 'Out of the Pit: The Capital Accumulation of Cecil Rhodes', *Journal of Imperial and Commonwealth History*, volume 10, number 1 (Oct. 1981), 25–43.

NGUGI WA THIONG'O, *Decolonising the Mind: The Politics of Language in African Literature* (London: James Currey 1986).

NIETZSCHE, F., *The Genealogy of Morals: An Attack*, trans. F. Golding (1887; New York: Doubleday 1956).

ODENDAAL, A., *Black Protest Politics in South Africa to 1912* (Totowa: Barnes and Noble 1984).

OGUNGBESAN, K., 'The Long Eye of History in *Mhudi*', *Caribbean Journal of African Studies*, 11 (1978), 27–42.

OMER-COOPER, J., 'Aspects of Political Change in the Nineteenth-Century *Mfecane*', in *African Societies in Southern Africa*, ed L. Thompson (London: Heinemann 1969), 207–29.

OWEN, R. and B. SUTCLIFFE, eds., *Studies in the Theory of Imperialism* (London: Longman 1972).

Pall Mall Budget, 'Review of *She*', 25 (6 Jan. 1887), 28.

PARKER, SIR G., *The Judgment House* (London: Methuen and Co. 1913).

PARRY, B., *Conrad and Imperialism* (London: Macmillan 1983).

—— 'Problems in Current Theories of Colonial Discourse', *Oxford Literary Review*, volume 9, numbers 1 and 2 (1987), 27–58.

—— 'The Content and Discontents of Kipling's Imperialism', *New Formations*, 6 (winter 1988), 84–112.

—— 'Conrad and England', in *Patriotism: The Making and Unmaking of British National Identity*, iii. *National Fictions*, ed. R. Samuel (London: Routledge 1989), 189–98.

—— review article of A. Ahmad's *In Theory*, *History Workshop Journal*, 36 (1993), 232–41.

—— 'Resistance Theory/Theorising Resistance or Two Cheers for Nativism', in *Colonial Discourse/Postcolonial Theory*, ed. F. Barker, P. Hulme, and M. Iversen (Manchester: Manchester University Press 1994), 172–96.

—— 'Signs of Our Times: A Discussion of Homi Bhabha's *The Location of Culture*', *Third Text*, numbers 28 and 29 (autumn–winter 1994), 5–24.

—— 'The Postcolonial: Conceptual Category or Chimera?', *Yearbook of English Studies: the Politics of Postcolonial Criticism*, 27, Modern Humanities Research Association (London 1997), 3–21.

—— 'Narrating Imperialism: *Nostromo*'s dystopia', in *Cultural Readings of Imperialism. Edward Said and the Gravity of History*, ed. K. Ansell-Pearson, B. Parry, and J. Squires (London: Lawrence and Wishart 1997), 227–46.

—— 'Materiality and Mystification in *A Passage to India*', *Novel. A Forum on Fiction*, volume 31, number 2 (spring 1998), 174–94.

—— *Delusions and Discoveries: Studies on India in the British*

Imagination 1880–1930, foreword by M. Sprinker (London: Verso 1998).

—— 'Tono-Bungay: Modernisation, Modernity and Imperialism, or the Failed Electrification of the Empire', *New Formations*, 34 (summer 1998), 91–108.

PATON, A., 'Trooper Peter Halket of Mashonaland', in *Olive Schreiner and After: Essays in Honour of Guy Butler*, ed. M. van Wyk Smith and D. MacLennan (Cape Town: David Philip 1983), 30–3.

PATTESON, R. F., '*King Solomon's Mines*: Imperialism and Narrative Structure', *Journal of Narrative Technique*, 8 (1978), 112–23.

PAUL, D., ' "In the Interests of Civilization": Marxist Views of Race and Culture in the Nineteenth Century', *Journal of the History of Ideas*, volume 42, number 1 (Jan.–March 1981), 115–38.

—— 'Eugenics and the Left', *Journal of the History of Ideas*, volume 45, number 4 (Oct.–Dec. 1984), 567–90.

PAUL, E. F., 'Herbert Spencer: The Historicist as a Failed Prophet', *Journal of the History of Ideas*, volume 44, number 4 (Oct.–Dec. 1983), 619–38.

PEARSON, K., *National Life from the Standpoint of Science* (London: Adam and Charles Black 1901).

—— *The Ethic of Freethought* (London: T. Fisher Unwin 1888).

PECHEY, G., '*The Story of an African Farm*: Colonial History and the Discontinuous Text', *Critical Arts*, volume 3, number 1 (1983), 65–78.

—— ' "Cultural Struggle" and the Narratives of South African Freedom', in *Altered State? Writing and South Africa*, ed. E. Boehmer, L. Chrisman, and K. Parker (Hebden Bridge: Dangaroo Press 1994), 25–36.

PEEL, J. D. Y., *Herbert Spencer: The Evolution of a Sociologist* (London: Heinemann 1971).

PELEM, M., 26 Feb. 1919, document 29, *From Protest to Challenge. A Documentary History of African Politics in South Africa 1882–1964*, i: *Protest and Hope, 1882–1934*, ed. S. Johns, T. Karis, and G. M. Carter (Stanford: Hoover Institution Press 1972), 101–3.

PELLING, H., *Popular Politics and Society in Late Victorian Britain* (London: Macmillan 1979).

PHELPS, J. M., 'Sol Plaatje's *Mhudi* and Democratic Government', *English Studies in Africa*, volume 36, number 1 (1993), 47–56.

PHIMISTER, I. R., 'The Making of Colonial Zimbabwe: Speculation and Violence 1890–1902', University of Cape Town Centre for African Studies Seminar paper (1982).

PICARDIE, M., *The Cape Orchard* (Cardiff: Pant-teg Press 1987).

PIERCE, P., *Rider Haggard*, B.Litt. thesis (University of Oxford 1986).

PLAATJE, S. T., *Sechuana Proverbs with Literal Translations and Their European Equivalents* (London: Kegan Paul, Trench, Trübner and Co. 1916).

—— *Native Life in South Africa Before and Since the European War and the Boer Rebellion*, ed B. Willan, foreword by B. Head (1916; Athens: Ohio University Press 1991).

—— *Mhudi* (1930; London: Heinemann 1982).

—— 'Chief Moroka', in *The African Yearly Register. Being an Illustrated National Biographical Dictionary (Who's Who) of Black Folks in Africa*, ed. T. D. M. Skota (Johannesburg: R. L. Esson and Co. 1932), 60–4.

—— 'Journalism', special issue, *English in Africa*, volume 3, number 2 (1976).

—— and D. JONES, *A Sechuana Reader in International Phonetic Orthography (with English translations)* (London: University of London Press 1916).

PLUMER, LT. COL. H. C. O., *An Irregular in Matabeleland* (London: Paul, Trench and Trübner 1897).

PORTER, B., *Critics of Empire: British Radical Attitudes to Colonialism in Africa 1895–1914* (London: Macmillan 1968).

PRATT, M. L., *Imperial Eyes: Travel Writing and Transculturation* (London: Routledge 1992).

—— 'Transculturation and Autoethnography: Peru 1615/1980', in *Colonial Discourse/Postcolonial Theory*, ed. F. Barker, P. Hulme, and M. Iversen (Manchester: Manchester University Press 1994), 24–46.

RADZIWILL, PRINCESS C., *The Resurrection of Peter: A Reply to Olive Schreiner* (London: Hurst and Blackett 1900).

RANGER, T., *Revolt in Southern Rhodesia 1896–97* (London: Heinemann 1967).

—— 'The Rural African Voice in Zimbabwe Rhodesia: archaism and tradition', *Social Analysis*, 4 (Sept. 1980), 100–15.

—— 'The Invention of Tradition in Colonial Africa', in *The Invention of Tradition*, ed. E. Hobsbawm and T. Ranger (Cambridge: Cambridge University Press 1983), 211–63.

RASMUSSEN, R. K., *Migrant Kingdom: Mzilikazi's Ndebele in South Africa* (London: Rex Collings 1978).

RAVENSCROFT, A., 'Literature and Politics: Two Zimbabwean Novels', in *Olive Schreiner and After: Essays in Honour of Guy Butler*, ed. M. van Wyk Smith and D. MacLennan (Cape Town: David Philip 1983), 46–57.

'Reality and Romance', *The Spectator*, 61 (28 April 1888), 569–71.

'Review of *King Solomon's Mines*', *Public Opinion*, 48 (30 Oct. 1885), 551.

'Review of *King Solomon's Mines*', *Queen*, 78 (7 Nov. 1885), 512.

'Review of *King Solomon's Mines*', *The Academy*, 28 (7 Nov. 1885), 304–5.

'Review of *King Solomon's Mines*', *The Athenaeum*, 86 (31 Oct. 1885), 568.

'Review of *King Solomon's Mines*', *The Independent*, 37 (3 Dec. 1885), 13.

'Review of *King Solomon's Mines*', *The Saturday Review*, [Andrew Lang], 60 (10 Oct. 1885), 485–6.

'Review of *King Solomon's Mines*', *The Spectator*, 58 (7 Nov. 1885), 1473.

'Review of *She*', *Public Opinion*, 51 (4 Jan. 1887), 38.

RICHARDS, T., *The Commodity Culture of Victorian England: Advertising and Spectacle, 1851–1914* (London: Verso 1991).

—— *The Imperial Archive: Knowledge and the Fantasy of Empire* (London: Verso 1993).

RICHARDSON, R. and J. J. VAN-HELTEN, 'Labour in the South African Gold Mining Industry, 1886–1914', in *Industrialisation and Social Change in South Africa: African Class Formation, Culture, and Consciousness 1870–1930*, ed. S. Marks and R. Rathbone (London: Longman 1982), 77–98.

RIDLEY, H., *Images of Imperial Rule* (London: Croom Helm 1983).

RIGSBY, G. U., *Alexander Crummell: Pioneer in Nineteenth-Century Pan-African Thought* (London: Greenwood Press 1987).

RITTER, E. A., *Shaka Zulu: The Rise of the Zulu Empire* (New York: Putnam 1957).

ROBERTS, M., *The Colossus: A Story of Today* (London: E. Arnold 1899).

ROSEBERY, Lord, *Questions of Empire* (London: Arthur L. Humphreys 1900).

ROWBOTHAM, S., and J. WEEKS, *Socialism and the New Life: The Personal and Sexual Politics of Edward Carpenter and Havelock Ellis* (London: Pluto Press 1977).

RUTHERFORD, J., *Sir George Grey: A Study in Colonial Government* (London: Cassell 1961).

SAID, E., *Orientalism* (Harmondsworth: Peregrine Books 1978).

—— 'Third World Intellectuals and Metropolitan Culture', *Raritan*, volume 9, number 3 (winter 1990), 27–50.

—— *Culture and Imperialism* (London: Chatto 1993).

SAMKANGE, S., *On Trial for My Country* (London: Heinemann 1966).

—— *Year of the Uprising* (London: Heinemann 1978).

SAN JUAN, JR., E., 'On the Limits of "Postcolonial" Theory: Trespassing Letters from the "Third World" ', *ARIEL: A Review of International English Literature*, volume 26, number 3 (1995), 89–115.

SANDISON, A., *The Wheel of Empire: A Study of the Imperial Idea in Some Late Nineteenth and Early Twentieth-Century Fiction* (London: Macmillan 1967).

SCHALKWYK, D., 'Plaatje Reviewed', *Scrutiny* 2, forthcoming.

——and L. LAPULA, 'Solomon Plaatje, William Shakespeare, and the Translations of Culture', paper delivered at 'Shakespeare Postcoloniality' conference, University of the Witwatersrand, July 1996.

SCHREIBER, H. and G., *Vanished Cities*, trans. R. and C. Winston (London: Wiedenfeld and Nicolson 1958).

SCHREINER, O., *The Story of an African Farm* (London: Chapman and Hall 1883).

——*Dreams* (London: T. Fisher Unwin 1890).

——'In a Ruined Chapel', in *Dreams* (London: T. Fisher Unwin 1890), 98–111.

——'The Sunlight Lay Across My Bed', in *Dreams* (London: T. Fisher Unwin 1890), 133–82.

——'The Buddhist Priest's Wife' (1892), in *An Olive Schreiner Reader: Writings on Women and South Africa*, ed. C. Barash (London: Pandora Press 1987), 109–21.

——*Dream Life and Real Life* (London: T. Fisher Unwin 1893).

——*Trooper Peter Halket of Mashonaland* (1897; Johannesburg: A. D. Donker 1974).

——'The Woman Question' (1899), in *Olive Schreiner Reader: Writings on Women and South Africa*, ed. C. Barash (London: Pandora Press 1987), 63–100.

——*Woman and Labour*, preface by J. Graves (1911; London: Virago 1978).

——*Stories, Dreams and Allegories* (London: T. Fisher Unwin 1923).

——*Thoughts on South Africa* (London: T. Fisher Unwin 1923).

——*From Man to Man; or Perhaps Only . . .* (London: T. Fisher Unwin 1926).

——*Letters. Volume 1. 1871–1899*, ed. R. Rive (Oxford: Oxford University Press 1988).

——and S. C. CRONWRIGHT-SCHREINER, *The Political Situation* (London: T. Fisher Unwin 1896).

SCHREUDER, D. M., *The Scramble for Southern Africa, 1877–1895* (Cambridge: Cambridge University Press 1980).

——'The Imperial Historian as Colonial Nationalist: George McCall Theal and the Making of South African History', in *Studies in*

British Imperial History: Essays in Honour of A. P. Thornton, ed.
G. Martel (London: Macmillan 1986), 95–159.

SCHUMPETER, J., *Imperialism and Social Classes* (1919; New York:
Meridian Books 1955).

SCHWARZ, B., 'Black Metropolis, White England', in *Modern Times:
Reflections on a Century of English Modernity*, ed. M. Nava and A.
O'Shea (London: Routledge 1996), 176–207.

SCOTT, D., *Refashioning Futures. Criticism after Postcoloniality*
(Princeton: Princeton University Press 1999).

SEME, P., *The Regeneration of Africa* (New York: Columbia University
Press 1906).

SEMMEL, B., *Imperialism and Social Reform. English Social-Imperial
Thought 1895–1914* (London: Allen and Unwin 1960).

SENGHOR, L. S., 'Negritude: A Humanism of the Twentieth Century',
in *Colonial Discourse and Post-Colonial Theory: A Reader*, ed. P.
Williams and L. Chrisman (Hemel Hempstead: Harvester Wheatsheaf 1993), 27–36.

SHARPE, J., *Allegories of Empire: The Figure of the Woman in the
Colonial Text* (Minneapolis: University of Minnesota Press 1993).

—— 'The Unspeakable Limits of Rape: Colonial Violence and
Counter-Insurgency', in *Colonial Discourse and Post-Colonial
Theory: A Reader*, ed. P. Williams and L. Chrisman (Hemel
Hempstead: Harvester Wheatsheaf 1993), 196–220.

SHAVA, P. V., *A People's Voice: Black South African Writing in the
Twentieth Century* (London: Zed Books 1989).

SHELLEY, P. B., *Shelley's Prose*, ed. D. L. Clark (London: Fourth Estate
1988).

SHILLINGTON, K., 'The Impact of the Diamond Discoveries in the
Kimberley Hinterland: Class Formation, Colonialism and Resistance
among the Tlhaping of Griqualand West in the 1870s', in
*Industrialisation and Social Change in South Africa: African Class
Formation, Culture, and Consciousness 1870–1930*, ed. S. Marks
and R. Rathbone (London: Longman 1982), 99–118.

SHOHAT, E., 'Notes on the Post-Colonial', in *Contemporary Post-
colonial Theory: A Reader*, ed. P. Mongia (London: Arnold 1996),
322–34.

SHOWALTER, E., *A Literature of Their Own* (London: Virago 1978).

SIMONS, J. and R., *Class and Colour in South Africa 1850–1950*
(London: International Defence and Aid Fund for Southern African
1983).

SINHA, M., *Colonial Masculinity: The 'Manly Englishman' and the
'Effeminate Bengali' in the Late Nineteenth Century* (Manchester:
Manchester University Press 1995).

SOLE, K., 'South Africa Passes the Posts', *Alternation*, volume 4, number 1 (1997), 116–51.

—— 'Writing South Africa', *Alternation*, volume 5, number 1 (1998), 256–66.

SPENCER, H., *First Principles* (London: Williams and Norgate 1862).

SPIVAK, G. C., *The Post-Colonial Critic: Interviews, Strategies, Dialogues*, ed. S. Harasym (London: Routledge 1990).

—— 'Neocolonialism and the Secret Agent of Knowledge: An Interview with Gayatri Chakravorty Spivak', *Oxford Literary Review. Neocolonialism*, volume 13, numbers 1 and 2 (1991), 220–51.

—— 'Imperialism and Sexual Difference', in *The Current in Criticism. Essays on the Present and Future of Literary Theory*, ed. C. Koelb and V. Lokke (West Lafayette: Purdue University Press 1993), 319–37.

—— 'Can the Subaltern Speak? Speculations on Widow Sacrifice', *Colonial Discourse and Post-Colonial Theory: A Reader*, ed. P. Williams and L. Chrisman (Hemel Hempstead: Harvester Wheatsheaf 1993), 66–111.

—— 'How to Read a Culturally Different Book', in *Colonial Discourse/Postcolonial Theory*, ed. F. Barker, P. Hulme, and M. Iversen (Manchester: Manchester University Press 1994), 126–50.

—— 'Three Women's Texts and a Critique of Imperialism', in *Postcolonial Criticism*, ed. B. Moore-Gilbert, G. Stanton, and W. Maley (London: Longman 1997), 145–65.

—— 'Subaltern Talk: Interview with the Editors', *The Spivak Reader*, ed. D. Landry and G. MacLean (London: Routledge 1995), 287–308.

—— *A Critique of Postcolonial Reason. Toward A History of the Vanishing Present* (London: Harvard University Press 1999).

SPURR, D., *The Rhetoric of Empire: Colonial Discourse in Journalism, Travel Writing and Imperial Administration* (Durham: Duke University Press 1993).

STANLEY, L., 'Olive Schreiner: New Women, Free Women, All Women', in *Feminist Theorists: Three Centuries of Women's Intellectual Traditions*, ed. D. Spender (London: The Women's Press 1983), 229–43.

—— 'Feminism and Friendship: Two Essays on Olive Schreiner', *Studies in Sexual Politics*, 8 (University of Manchester Department of Sociology 1985).

STARFIELD, J., 'The Lore and the Proverbs: Sol Plaatje as Historian', University of the Witwatersrand African Studies Institute Seminar paper (1991).

STATHAM, F. R., *Mr Magnus* (London: T. Fisher Unwin 1896).

STEAD, W. T., *If Christ Came to Chicago! A Plea for the Union of All Who Love in the Service of All Who Suffer* (Chicago: Laird and Lee 1894).

STEDMAN-JONES, G., *Outcast London: A Study in the Relationship between Classes in Victorian Society* (Harmondsworth: Peregrine Books 1984).

STEVENSON, R. L., *Treasure Island* (London: Cassell 1883).

STOTT, R., 'The Dark Continent: Africa as Female Body in Haggard's Adventure Fiction, *Feminist Review*, 32 (summer 1989), 69–89.

STOWE, G., *The Native Races of South Africa* (London: Swan Sönnenschëin and Co. 1905).

STREET, B., *The Savage in Literature: Representations of 'Primitive' Society in English Fiction 1858–1920* (London: Routledge and Kegan Paul 1975).

SULLIVAN, E., 'Liberalism and Imperialism: J. S. Mill's Defense of the British Empire', *Journal of the History of Ideas*, volume 44, number 4 (Oct.–Dec. 1983), 599–617.

SUTTON, D., 'Liberalism, State Collectivism and the Social Relations of Citizenship', in *Crises in the British State, 1880–1930*, ed. M. Langan and B. Schwarz (London: Hutchinson and Co. 1985), 63–79.

'The Fall of Fiction', *Fortnightly Review*, 44 (1 Sept. 1888), 324–36.

THEAL, G. M., *A History of South Africa from 1795 to 1872*, vols. i and ii (4th edn.; London: George Allen and Unwin Ltd. 1915).

THOMAS, N., *Colonialism's Culture. Anthropology, Travel and Government* (Cambridge: Polity Press 1994).

THOMAS, W., *Mill* (Oxford: Oxford University Press 1985).

THOMPSON, L., ed, *African Societies in Southern Africa* (London: Heinemann 1969).

—— and M. Wilson, eds., *The Oxford History of South Africa*, ii (Oxford: Oxford University Press 1971).

TORGOVNICK, M., *Gone Primitive: Savage Intellects, Modern Lives* (Chicago: University of Chicago Press 1990).

TRAPIDO, S., ' "The Friends of the Natives": Merchants, Peasants and the Political and Ideological Structure of Liberalism in the Cape, 1854–1910', in *Economy and Society in Pre-Industrial South Africa*, ed. S. Marks and A. Atmore (London: Longman 1980), 247–74.

TROTTER, D., 'Modernism and Empire: Reading *The Waste Land*', *Critical Quarterly*, volume 28, numbres 1 and 2 (spring–summer 1986), 143–53.

—— 'Colonial Subjects', *Critical Quarterly*, volume 32, number 3 (autumn 1990), 3–20.

TURRELL, R., 'Rhodes, de Beers, and Monopoly', *Journal of Imperial and Commonwealth History*, volume 10, number 3 (May 1982), 311–42.

—— 'Kimberley: Labour and Compounds, 1871–1888', in *Industrialisation and Social Change in South Africa: African Class Formation, Culture, and Consciousness 1870–1930*, ed. S. Marks and R. Rathbone (London: Longman 1982), 45–76.

VAN ZYL, J., 'Rhodes and Olive Schreiner', *Contrast*, volume 6, number 1 (Aug. 1969), 86–90.

VERA, Y., *Nehanda* (Harare: Baobab Books 1993).

'Vindex', *Cecil Rhodes: His Political Life and Speeches 1881–1900* (London: Chapman and Hall 1900).

VIVAN, I., ed., *The Flawed Diamond: Essays on Olive Schreiner* (Coventry: Dangaroo Press 1991).

VOGELSBURGER, H. A., *'King Romance': Rider Haggard's Achievement* (Salzburg Studies in English Literature, 92:3 1984).

VORZIMMER, P., *Charles Darwin: The Years of Controversy* (London: University of London Press 1972).

VOSS, A. E., 'Sol Plaatje, the Eighteenth Century, and South African Cultural Memory', *English in Africa. Revisions. 21st birthday issue*, volume 21, numbres 1 and 2 (1994), 59–76.

WALKER, C., ed., *Women and Gender in Southern Africa to 1945* (Cape Town: David Philip 1990).

WALMSLEY, H. M., *The Ruined Cities of Zululand* (London: Chapman and Hall 1869).

WALSHE, P., *The Rise of African Nationalism in South Africa: The African National Congress 1912–1952* (Berkeley: University of California Press 1971).

WALTER, B., 'The Romance of Protest: Sol Plaatje's *Mhudi*', in *Literature, Nature and the Land. Ethics and Aesthetics of the Environment. Papers given at the annual conference of the Association of University English Teachers of Southern Africa, University of Zululand, 7–10 July 1992*, ed. N. Bell and M. Cowper-Lewis (1993), 193–9.

WARE, V., *Beyond the Pale: White Women, Racism and Imperialism* (London: Verso 1992).

WARREN, B., *Imperialism: Pioneer of Capitalism* (London: Verso 1980).

WATSON, W., *Selected Poems* (London: The Bodley Head 1903).

WEEKS, J., *Sex, Politics and Society: The Regulation of Sexuality since 1800* (London: Longman 1981).

WELLS, J. C., *We Now Demand! The History of Women's Resistance to Pass Laws in South Africa* (Johannesburg: Witwatersrand University Press 1993).

WIESCHHOFF, H. A., *The Zimbabwe–Monomotapa Culture in Southeast Africa* (Menasha: George Banta 1941).

WILHELM, P., '*Peter Halket,* Rhodes and Colonialism', *Olive Schreiner,* ed. C. Clayton (Johannesburg: A. D. Donker 1983) 208–12.

WILLAN, B., 'An African in Kimberley: Sol T Plaatje, 1894–1898', *Industrialisation and Social Change in South Africa: African Class Formation, Culture and Consciousness 1870–1930,* ed. S. Marks and R. Rathbone (London: Longman 1982), 238–58.

——*Sol Plaatje: South African Nationalist* (London: Heinemann 1984).

——ed., *Sol Plaatje: Selected Writings* (Athens: Ohio University Press 1996).

WILLIAMS, P. and L. CHRISMAN, eds., *Colonial Discourse and Post-Colonial Theory: A Reader* (Hemel Hempstead: Harvester Wheatsheaf 1993).

WORMELL, D., *Sir John Seeley and the Uses of History* (Cambridge: Cambridge University Press 1980).

YOUNG, R., *White Mythologies: Writing History and the West* (London: Routledge 1990).

ZWEIG, P., *The Adventurer* (London: J. M. Dent 1974).

Index